▲ ▲ ▲

FEED YOUR CHILD RIGHT
from Birth through Teens

▲ ▲ ▲

▲ ▲ ▲

FEED YOUR CHILD RIGHT
from Birth through Teens

▲ ▲ ▲

A PEDIATRICIAN'S NOTES ON NUTRITION, EASY-TO-PREPARE RECIPES, AND HEALTHY SNACKS

Albert C. Goldberg, M.D.

M. Evans and Company, Inc.
New York

M. Evans and Company, Inc.
216 East 49th Street
New York, New York 10017

Library of Congress Cataloging-in-Publication Data

Goldberg, Albert.
    Feed your child right from birth through teens / by Albert Goldberg.
        p. cm.
    Includes bibliographical references.
    ISBN 0-87131-899-7
        1.   Infants—Nutrition. 2.   Children—Nutrition. 3. Nutritional disorders in children—Prevention. I. Title.
RJ206.G55 2000
613.2'083—dc21   99-054841

Book design by Rik Lain Schell

Printed in the United States of America

9   8   7   6   5   4   3   2   1

CONTENTS

▲ ▲ ▲

Introduction   vii

PART I: FEED YOUR CHILD RIGHT

1. Feeding Your Infant   1
2. First Foods   15
3. Making Your Own Baby Foods   30
4. Feeding Your Toddler or Preschooler   37
5. The Foods Children Need, Part 1   50
6. The Older Child's Diet   71
7. The Foods Children Need, Part 2   84
8. The Adolescent's Diet   93

PART II: NUTRITION 101

9. The Chemicals of Life   107
10. Carbohydrates   109
11. Protein   115
12. Fats (Lipids)   120
13. Fiber   126
14. Vitamins   130
15. Minerals   146
16. The Food Guide Pyramid   163

PART III: RESOURCES FOR PARENTS

17. Recipes   173
18. Fast Foods   217
19. Reading Food Labels   221

Acknowledgments   283
Index   285

to Keith Goldberg,
12/11/61–6/14/62,
who inspired me to become a pediatrician

▲ ▲ ▲

Feed Your Child Right from Birth through Teens is a nutrition book that contains more than nutritious soups, sandwiches, and snack recipes that kids like. I've slipped in an elementary education in nutrients— just the basics—that can help parents find their way through the thicket of good nutritional information, the hype and the misinformation that's out there. I've also included charts and specific guidelines on the nutritional needs of children at various ages. This book contains everything a parent needs to know to design an optimal diet for the well child from infancy through the teenage years. Although I am writing this book for children, it will surely have an effect on the eating habits and good health of grown readers. When you find out about sodium, for instance, whether or not you're a parent and no matter what your age or family medical history, I believe you'll be grateful for my Five-Step Program in Part I for cutting down the amount of salt in your food. It is important to make changes in manageable steps, and come up with foods that children will accept and incorporate into their diets.

There is a special need for a practical nutrition book that contains truth rather than wishful thinking or armchair reasoning passed off as "science." This, along with suggestions that a busy parent can follow, makes *Feed Your Child Right from Birth through Teens* such a book. To my knowledge, this is the only book that addresses the daily nutritional health issues of children in a specific, scientific and friendly way.

In addition to parents, this book will be of special interest to nursery schools, elementary and high school teachers, coaches, all health care providers, family physicians, pediatricians, and nurses who work with children, including pediatric and family nurse practitioners. One of the most important duties of health practitioners is teaching families what they can do to prevent future health related illness. Most of the nutritional guides available to family practitioners bypass the special nutritional needs of children. Of those books designed for children, the recommended foods, meals, soups and sandwiches not only conflict with scientific nutritional information, but often promote foods shown to be poor nutritional choices. For example, the high fat, salt, and sugar peanut butter sandwich seems to appear alongside the high-salt soups as a recommended food choice in most children's nutrition guides.

Many readers will not read this books straight through; therefore I have repeated important points in different sections of this book. These repetitions are deliberate to make certain that the reader who reads a book from back to front, as I often do, does not miss this information.

There are other types of nutrition books available to health educators and families and are promoted by the "Health Food Store" industry. These books contain the most misleading information imaginable. They put the fear of God into anyone who buys mainstream foods. They claim that pesticides and poisons are around every corner, while the foods they recommend are supposed to contain healing properties. These books are filled with claims that their recommended food choices prevent all sorts of illnesses and promote high immunity, along with other unsubstantiated information. These books state that in order to maintain optimal health one must consume multiple supplements (purchased in "Health Food Stores") to counteract all our environmental toxins. Our U.S. Constitution gives every citizen the right of freedom of speech, therefore, it is legal to write and publish any type of information, be it true or false.

Read my comments on the nutritional value of peanut butter in Part I. You may be surprised. Ice cream, which we all love, is commonly treated as a food rather than an extremely high fat candy, while pizza is passed off as a "nutritious" food without regard to its excessive salt and fat content. The food industry bias dominates these books. In *Feed Your Child Right from Birth through Teens*, the nutritional counterparts to these snack foods are presented in Part I and again, in greater detail, in Part III.

Although most of my suggestions and anecdotes come from my years of experience nurturing thousands of children (and their parents), I have recruited the experience of many other experts in nutrition. I've footnoted the sources of many statements I've made that were based on the research or experience of other investigators. This will help those readers who wish to probe deeper into clinical nutrition with a concrete starting point. With the World Wide Web at our fingertips, obtaining original articles is now much easier. But beware; the Web is also filled with highly flawed advice. Learn about the lists of reputable online sites for nutritional information. Ask your pediatrician for help. If your doctor is unfamiliar with such a list, have him consult a local Pediatric Residency Program Director. Doctors in your medical community often maintain an updated list as well. The Council Against Health Fraud operates an important website called Quackwatch (www.quackwatch.com). This is an excellent resource for parents, teachers, coaches, nurses and physicians. I deliberately omitted other websites because they may become obsolete or undependable.

Nutrition has been an area of great interest to me since medical school. I knew what a unique position I was in as a pediatrician to influence and educate patients in practical nutrition. As a college student I visited Rodale's farm in Pennsylvania and learned about his organic farming. Rachel Carson's *Silent Spring* gave me further insight into the long-term effect of what we eat. But it was after reading Nathan Pritikin's *Live Longer Now* that I realized how much more I needed to learn about diet and its effect on health and disease. Nutrition, as taught in medical school, was a small part of the biochemistry and physiology curriculum. I learned what was scientifically known at the time about digestion of foods, carbohydrates, fats, proteins, minerals and vitamins. These classes gave me a fundamental understanding of how our body works and the tools to understand the merits of a good diet as well as the pitfalls of fad diets.

For the past twenty years I've worked in many countries, including Honduras, Ecuador, Chile, Argentina, Venezuela, Peru, and Vietnam, where poverty, ignorance, social disintegration and war have contributed to nutritional diseases. In Central and South America I've seen and treated all the classical nutritional diseases including rickets, scurvy, pellagra, and kwashiorkor. In Asia, I've witnessed the nutritional changes taking place in China where the introduction of the Western diet has made heart disease a new leading cause of death in their country. I have learned from practical experience that it is not easy to alter a person's food choices. Change involves much more than presenting nutritional information or making healthier food available. There are many complex issues involved in food choice or selection, such as one's religion, cultural background, ethnicity, one's inherited temperament, and of course the availability of competing sugary or salty snacks.

In 1967, as medical director and nutritional advisor of the first Head Start Program in Marin County, California, I developed its initial medical and nutrition program. This experience taught me how diet can improve minds as well as bodies. It is unfortunate that the well-intentioned school lunch programs subsidized by the U.S. Department of Agriculture that have since followed have turned into a dumping ground of high fat, high sodium, and low fiber foods.

▲   ▲   ▲

As a father of five and a pediatrician in private practice in Marin County, California for over thirty years, I've been in a good position to witness how the average American family's diet stacks up. There has been a major shift in our children's dietary habits.

At the turn of the century, malnutrition—the lack of certain vitamins and minerals—was a problem second only to infection in this country. The dietician or nutritionist was called upon to assist physicians in the dietary control of diseases after they had already developed to an advanced stage. Today malnutrition is more likely to be a case of *overconsumption* of certain nutrients. Too much has replaced too little: Too much fat, too much salt, too much ultra-processed food.

In the past, traditional nutritional advice was given to optimize a child's growth and development. It was believed that if the child were growing taller and maintaining appropriate weight, good nutrition was achieved. Sufficient dairy, eggs, poultry and meats were emphasized along with the American "four foods group" diet. Today, pediatricians know that nutrition goes far beyond these simplistic concepts.

Pediatricians also know that nutritional mistakes can have serious consequences for youngsters. Although the immediate causes of death in children are no longer due to lack of nutrients, between 30 and 40 percent of our children are even now developing blood vessel diseases that will slowly kill them. These vascular diseases begin with consumption of too much fat, too much salt, insufficient fiber and antioxidants.

Parents and physicians share concern over the pesticides used in growing fruits and vegetables, plus the new and old additives incorporated into our convenience foods. The attentive pediatrician considers these additives not only when giving nutritional advice, but also when analyzing a child's symptoms. For example, when we see a child with recurrent headaches, we are likely to consider what might be wrong with his diet along with other possibilities. Foods containing MSG or nitrites: hot dogs, lunchmeats, or Top Ramen soups are examples of common headache producing foods and are discussed in greater depth in the section covering foods associated with headaches.

More and more I talk to parents about their children's healthy diet—and this is good, because consumers have become much smarter than we were a generation ago about eating properly and reading food labels. But it's difficult to keep current with all the mis-information constantly being fed to us by a self-serving food industry.

Although food labels have improved, they are of limited value for understanding children's nutritional needs and at times downright confusing even to the well educated. Furthermore, new foods are regularly added to our already superfluous choices—50 percent of what we see on the shelves of our supermarkets didn't even exist twenty-five years ago. Frozen pizza and chicken nuggets, Gatorade, sports or energy bars, instant breakfasts, and of course the constant introduction of new dry cereals are all fairly new phenomena. Kids seem to prefer these foods. How do we know if they're any good or even more important, are they harmful? And what can we provide that is nutritious, easy to prepare and that the child will like? An entire section of this book, Part III, is devoted to help you make informed choices at the supermarket. Readers will find the answers to these and many other frequently asked questions about what kids should eat and don't eat.

▲ ▲ ▲

Feed Your Child Right from Birth through Teens is organized into three parts. Part I includes the nutritional needs of infants, children and ado-lescents. I discuss the nutritional needs of infants, children and adoles-cents, the real world of appetite and lack of appetite, of stubbornness and curiosity, of food habits good and bad, of food fads and fad diets. Each chapter in this section focuses on children of a certain age, and each spotlights foods of particular value enjoyed at that age. For instance, the chapter "Feeding Your Infant" explores the art and sci-ence of breastfeeding, formula selection, preparation, and feeding for infants **from birth through the twelfth month.** Regular cow milk, skim milk, evaporated milk, and goat milk are not usually recommended for children under a year old. Readers find out why in this chapter.

Chapter Two continues with "First Foods." At **four to seven months**, babies may require more calories than breast milk or formula provides, and parents may introduce semisolid foods. I suggest what's appropriate and what's not. Foods that are potential allergens are flagged, and the over and under diagnosis of wheat and milk intolerance is discussed as is the infant's special need for iron at this age. Fruits, vegetables, cereals and liquids other than milk are featured. In this chapter I show how food manufacturers subliminally suggest to parents that juices need to be introduced into an infant's diet.

The remainder of Part I covers the diets of toddlers, preschoolers, older children, and adolescents. Most children begin to eat table foods between **one and two years of age**. Picky eating may show itself, and here's when food habits—good and bad—begin to form. The folly of giving juice, crackers, raisins and grapes—"I know it's not great food, but it's better than nothing," is explored and how this is often the first step to a poor diet. Here I offer helpful suggestions gleaned from years of experience to help parents through these difficult months. Salt and sugar are featured, along with the complex carbohydrates such as potatoes, corn, wheat, grains, legumes and crucifers, some of the basic foods that should form the heart of your youngster's expanding diet. As in all the chapters, easy to prepare recipes for dishes that your whole family will enjoy are included.

The preschool child tastes independence! You may yearn for yesterday's picky eater when your child begins demonstrating rigid preferences and prejudices toward foods that some **two- to six-year-olds** do. The solutions are simple, but often not obvious.

The child is independent at this age. Parents are no longer able to control every bite the child takes and begin to worry whether he's eating enough, eating too much, or eating the right things. This chapter is big on snacks—lots of them, good ones, ones to make at home—with guaranteed-to-please recipes included. Avoid mealtime fights and stress. Mealtimes should be pleasant, and a relaxing time of day. It's a time for comparing notes with spouses and being a role model for your children. A parent's job is to buy and prepare wholesome foods. The child's job is to decide how much to eat. Don't turn into a "short-order cook" and prepare special meals for each member of the family. Learn how to smile and say, "This is what I prepared for dinner. If you don't wish to eat it now I'll save it for you in case you get hungry later." Your child won't starve if he chooses to leave the table to play, but be sure not to let him fill up on crackers, cookies, milk, juice, raisins and bananas!

School age, Preteen, and Teenagers: Your children's socialization is likely to have a profound effect on their eating habits. Your careful attention to balanced meals, nutritious snacks, conscientious shopping and all the good this has done may meet its gravest challenge during your children's school years. This chapter considers the school-agers' and teenagers' special nutritional needs, vegetarianism, the needs of children who get into sports, how menstruation affects nutritional needs, and the special nutritional requirements of pregnant teenagers. This chapter highlights the importance of snacking and debunks the concept of three square meals. If you can make nutritious breakfasts available at home, even nutritious breakfasts that can be eaten on the fly, you go a long way toward meeting the challenge. If you can offer a nutritious box of favorite snacks to your child or teenager, this will better serve him or her than the ever-present vending machine filled with high-fat granola bars, ice cream, burritos, hot dogs, chips, nachos or the highly processed salted chicken or turkey sandwich. The anything-but-nutritious lunches most school cafeterias serve provide fertile territory for those activists who read this book and wish to make constructive suggestions to those responsible for school lunch programs. My ideas for easy-to-prepare delicious and truly nutritious lunches and suppers are also featured.

▲ ▲ ▲

Part II takes a close look at the specific nutritional needs, likes and dislikes of children as they grow. I call this part "Nutrition 101." That sounds less threatening than "Biochemistry 101." "The Chemicals of Life" is a primer to help understand the basic nutritional needs of infants, children, and adolescents, and what foods will fulfill those needs. Also, I discuss foods detrimental to children's health, and how the food industry hypes its products with blatantly deceptive advertising copy and empty claims.

Part II devotes a chapter each to carbohydrates, proteins, fats, fiber, vitamins and minerals, with tables in all these categories to help the reader estimate the individual nutritional needs of infants, children, teenagers, and young adults—without being a mathematical wizard. In addition, in each of these categories I offer anecdotes and reminiscences, nutritional facts and fiction, and a cornucopia of foods high in the various nutrients but low in fat and salt. Among these are occasional child-tested delicacies—easy to prepare, nutritious, and delicious—to illustrate how good nutrition appears on the plate. Become familiar with my Children's Nutritional Pyramid. See how your choices fit your healthier way of living. Select a truly balanced diet for your child.

▲ ▲ ▲

Part III contains nutrition facts and recipes. This section is a guide on how to read the Nutrition Facts as they are on food labels, and kid-tested recipes. The recipes section is loaded with practical nutritional pearls. They include:

On-the-fly breakfast suggestions and recipes.
Nutritious snacks that can be used as a substitute for lunch or dinner.
The art of seduction: preparing meals the way children like them.
The art of compromise. (This isn't a perfect world!).
Food suggestions at the Chinese, Italian, or Mexican fast food restaurant.
Foods that should be avoided except on very special occasions.
Methods on how to modify your favorite unhealthy recipe. How to change it to a healthy one and *still* love it.

The Guide to Eating Out With Children, the Fast Food Restaurant and learning the Art of Compromise is a fitting conclusion to my book. This section is filled with suggestions on how to deal with food choices when eating outside the home. As a parent, I know it's neither fair nor wise to "outlaw" foods. That is why I have devoted an entire section to help you and your child face the world of foods outside your home.

You will find yourself returning to this book over and over again. It will help you sort through hype from mainstream food industry and health food industry. But most of all, it will help parents feed their child right.

Albert C. Goldberg, M.D.

PART I

▲ ▲ ▲

FEED YOUR CHILD RIGHT

CHAPTER ONE

FEEDING YOUR INFANT

▲ ▲ ▲

Breastfeeding provides the best nutrition for an infant, and the practice is gaining in popularity as more information reaches parents. Breast milk is truly a magic food, and your breast milk is unique to your baby. It is more variable and valuable than what is suggested in scientific tables found in standard nutrition books.

Diet affects the composition of breast milk. A vegetarian's breast milk is different in fatty acid pattern from that of a non-vegetarian. Breast milk also changes depending on the age of the baby—the breast milk produced by the mother of a preterm infant is more suited to the needs of her baby and is not the same as the milk from the mother of a full-term infant. At nine months of age the breast fed baby is receiving milk which is different from the milk received at one week and depending on what the mother eats, the milk may taste differently from day to day, compelling the infant to adapt to new tastes. This prepares your baby's palate for when you introduce semisolid foods. Milk expressed in the first few minutes of nursing, called *fore milk*, has a lower fat content than *hind* or later milk. That is one important reason why many infants need to nurse longer than a few minutes at a time. One mother may nurse briefly a few times a day and the baby rapidly gains weight while another mother may have to nurse two to three times as long and more often to provide as many calories to her infant. If your infant nurses less than the time suggested by your "how to nurse" books, and your baby is thriving, don't fret! Breast milk varies tremendously from mother to mother.

Breast milk is high in saturated fats and cholesterol and there is good reason for this. Many parents look at the listed ingredients on a can of infant formula and wonder why it contains so much saturated fat, cholesterol, and sugar, since they have been told repeatedly that fats, cholesterol, and sugar should be avoided in their diets. *Babies are different. They are not merely small adults! Babies need saturated fat, cholesterol, and sugar.* Ample amounts of these nutrients are essential in these early months because of the baby's high energy needs and rapid growth of the brain and nervous system. Infant nutrition becomes even more complicated, because the amount and types of unsaturated fat and fatty acids found in breast milk are different from what is found in other animal milks such as cow or goat milk. This is one of the reasons it is so important for parents to have some understanding of the more complex nutritional needs of children and to respect the possibility that there are probably many more nutritional unknowns to be discovered.

Most parents are not aware that infants breast fed for greater than six months may be 5 to 9 IQ points smarter than matched formula fed infants.* Certain types of fatty acids (docosahexaenoic acid or DHA and arachidonic acid or ARA) found in breast milk may have a part in this and hopefully they may soon be added to commercial formulas. There are intestinal maturing factors found only in breast milk and *colostrum*, the first milk present at birth, that protect the infant from food allergies and intestinal infections. This may be reason enough to try nursing, even if you must stop early to return to work or for other personal reasons. Keep in mind the option of using a high quality electric breast pump to prolong nursing. This will allow your baby to receive the benefits of breast milk while you are away and also give other family members added opportunities to feed and bond with the new baby.

Although breast milk contains a lot of fat, it must be absorbed by the baby to do any good. Lipase is an enzyme which digests fat; it comes primarily from the pancreas. At birth and for the first few weeks of life, pancreatic lipase is in short supply, possibly due to the immaturity of the pancreas. Pancreatic lipase can't be given by mouth

---

Lancet, 1992-339: 261-64.

to correct this deficiency because it would be destroyed by the stomach acid before reaching the intestine. Breast milk contains a lipase which resists stomach acid and which aids pancreatic lipase in the digestive process. Neither cow nor goat milk contain this unique enzyme. So it is possible that this extra lipase helps breast fed infants to absorb more fat. Another lipase, called lingual lipase, comes from the base of the infant's tongue and is produced in response to sucking. This may help to explain why babies, particularly in the first few months of life, want to continue sucking even after they have finished feeding. This *nonnutritive sucking* has been used as a rational justification for offering a pacifier to a newly born infant.*

The salt content of breast milk is only 150 mg per liter, whereas cow milk contains 500 mg per liter or over *three times as much salt*. It is unknown whether this extra salt intake from cow milk could set a baby up for high blood pressure later in life, but this remains a worrisome consideration. About 20 percent of infants are salt sensitive. This is one area of research that desperately needs to be studied by a major university, but in the meantime, with lack of scientific proof to guide us, the low salt content of breast milk should be our model. I trust nature's model better than the food industry or nutritionists who suggest salt may not be a bad addition to an infant's or child's diet!

Parents are led to believe that lots of minerals and calcium are good for young children, but cow and goat milk have a much greater mineral content than human milk, and this could harm an infant. The high calcium content in cow milk, (1200 mg vs. 300 mg in breast milk!) is too great a load on the infant's immature kidneys and should be avoided until the baby is over twelve months old. Most store-bought formulas contain about 500 mg of calcium per liter. Another reason to avoid cow milk during the first year of life is its high phosphorus content—six times that of human milk. In rare cases, such a high phosphorus content can drop calcium levels in the blood, causing newborns to have seizures.

---

*Nursery nurses promote the pacifier because it calms the hungry infant. It is used in the noble spirit of letting the tired or often exhausted mother get some needed rest. What is not appreciated is that as a consequence of this, the mother's breasts are not stimulated sufficiently, and as a result there is often a delay in milk production. The seemingly benign and benevolent act of giving the pacifier (or bottles of water) during the few days following birth is often responsible for "nursing failure." Please restrain from the temptation of using a pacifier until your milk production is enough for your infant to achieve adequate weight gain.

The iron content of breast milk may appear to be tiny at only 0.5 mg per 100 ml. However, almost 50 percent of this iron is absorbed, making it the most usable iron available. Cow milk contains nearly the same amount of iron but, by contrast, only 10 percent is absorbed. Infants who drink low iron cow milk often become iron deficient by 10 months! For this reason most cow milk formula is fortified with 10–12 mg of iron per liter. *Contrary to popular myth, this added iron will not lead to iron overload, bowel discomfort, spitting up, colic, or constipation.*

Trace elements found in breast milk are different in type and concentration compared with cow or goat milk. As an example, there is less zinc in human milk than in cow milk, but a baby can use almost 60 percent of it. The zinc present in cow milk, although higher in milligrams is only about 45 percent available for use. Adequate zinc is needed to enhance infant growth. Also, a baby who gets too little zinc may be very cranky or suffer from an eczema-like rash on hands, feet, face, and the genital region. Zinc is added to commercial formulas to correct for this deficiency.

A look at the vitamin content of breast milk and formula reveals some interesting comparisons. Both human and cow milk are rich in vitamin A and vitamin B Complex. Cow milk is low in vitamin C. For this reason, babies fed cow milk alone need supplements. Well nourished mothers produce milk sufficient in vitamin C. Cow milk has no vitamin D. Because of this, rickets was a common occurrence in the past and still is in countries where milk is not fortified with vitamin D. This vitamin is also in low supply in breast milk. Vitamin supplements may be a good idea for babies who get little sunlight.*†

Goat milk is low in folic acid (folate), and because of this infants fed only goat milk often develop a severe anemia called megaloblastic anemia. Goat milk has achieved fad status in some circles because of its supposed likeness to breast milk. Parents who are concerned about their infant's slow weight gain, irritability, or frequent infections, are tempted to try goat milk as a remedy. But for reasons pointed out above, it is better to defer offering goat milk during the first year.

---

*There is more detailed information on vitamins in Part II. Please refer to this section.

†Rickets is a disease of children, characterized by softening of the bones as a result of lack of vitamin D. Refer to Part II for more information on how sunshine helps the body manufacture vitamin D.

Another vitamin that is low in human milk but needed for blood clotting is *vitamin K. Breast fed infants are prone to a bleeding disease which in rare cases results in sometimes fatal bleeding into the brain.* Fortunately, this can be prevented by giving the infant vitamin K either by mouth or by shot. Vitamin K is now given by a nurse to almost all infants shortly after birth. Cow milk formulas are fortified with extra vitamin K so babies on formula are actually less susceptible to this disease than those who are breast fed.

Vitamin E is found in greater amounts in human milk than in cow milk. Skimmed cow milk contains no vitamin E. Infants fed only non-fat milk develop what is called *"failure to thrive,"* infections, extremely dry skin, and blood problems.

Besides the immune, growth, and brain development factors found in breast milk, I'm certain that it contains many other yet undiscovered nutritional factors that nature created during our evolution. I strongly suggest that mothers continue to nurse for at least six months whenever possible, or better yet, up to one year.

It is the art of nursing rather than the chemistry of breast milk that is of importance right away to a new mother. The nurturing aspect of nursing has a potent emotional effect upon the bond between infant and mother. Unfortunately, there are a lot of worries around breast feeding, and many myths exist. Therefore, the aid of a well-trained helper is the most important first step in nursing. Beware of the helper who suggests pacifiers, sugar water or putting the infant on an "every 2 to 3 hour schedule" during the first week of life. *This advice usually leads to insufficient sucking, which in turn leads to a delay in milk production, and in turn leads to a frustrated exhausted mother who turns to a formula.* At that moment the infant gobbles down the formula and the mother concludes that the infant has chosen not to nurse. Often, the physician agrees and thus pays only lip service to nursing. There are now a group of specialist nurses, *lactation consultants,** who truly understand the art and science of nursing, and I recommend that one be consulted on the day of your infant's birth. Different opinions and techniques can be very confusing to the new mother. A breast-feeding specialist, along with your pediatrician, can help you establish a plan for the early weeks of nursing that is specific to your baby's needs and nursing style.

---

* Ideally an I.B.C.L.C. (International Board Certified Lactation Consultant).

PRACTICAL NOTES ON THE PREPARATION OF INFANT FORMULAS

Infant formulas are available in three forms. The ready-to-use form is believed by many pediatricians to be the easiest and most convenient to use, but is also the most expensive. Always wash your hands before preparing a bottle. Rinse and dry the top of the formula can before you open it. After pouring the prepared formula into the infant's bottle, place the can in the refrigerator with a foil top or plastic cap to cover the opening. The next time you use this container, the formula will be very cold. To bring this cold formula bottle to room temperature, it needs warming* in a water bath. This is time consuming and appears to me to negate the original selling point.

Concentrated liquid formulas are prepared by mixing the concentrate with an equal amount of clean warm tap water. The warm water plus the cold formula concentrate produces the ideal room temperature bottle. It is usually unnecessary to boil the tap water. Discuss this point with your pediatrician, because he is most acquainted with the safety of your water supply. Prepare only one bottle at a time and use it immediately. Discard what the infant does not finish. Do not save partially consumed bottles for more than an hour.

My favorite, and the least expensive infant formula is a powdered formula. All you need to do is put a scoop (a tablespoon) of powdered formula into two ounces of clean warm tap water (or 2 scoops/4 oz. of water): shake and serve! If you wish to bring a bottle along on a short or long trip, a prepared bottle will "go bad" if it is unrefrigerated. Powdered formula is ideal for travel because no refrigeration is needed nor is there a problem with spillage. Bring along two bottles: in one bottle put the usual needed amount of powdered formula. In another bottle put the measured water. Combine the two just before serving. What could be easier or safer?

---

*Do not warm bottles in the microwave. Warming of the bottle's contents is uneven and the formula continues to cook for about a minute after removing the bottle from the microwave. An infant's tongue and mouth could easily be scalded by a bottle heated this way.

Formulas should be reserved for those who truly can't nurse or for those who choose not to nurse only after being taught about the nutritional advantages of breast milk. The final decision for or against breast-feeding should rest with the mother. In the meantime, don't think breast feeding is another fad. It has been tested for thousands of years and has followed the evolution of our species.

When a mother doesn't want to breastfeed—or can't—the second choice is a store bought formula of cow milk base, or sometimes a soy formula. Ideally, your baby's doctor should prescribe the specific formula, technique of preparation, and appropriate schedule for bottle feeding. These directions should be based on your baby's own nutritional and digestive needs.

Formula hasn't always been a risk-free second choice. By ignoring the composition of breast milk as a model, company nutritionists created formulations that sickened some infants. The lesson: in determining infant formula's nutritional specifications, a formula should match as closely as possible the functional composition of human breast milk. The dictum *eat a variety of foods* to protect against nutritional unknowns, does not hold for the infant who relies solely upon a single food (formula). There is no room for error when our children are the experimental creatures. Your pediatrician needs to be especially knowledgeable about formulas and not consider them all to be alike. The American Academy of Pediatrics and the FDA are constantly examining the make up of breast milk in order to make recommendations for reformulating commercial formulas. The Infant Formula Act of 1980 (revised in 1986) directs the FDA to ensure the safety and nutritional quality of infant formulas.

Here are a few more bottle feeding tips:

▲ Select a nipple that is available in most drug stores. Infants become attached to the nipple they are started on and often refuse to use another type. I can recall horror stories from parents who were up all night going from one pharmacy to another searching for the only type nipple their infant would take.

▲ The plastic bag type bottles, such as Playtex, do not prevent air swallowing. Infants swallow air regardless of the bottle type and this is normal. Colic or gassiness is not prevented by this type of bottle.

▲   Bottles do not need to be boiled or sterilized. They can be cycled through the dishwasher or washed and rinsed well by hand using a bottle brush. Extra rinsing is important in order to remove all residual detergent.

▲   Boiling nipples will destroy them. Wash them thoroughly by hand with soap and water and allow the nipples to air dry in a cup or bowl.

▲   Both glass or plastic bottles are okay, but I prefer the plastic ones since they won't break when the baby throws one across the room.

The Art of Breastfeeding

IN THE BEGINNING

The first milk is *colostrum*, which is present at birth. It is small in quantity, but rich in calories, which protects the infant from low blood sugar and jaundice. Colostrum is rich in immune substances that protect the infant from some infections. Many of these immune factors continue to be passed on to the baby as long as you nurse. This does not mean that the breast fed baby will never catch a cold. Any cold the mother does catch is one for which the baby probably has no immunity as it takes about two weeks for antibodies to be produced by the mother. Infants are still susceptible to infections whether breast fed or not, particularly at six months of age and beyond. This is when most of the antibodies that entered the baby through the placenta are used up. Unfortunately, six months is a time when many mothers elect to stop nursing. At a year of age the baby's own antibodies have begun to reach protective levels, but resistance to infection does not dramatically improve until after four years of age.

The first twenty-four hours of the baby's birth is getting acquaint-ed time and is different from all other days, not only for you, but for the baby as well. *The first one to two hours* the baby will be more alert than you might expect, looking at you with searching eyes. Enjoy these moments. Yes, *the baby does see*, even in color, contrary to what you might have heard. Many infants want to nurse immediately—let the baby try. Other infants prefer to cuddle and get acquainted. Some mothers say they instantly fell in love with their baby, while others bond more slowly over the following year. Both reactions are normal. *A few hours after birth, infants often go into a deep sleep* and are not interested in nursing for a few hours. When the baby shows interest in breastfeeding—by making mouthing or sucking motions, *don't use a pacifier, use your breasts!* I have nothing against pacifiers, but I do not believe they should be used the first few weeks because many mothers may miss feeding cues and use a pacifier instead of breastfeeding. This practice often leads to a slow weight gaining baby. Sore breasts are not necessarily caused from prolonged breastfeeding, but are usually caused by not placing the infant properly on the breast. A knowledgeable nurse or doctor should assist you. *The cradle position is usually the most comfortable and best, to avoid soreness during the first week.* This position is also comfortable for the postcesarean-section birth. Cesarean incisions are very low, which makes the cradle position a good choice.

Let the baby breastfeed anytime the infant cries during the first few days—you cannot "spoil" your baby. *Some babies enjoy nursing every fifteen to thirty minutes during "awake periods."* Most would rather breastfeed every one to three hours during the first ten days. *As long as your breasts are not tender, the length of time you breastfeed is best decided upon by you and your baby.* The first week, breastfeed on one breast until the infant stops sucking or falls asleep. Do not interrupt the baby's sucking rhythm. If you interrupt a good feeding in order to place the baby on the other breast, the infant usually falls asleep during the transfer and it is extremely frustrating to the mother to try to get a sleepy infant to latch on again. Later, after your milk arrives to replace the colostrum on the third or fourth day, nurse both breasts during a feeding if possible.

Much is made of burping a baby because most nurses and doctors have been trained to care for the bottle-fed infant. Breast fed infants seldom need much burping the first three to four days. *Fifteen to thirty seconds is usually more than enough time and the infant does not need to make that "burp" sound.* It is common for infants to spit up mucous or vomit the first two days. Although this is scary for the parents, it is normal as long as the vomiting does not persist. It has little to do with the burping ritual.

Your regular milk comes in on about the third or fourth day after birth, if the baby is encouraged to nurse eight to twelve times a day. In general, the more your infant suckles, the more milk you produce. For this reason, avoid bottles of water unless absolutely necessary. Babies are born puffy or water-logged and usually have enough tissue water to fulfill the infant's needs for the first three days. Studies have shown that jaundice is not prevented in full term babies by giving extra water. Quite the opposite, there is usually less jaundice in the baby who breastfeeds and is not supplemented with water.* Babies who get water bottles the first few days are also more, not less, likely to become dehydrated between days five and six. That is because these infants aren't on the breast often enough and as a result the arrival of mother's milk is delayed. This is a common problem now that mothers and babies are discharged from the hospital within 24 hours after birth. A knowledgeable visiting home nurse is especially important when a breastfeeding mom goes home early, but many of the home care nurses are only well-trained to evaluate the mother's postpartum condition, and are not lactation specialists. Have your pediatrician help you find and make arrangements with a certified lactation specialist to come to the hospital or your home by day two.

If your baby is premature or has a special problem, these generalizations may not hold. The above information is for the healthy full-term newborn.

Keep this rule of thumb in mind. A crying baby should be treated as a hungry baby during the first seven days after birth. *Even if the infant just nursed ten minutes before, nurse again, and if the crying persists, nurse again!*

The above rule is for the first week. After two weeks of age, a baby who is gaining weight well may have many other reasons for fussiness. When the infant is over two weeks old, first try rocking, holding and talking to soothe the infant, especially if he or she was fed in the past hour.

Here are a few hints to prevent tender breasts:

---

*Yellowness of the skin and/or the whites of the eyes.

▲   Use a hair dryer to blow dry your breast for about 20-30 seconds after each breastfeeding. This is very soothing and helps healing or tender breasts.

▲   Be sure the infant takes more than the tip of the nipple into its mouth. Remove the infant from the breast by first breaking the suction with your finger.

▲   Correct position is critical. Call a lactation specialist immediately if you even think you might be having any breastfeeding problem. Do not delay. Small problems are easier to solve than big ones.

▲   Don't allow yourself to become frustrated. Some infants are not very interested in breastfeeding the first twenty-four to thirty-six hours.

▲   Fatigue and poor nutrition are enemies to good breastfeeding. Rest and good eating are essential. This is not the time to go on a crash diet. *A new mom needs a helper*—she doesn't need a nurse! If your budget can afford it, hire a helper. The helper should take care of running the home, the cleaning, shopping, preparing food, laundry, and giving that two-year-old sibling some special attention. If grandma is not an option, enlist a relative or close friend to help. The feeling of isolation and facing the responsibility of running a household in addition to caring for an infant is often overwhelming and has a profoundly negative effect upon successful breastfeeding.

▲   A nipple shield (Madela brand) may be needed for inverted nipples, as well as a high quality electric breast pump. Consult a lactation specialist at least one month before the delivery of your baby if you have inverted nipples or if you are not certain. There are many things that can be done early to keep this from becoming a problem. The lactation specialist has devices that can be worn under the bra and over the nipple, during the month prior to delivery. She will let you know, after examining your breasts, if you need them.

Pediatricians are often nonscientific in the manner in which they first select and later switch formulas. Since many infants are irritable or colicky beginning at two weeks of age through three-and-a-half months of life, a ritual of formula changing usually begins when the baby is about ten days old. By that time the desperate calls begin with predictable regularity. Instead of carefully explaining the causes of *colic*,* the physician often elects to take the shortcut and *changes the formula*. This usually keeps the telephone quiet for another two or three days!

What happened to me when I cared for my oldest daughter is typical. At the time I was in my third year of medical school and I was about to learn my first practical lesson in pediatrics. She was breast-fed for four to six weeks. In those years most infants were bottle fed. If the mother breastfed, it was rare to continue beyond three months. My daughter was a skinny and irritable infant. Her knees were always red because they were in constant motion. She cried often, starting at ten days of age, and with such persistence, at first in the middle of the night, and later beginning at 4 or 5 P.M., that we were asked to move from our apartment because the neighbors couldn't stand the noise!

Even hours after breastfeeding or taking her formula, she would spit up. Our pediatrician suggested that my wife stop eating dairy, chocolate, "gassy vegetables" and spicy foods. For a couple of days we thought our daughter was improving, but by the weekend she was back at it. Like clockwork, as soon as I came home at around 5 P.M. she started crying and fussing until after midnight. We were then instructed to try a formula. But our daughter continued to draw up her legs, turn red and cry, pass gas, and cry again. Next a soy formula was suggested. "This may be easier to digest," he explained. The colic continued. Another brand of soy formula was then recommended with

---

*Nobody has yet determined, with certainty, the cause of colic. This periodic fussiness appears at about two weeks of age and often persists to three and one half months. Colic peaks around six weeks of age and then gradually becomes less intense. Most infants have a daily "fussy" period between 5 P.M. and 11 P.M. During this time the infant cries, turns red in the face, draws up his or her legs, passes gas, and appears to be in pain. The source of the pain is unclear, but most parents believe the pain arises in the gastrointestinal tract and therefore call it a bellyache or think it is constipation. For this reason parents blame the pain on diet, if it is a breast-fed baby, or the formula, in formula fed infants. There is little proof that milk formula, with or without iron, is the culprit. Nevertheless changing formulas is the traditional advice, if for no other reason than to "buy

similar disappointment. Maybe she's constipated, I reasoned. The elderly lady down the hall suggested a "suppository" or inserting the "end of a thermometer." We were willing to try almost anything and did this unhealthy maneuver for a few days. At first I thought we were on to a cure, but it soon became clear that the relief was not long lasting. "Perhaps the baby can't handle the iron in the formula," was the next week's telephoned advice. I later learned there was about as much iron in the soy formula he recommended as was in the last formula. The spitting and crying persisted after what I thought might have been a one or two day reprieve. The next suggestion seemed to help the most. Our doctor showed us how to swaddle her, and this did have some calming effect. He also suggested that we have her sleep in her infant seat to prevent reflux, and prescribed an antacid and anti-gas drops. In those days gasoline was cheap, so I would buckle her in her car seat and drive around the block for an hour. This motion had a calming effect. I promised the landlady I'd do this nightly, but she still asked us to leave our second apartment. We had three different apartments that first year of our daughter's life.

With all the scientific progress we have made over the past decade, no treatment surpasses holding and walking a colicky infant. There is little evidence that changing formulas or putting a nursing mother on a dairy-free, non-gassy, or non-spicy food diet helps colic, but such advice continues to be freely prescribed.

WEANING THE BABY

When you are ready to wean your baby, try the following method to make the change painless for you both. It takes about two weeks to complete the weaning process. For ten days to two weeks before you

---

time" until the infant is over three months old. Then miraculously the baby is able to tolerate breast milk even if the mother eat beans, cabbage, or drinks cow milk. The formula-fed infant now tolerates formulas that were stopped earlier. The scientific community doubts that allergy to milk or lactose intolerance is the cause of this periodic fussiness or "colic." Nothing better than walking your infant during these hours has been invented, but swings, music, vibrating beds, and other devices have been helpful. Many medicines have been tried. Sometimes they seem to work, but the placebo effect may be the cause of temporary improvement. There are a host of other things that can be done to help parents through this stressful period. Be sure to let your pediatrician know if your child has symptoms of colic.

INFANT

plan to stop breastfeeding, breastfeed your baby only when your breasts feel uncomfortably full. Then let the baby nurse for *no more than forty-five seconds on each breast.* This should relieve your breasts' uncomfortable feeling of fullness. Then immediately offer the infant a bottle or cup of formula. If your baby is over a year old, offer whole milk. Whenever your breasts need relief, let the baby nurse forty-five seconds or *less*, and once again offer cup or bottle as before. Continue this for a couple of days and soon you'll feel little discomfort during the usual feeding times as your breasts produce less and less milk. Over the following days continue to breastfeed briefly, but stop as soon as your breasts feel comfortable. This will now take much less than forty-five seconds. All other times, when your baby is hungry, feed the baby with a cup or bottle. If you were in the habit of breast-feeding the baby before bedtime, hold the baby in your arms and offer a cup or bottle instead. You should continue this closeness and nurturing attention during these feedings. When you no longer feel discomfort during the day, consider the baby weaned.*

If you wish to keep breastfeeding before work, after work, or weekends, because you enjoy the closeness and comfort of nursing, do so. Your infant will come to rely more and more on formula or milk for his or her nutritional needs. Like before, your baby will decide how much milk is needed. In some cases, a parent may need to limit milk or formula if a baby is gaining weight too fast, but check with your pediatrician or health care provider before cutting back.

When the baby is twelve months old gradually change the baby's formula to whole milk. Doing this abruptly may lead to constipation. Instead, offer the baby a bottle of half formula and half whole milk for about a week. Gradually add more whole milk and less formula to the bottle until the bottle contains only pasteurized whole vitamin D milk. If the baby was on a special formula before, such as soy formula, follow the same instructions as above. Most infants will tolerate this change to whole milk without incident, but first discuss with your own pediatrician about how best to make the change.

---

*There are many other methods of weaning, depending on age, and culture, to a bottle or cup. *The Nursing Mother's Guide to Weaning* by Kathleen Huggins, R.N.,M.S. & Linda Ziedrich. The Harvard Common Press, Boston, Mass. is an in-depth, easy to read guide.

CHAPTER TWO

FIRST FOODS

▲ ▲ ▲

At four to seven months, the baby may require more calories than breastfeeding provides, and you may decide to introduce *semisolid* foods. The bottle fed baby may also be interested in exploring different tastes and textures. Feeding the infant may also afford the father a chance to bond or fall in love with his baby.* Many people believe that introducing semisolid food at two to three months, especially at the last feeding of the evening, will cause an infant to sleep through the night. After all, it seems logical that the increase in calories will keep the baby full longer. Unfortunately, armchair reasoning has to give way to careful studies which show that semisolid foods in the diet have little or no effect on the age at which an infant begins to sleep through the night.

Because the rapidly growing infant needs iron to build muscle and red blood cells, *I recommend an iron-fortified cereal* such as baby rice and oatmeal cereal. I usually recommend these two because I've never encountered any allergic reaction from either of them in over thirty years of pediatric practice. On a practical level, these commercially available dry cereals are a convenient way to get your baby used to taking semisolid foods by spoon. Infants fed iron-fortified com-

---

*This should not be interpreted to mean that fathers need to feed their baby to fall in love with them. We know that many fathers fall in love with their baby without ever feeding them.

mercial formula usually get sufficient iron from this source; however, iron rich foods are needed the first year and beyond to fulfill the needs of a rapidly growing infant.

Because eating habits begin early, I strongly encourage parents to introduce nutritionally important foods early. Don't be afraid to introduce other cereals, such as barley, rye, and wheat but mixed high-protein cereals should be reserved for last. Avoid putting cereal or foods in a bottle as it delays a baby's adjustment to textures. Some parents do this and go on with chores. Instead, *hold or attend* your infant during feedings. Your baby needs this attention and social contact. After all, feeding an infant is more than nutrition. If you are too busy to feed semisolid food to your infant, delay that part of the feeding until you have time *to relax and nurture* him. Enjoy him/her during this special period in his life.

Experiment with textures, first by adding breast milk or formula to the dry cereal to make a thin gruel and then gradually make it thicker if the infant tolerates it without gagging. I'm not aware of any scientific studies that examine the long term consequences of early versus later exposure to different tastes or textures. One good reason for starting semisolids in the first place, is to give the non-breast-fed baby a variety of foods as a safeguard against the nutritional unknowns.*

Many parents want to know exactly how many teaspoons of food to give their child and wonder how to tell whether the baby is getting enough or too much. The answers you will find in most baby books is intentionally vague. That is because babies vary so much in their specific needs. All those charts and calorie formulas are guidelines that are seldom necessary to use. Look at your child. Is he or she too thin? Then offer more food or increase the frequency of feedings. Too plump? Then decrease amounts a little. If you are uncertain, the safest thing is to discuss this important issue with your pediatrician or health provider during a "well child" checkup where the baby can be observed in person.

---

*The maxim "Eat a variety of foods" is difficult to follow if your only food source is breast milk. Fortunately, breast milk is a near perfect food for infants. If an infant's total diet is commercial formula, a vital nutrient may be missing. So until we learn a lot more about how to make a perfect formula, it may be wise to add a variety of semisolid foods to an infant's diet beginning at four to nine months of age.

Be selective in choosing your cereals. In the 1970s, natural cereals and granola swept the nation. Seeds, nuts, and dried fruits were all the rage. A Swiss product called Familia gained favor as an introductory cereal because it contained natural ingredients. It had all those seeds and nuts, but they were finely ground and thus seemed suitable for babies. Many nutritionists made it their first choice. Poor babies. What followed was a small epidemic of rashes and eczema among infants who ate Familia. Allergists (and most pediatricians) could have warned those nutritionists that *seeds and nuts are potent allergens, especially so in infants* under a year old.

A Word About Food Allergies

Several years ago, I saw a baby who had been fed peanut butter as one of her initial foods. She came to me with eyelids and face swollen and covered with hives. She survived, but she may be dangerously allergic to any food that contains peanuts for the rest of her life. More on peanut butter later.

Other foods associated with allergy in infancy are *strawberries, raspberries, fish, shell fish, lobster, shrimp, crab, cinnamon, almonds, walnuts, and eggs* (both egg white and egg yolk should be avoided by infants until over one year). This is one of those revised recommendations. Nutritionists formerly recommended egg yolk because it is rich in iron. What they didn't realize was that iron phosphate, the particular kind of iron found in egg yolk, is absorbed poorly.

For infants with a strong family history of allergies, introduction of all the foods mentioned above should be delayed even longer. Discuss this with your pediatrician before introducing these foods.

Another food to be avoided until the baby is over a year old (although not an allergen) is *honey, as it has been linked to infant botulism.* Botulism causes muscle weakness in infancy, often beginning with facial weakness, droopy eyelids, or the loss of ability to sit. Constipation is another early sign of infant botulism. If not treated early it can cause paralysis of the muscles needed for breathing. Although this is a rare condition, should you ever suspect it in your infant, call your physician immediately and tell him or her of your concern.

Wheat and Milk Intolerance

In the 1960s, when an infant had persistent diarrhea, a popular diagnosis was celiac disease or gluten-induced intolerance. The baby was immediately taken off any wheat products (and foods containing *gliadin*—the protein found in wheat, rye, oats, barley, and buckwheat which is responsible for this illness). In fact, celiac disease is a somewhat rare illness. Now we know that certain viruses can cause prolonged diarrhea, and the parasitic infection *giardiasis* mimics many of the symptoms of celiac disease, with foul-smelling bowel movements, gas, and abdominal pain. Most of those infants in the '60s weren't wheat or gluten intolerant at all. They were temporarily intolerant to wheat, milk, and juice as a result of an intestinal infection. The key word is *temporary*. Today milk sugar and protein intolerance are diagnosed as promiscuously as wheat intolerance used to be. Milk sugar (lactose) intolerance in infancy is highly unusual except briefly after a viral diarrhea. Nevertheless many babies are unnecessarily taken off milk formula and put on a soy formula for their entire first year. It appears that parents, grandparents, and some physicians blame milk or teething for any unexplained crankiness or fever in infancy.

Traditional advice is to introduce a new food and then wait three to seven days before introducing another. The theory is that any allergic reaction will show up during that interval, and the offending food could be identified and eliminated. In all my many years of private practice, I have not found this advice to be of any practical help as long as you avoid the highly allergenic foods, such as peanut butter, nuts, seeds, chocolate, cinnamon, eggs, berries, lobster, crab, shrimp, and shell fish. Infants tolerate most other foods extremely well.

About Fruits and Vegetables

Another common recommendation is to start fruits before vegetables. There is little scientific information to support which order is best. Pediatricians do almost as well as grandmothers when it comes to choosing first foods. Almost all schedules are speculative, intuitive or anecdotal.

Apples and pears are popular fruits, and most babies tolerate

INFANT

them quite well. Cooked carrots, squash, yams, and potato are foods I personally recommend to my patients. If these are tolerated I suggest adding peas, strained spinach, beets, beans, broccoli, and brussels sprouts. However, I'm not dogmatic about the order in which foods are introduced. The choice is yours. That's part of the fun of being a parent.

I have more concern about the practice of adding a little salt or sugar to the baby's food, whether done by the commercial baby food company or the parent:* In Europe, Asia, Central and South America, parents introduce soups at an early age. They put all these vegetables in a broth and mash or blend it into a soup. Infants usually love this and as the baby matures, the soup takes on a more lumpy, stew-like texture. This is a major problem because *these soups too often contain added salt plus the amount in the broth.* To avoid this, use a non-salt broth and forget the pinch of salt that makes it tasty to your palate! Experiment with textures. Babies without teeth may gum lumpy food easily, while some infants with teeth may gag on the same foods. As the baby matures, more and more textures will be tolerated until "grown-up" food cut in small pieces will be eaten exclusively.

When foods aren't pureed, you may notice partially digested material in the bowel movement. This is especially true for corn or raisins and is quite normal. Stool color also changes with different foods. Don't be alarmed if the bowel movement is green. The only colors of concern in bowel movements are red, jet black, or cream-clay. Red and black may suggest bowel bleeding, while the clay color may be associated with a liver problem. However, colors often reflect the color of the foods eaten such as beets, peas, or spinach. Spinach, by the way, is an excellent natural laxative for infants as well as adults—it's not, however, the fabulous source of iron it's reputed to be. The baby doesn't absorb the iron in spinach as well as in many other iron-rich foods.

Protein and Your Infant

Today, health conscious parents, who know that meat, fish or chicken are good sources of protein, wonder if they shouldn't be providing those foods to their baby. They often think of milk as a calcium

*Hypertension, 1997;29:913-917,930-936 Dietary Nutrients Early In Life Influence Later Blood Pressure.

food and forget that it is also very rich in protein. In fact, a thirteen-pound infant requires only 12–13 grams of protein daily, which is easily provided by nursing or feeding three 8 oz. bottles of formula a day. The reason for suggesting the introduction of the above foods is not necessarily because of their protein content, but because they are an excellent source of the much needed mineral iron. The fatty acids ARA and DHA (see "Nutrition 101" for more in-depth details) are also found in fish and are important in eye and brain development. My mother used to tell me that fish was a "brain food" and encouraged me to eat it as a young child. Now it appears that she may have been correct. But remember, fish is a potent allergen, so wait until your baby is over one year old before introducing it. Before then, a nursing mother who consumes more fish will increase the ARA and DHA content of the breast milk.

After one year of age, when the baby switches to cow milk, more protein will be provided than mother's milk or formula. In fact, three 8 oz. cups or bottles of cow milk a day contain enough protein for infants up to 30 pounds. So there's really no need to worry about insufficient protein. Because cow milk is iron-poor, it's important to introduce iron-rich foods, as explained earlier, and to make vegetables a significant part of the daily diet. *I don't recommend* ham, bacon, sausage, hot dogs, or lunch meats because of their high salt and fat content. There are better choices to obtain important nutrients than from these "holiday foods." *Partially cooked meats are dangerous* because thorough cooking is needed to kill contaminating bacteria or parasites that can cause deadly diarrhea by E. coli, salmonella-shigella, and campylobacter, as well as the diseases toxoplasmosis, trichinosis or tapeworms.

Some nutritionists recommend beef or chicken liver as a good source of iron and vitamins. It is true that liver contains many important nutrients, but I no longer recommend liver as a nutritional source. As a detoxifying organ the liver may contain a high concentration of all sorts of environmental poisons. There are safer ways to obtain these nutrients. I don't feel good about feeding liver to infants or children, and that includes the popular liverwurst sandwich.

OTHER CAUTIONARY NOTES

Plain pasteurized *yogurt and cottage cheese are fine foods, but since your less than one-year-old infant is already consuming a lot of milk, he or she doesn't need either from a nutritional standpoint. Concentrating on vegetables is preferable and healthier.*

Do not give your baby raw carrots, popcorn, peanuts, grapes, or other similarly hard to chew foods. I don't recommend popcorn or peanuts until the child is four years old or older. An infant can choke to death on a grape, or inhale a tiny bit of food into the lungs and end up with pneumonia. The hot dog remains the most common cause of choking death.

I've heard of letting a baby teethe on a cold carrot, but the carrot won't dissolve in the throat if the infant is choking on it. A piece of zwieback or unsalted rice cake is preferable for teething foods. Teething rings are of little value and sales are aimed mostly to keep anxious parents occupied.

Some parents let infants eat crackers as finger foods. This is okay as long as you check the contents for salt and fat. Graham crackers are high in sugar or honey. It sticks to the older child's teeth and contributes to early cavities. Many commercial crackers contain 40 percent of their calories from fat and are loaded with salt. Although I'm not worried about the fat content during infancy, this is when habits begin. It has been demonstrated that a low-salt diet in infancy protects against the development of high blood pressure later in life.* High blood pressure later in life may well be the price we pay for too much salt in childhood.

---

*Hypertension, 1997; "Dietary Nutrients Early In Life Influence Later Blood Pressure." This study warns us that a high sodium diet "in utero (during pregnancy) and in infancy may be more important in relation to cardio-vascular disease than exposures in adulthood, as 'programming' of different systems and organs in the body occurs very early in life."

Food Notes on Liquids Other Than Milk

It's nutritionally more sound to give the baby water than juice.* If you choose to give juice, be certain that it is pasteurized if not fresh, and limit it to once a day only. If your baby totes a bottle around all day for security, do not put diluted juice in it. *Use pure water.* Tap water is fine. If your water is not fluoridated and you don't use a fluoride supplement, bottled fluoridated water is a good option. It is healthier and won't destroy the infant's teeth or appetite for healthier foods.

I've seen many two-year-olds whose teeth were nearly rotted away from the ever-present bottle of diluted apple juice. And premature loss of primary teeth can lead to damage in the permanent teeth. Because milk sugar (lactose) promotes cavities, rotting teeth is seen in nursing babies over a year of age when the mother uses her breasts as a pacifier.

Orange and other citrus juices can cause a contact rash around the mouth. The fresher the juice, the more *peel oil* is present in the juice. It is the peel oils that cause the irritation to the skin around the mouth, not citric acid. *This is not allergy.* Tomato sauce also contains a lot of peel oil, and also may cause skin irritation. If you wash the infant's face immediately after feeding foods with high peel oil content, these rashes may be avoided or decreased. Peel oil concentrations are controlled in the commercial production of all juices. Today formulas are fortified with vitamin C, and many non-citrus juices are too. Breast milk contains sufficient vitamin C to protect your infant from scurvy.

In the early 1970s, I had an epidemic of yellow-orange babies in my practice. It wasn't jaundice—the whites of their eyes were clear, and the babies were vigorous—it was too much beta-carotene from carrot juice. Once they drank less carrot juice, the color disappeared. The color does not harm the baby. The real problem with carrot juice is that an important nutrient, fiber, is discarded during processing. Health conscious parents often try to avoid processed foods, and inadvertently do the processing themselves. There are now juicers

*Although 70 percent of parents with infants six months and under say they give juice to their babies, there is no nutritional need for it. Fruit juice lacks the protein, fat, calories, calcium, vitamin D, iron, and zinc needed to support normal development in infancy and childhood. The vitamin C in fruit itself is a more nutritious source than juice, and mother's milk has plenty of vitamin C as well. Infant formulas are fortified with vitamin C.

available that retain the fiber and those are the preferred types.

Prune juice is well tolerated by most infants and toddlers and is high in iron, but I haven't found it to be especially effective for constipation. Prunes or plums seem to have better results as natural laxatives for infants and children. If you prepare your own, look for prunes (at most health food stores) that don't contain sulfur as a preservative.* If your child needs a natural laxative, figs, brown rice, spinach, and peas are excellent additional helpers.

Cola drinks, diet soda, Kool Aid, Hi-C, Gatorade, sports drinks, and punch have no place in an infant's diet. Carbonated beverages do not "settle" an upset stomach, and Gatorade is not good for an infant with diarrhea. Sodas contain lots of phosphate, a compound that promotes calcium loss. This is hardly a time in an infant's development when that should happen.

Don't feed non-pasteurized eggnog or raw egg, honey, and banana blended as a milkshake—an "old wives" solution for putting weight on infants. Raw eggs often contain the salmonella germ and are also very allergenic. Raw egg poses far more danger to the infant than low weight.

It's fine to give traditional breakfast foods for dinner and the vegetables, meat, and potatoes for breakfast. Most arrangements are cultural. Many Asian babies eat fish and rice for breakfast. The main meal in South and Central America is lunch. Furthermore, foods can be given more than once a day. In fact, many infants go on jags—preferring a particular food for days or weeks, then suddenly reject the food entirely and demand something they wouldn't touch the week before. Don't let such temperamental tastes discourage you from reintroducing a rejected food on another day.

Commercially prepared baby foods are now being promoted as first-step and second-step foods. The latter is often referred to as junior foods. The difference between these foods is texture, not nutritional value. They are designed to help the infant achieve a smooth transition to table foods. Generally second step foods are started at about seven to eight months of age; however, the age at which infants accept the more coarse texture is highly variable. Some children resist these lumpy foods until the end of the first year or even later. Do not feel that you must switch from strained foods.

---

*Sulfites can cause minor and sometimes severe allergic reactions.

You and your infant will decide how much of each food is appropriate. Don't force a baby to finish the jar or an arbitrary portion you've prepared. As a new father, I remember the games I made up to get that last teaspoon of food into my daughter's mouth. "Here comes the airplane into the hanger!" And just as I was congratulating myself on my slick maneuver, she'd gag and throw up the entire meal.

Salt: Is it Truly the White Death?

Salt, or sodium chloride, is one of our oldest food preservatives, used in commercially prepared foods as an inexpensive way to inhibit molds, retard spoilage, and provide smooth texture and quick-cooking properties. It's also a necessary mineral in our diet. On food labels, the words *sodium*, *soda*, or the chemical symbol for sodium, *Na.*, all signify salt. An infant's preference for salt does not emerge until four months, but how much is innate and how much is learned remains uncertain—quite unlike our taste for sugar, which we seem to be born with.

*Too much salt in childhood is an extreme dietary hazard, and has been linked to the development of hypertension (high blood pressure) in teenagers and adults.** A high salt diet beginning in infancy is a major cause of high blood pressure in adulthood. In a Dutch study, newborns who were fed, in addition to breast milk, formula and foods providing 22 mg of sodium a day had lower blood pressures than those fed diets with 58 mg a day. Fifteen years after the study ended, the difference in blood pressure was still there.†

While high blood pressure seems to run in some families, lots of salt helps encourage this undesirable family trait. Whether or not

---

*In the past few years there have been a few studies, mostly subsidized by the food industry, claiming that the effect of sodium as a cause of high blood pressure has been greatly exaggerated. The researchers are from reputable universities, but these seriously flawed studies have been very short term. Totally ignored in these studies are infants, children and young adults. Newspapers, magazines and "health journals" have been publishing outrageous distortions under headlines suggesting salt should be used more liberally and that our prior understanding of salt or sodium is now obsolete dogma. No wonder most people are confused when presented with such disinformation. Chefs from major restaurants are already featuring dishes enhanced with flavors from exotic "healthy" salts.

†*Journal of Hypertension,* 14 (suppl.): S210, 1996.

there is any history of high blood pressure or stroke in your family, I recommend you limit your child's salt intake—and your own.*

The amount of salt in a diet should approximate a ratio of salt in milligrams (mg) to the number of calories in your diet. Therefore, a 700-calorie diet should have salt limited to about 700 mg of sodium, while a 2000-calorie diet should limit salt intake to 2000 mg or two grams.† Avoid foods with more than 350 mg of sodium per serving. The right amount of salt needed by children through adulthood can be found *naturally* in fresh vegetables, grains, meats, poultry, and fish. But in fact, many children consume over 5000 mg of salt daily while adults often consume from 10,000–12,000 mg *daily* between what's natural in the food, what the food industry has added to the food, and what we add ourselves from the salt shaker in the kitchen and at the table!

When selecting a food, note the amount of calories. Then check the label for sodium content.‡ If the sodium content in milligrams is far above the number of calories, search the shelves for a brand that contains less salt. There are many canned soups available now that have a reduced or low salt counterpart. Bread and cheese are very high salt foods. Check the labels—you'll be surprised. Take time out one day to calculate how much salt you actually consume in a day. The figure may be shocking!

For most Americans, 10 percent of the sodium in their diet occurs naturally in food, 15 percent comes from the salt they shake on while cooking or at the table, and 75 percent is added to food during processing. A bowl of canned chicken noodle soup can deliver 900 mg of

---

*High blood pressure is a serious matter. What a child eats sets the stage for high blood pressure later in life. It can eventually lead to *heart failure*, a condition where the heart gets larger and weaker and is less able to pump blood. High blood pressure can also lead to *aneurysms*. Aneurysms are small blisterlike areas in the blood vessels of the brain which can burst, causing death or permanent disability. Kidney failure is another result of high blood pressure. As blood vessels in the kidney narrow, they are less able to supply the kidney with blood. This could lead to permanent kidney damage. High blood pressure also speeds the hardening of arteries. Healthy arteries are elastic. When the arteries to the brain, heart and other organs become less elastic or hard, they are less able to carry blood and the result is early aging or premature death of those organs.
†One half-teaspoon of salt equals 2000 milligrams or two grams.
‡A cup of cottage cheese, a small bag of pretzels, and a salad with Italian dressing is more than the adult recommended daily limit of sodium—2400 mg! A glass of tomato juice contains 880 mg and the parmesan cheese sprinkled on top of a pasta dinner adds about 500 mg.

sodium—for a child, that's over a day's worth of sodium and that's why it's so important to check the Nutrition Facts label.

If you can save your child from the habit of craving a relatively high salt diet, you may save him or her from future heart disease or stroke, or an earlier death. I personally know many middle aged men and women who ignored this advice and have suffered a possibly

FIVE STEPS FOR MODIFYING SALT INTAKE

1. *Empty the salt from the shaker on the table, and refill with an herbal substitute.*

2. *Gradually use less salt in cooking*—don't use it at all in cooking water. *Start with half the salt a recipe calls for. After a few months, omit salt for cooking entirely.*

3. *Notice salt or sodium content on food labels. Canned foods are very high in salt (unless specifically stated as, "reduced salt, low salt or no salt added"), followed by frozen foods; but some fresh foods are too—like tomato and celery—therefore don't add salt to such dishes.*

4. *Don't keep highly salted foods in the house. Don't buy crackers, chips, salted nuts, bacon, sausages, lunch meats, dehydrated soups, tomato or V-8 juice, most canned soups, pickles, relishes, barbecue sauces, lox, herring, many processed cheeses and especially cheddar cheeses, or Jell-O. Treat yourself to such foods only on special occasions in small amounts, when you're away from home.*

5. *In a year's time you won't believe how different foods taste, or that you ever purposefully put salt on your corn on the cob! Restaurant food may seem very salty, unless you ask that the chef use very little salt and no MSG.*

preventable brain damaging stroke.*

Improve your odds by modifying your own salt intake. The following is a five-step program for the gradual reduction of salt in your family's diet. It takes most adults about a year to withdraw from the salt craving. Go slowly and you won't feel deprived—it will take the children much less time—but in either case it's a minor and brief deprivation in the big scheme of things, and worth it.

What About Sugar?

The impact on behavior from eating sugar and various foods has been a topic of both interest and concern to parents. Sugar isn't nearly the bad guy it's been made out to be as popularized by many books written during the 1970s. Sugar isn't a "slow poison," and doesn't cause cancer, diabetes, or heart disease, as some have claimed, nor is there evidence it causes behavior problems,† such as hyperactivity.‡ There is now considerable evidence that the concern about sugar consumption as reflected by the media was in error. The myths surrounding sugar and health, including the myth of the "sugar high" or that it causes hyperactivity, has been slow to disappear. These

---

*A stroke is a "brain attack" and its mechanism is similar to a heart attack. Blood vessels to the brain either burst or become blocked. The stroke is referred to as a hemorrhagic stroke if it is caused by a burst blood vessel to the brain, or an ischemic stroke if it is due to a blocked blood vessel. Ischemic stroke is the most common. In both cases, damage to the brain is caused by lack of oxygen and blood glucose. Oxygen and glucose are essential nutrients carried to the brain by blood vessels. Brain cells quickly begin to die without these nutrients. The results may be impaired speech if the brain cells in the speech center die; paralysis of the arms or legs if the motor brain cells die; blindness if the vision center brain cells die or coma and death if the stroke is severe enough to cause the death of enough vital brain cells. A diet low in sodium and fat plus regular exercise greatly reduces the risk of stroke. Although stroke is usually an event that occurs in adulthood, its roots (poor eating and exercise habits) are developed during childhood.

†"Facts and myths about sugar." Department of Nutritional Sciences Faculty of Medicine, University of Toronto, Ontario, Canada. *Bol Asoc Med P R* 1991 Sept; 83 (9); 408–410. "Effects of diets high in sucrose or aspartame on the behavior and cognitive performance of children." Department of Pediatrics, Vanderbilt University, Nashville, Tenn., *N Engl J Med* 1994 Feb 3; 330 (5): 301–307.

‡"Effect of sugar on aggressive and inattentive behavior in children with attention deficit disorder with hyperactivty and normal children." Wender, E. H., Solanto, M.V.: Schneider Children's Hospital, Long Island Jewish Medical Center, New Hyde Park, New York 11042. *Pediatrics* 1991 Nov: 88 (5): 960–966.

INFANT

myths are misleading and harmful. We need to place sugar in the diet in perspective. Small amounts of sugar have an important place in nutrition. For example, the only fuel the brain uses is sugar. There is some evidence showing sugar to have a calming effect on normal and hyperactive children.* Too much sugar, on the other hand, like too much of anything, is detrimental to our health and eating too much sugar *does* contribute to tooth decay, obesity, constipation, and malnutrition.

When I was seven or eight years old I informed my close friend David that the Stork Myth was scientifically non-supportable and offered a more plausible explanation. He rejected my offer of truth and beat me up to boot! David is now a pediatrician in New Jersey and I dare not offer him any more truths since he's still bigger than I am.

When we think of sugar, we generally imagine that white crystalline product—but that's just the tip of the sugar iceberg. Sugar exists in most foods we eat: juice, soda, jams, cookies, chocolate, crackers, hot and dry cereals, pies, ice cream, chili, pizza, Jell-O, hot dogs, bacon, ham, salami, and cold cuts, stuffings, breads, soups, mayonnaise, catsup, salad dressing, fruit flavored yogurt, canned vegetables, beans, and virtually all frozen foods, to name just a few. The average American consumes approximately 120 pounds of sugar a year.

Besides refined cane and beet sugar, chemically known as sucrose, check food labels for refined fructose, glucose, dextrose, lactose, levulose, maltose. All of these refined sugars have been stripped of their mineral, vitamin, and fiber content. They are good as a sweetener and for calories; whereas nutritious foods such as oranges, strawberries, cantaloupe, apples, plums, papaya, mango, and dried fruits are all high in sugar but retain the important vitamins, minerals, and fiber. Other refined sugars are corn syrup, molasses, maple syrup, and honey. "Sugarless" desserts and ice cream are sometimes deceptively loaded with honey or "real maple syrup." Although many parents or children may prefer a particular type of sugar, the body uses all sugars in essentially the same way. None of these sugars are nutritionally better than cane sugars, and brown sugar, raw sugar, honey, or molasses are not any healthier than other sugars.

---

*"Effect of nutritional supplements on attentional-deficit hyperactivity disorder." Dykman, K. D., Dykman, R. A. *Integr Physiol Behav. Sci* 1998 Jan–Mar; 33 (1) 49–60.

Apple juice is probably the greatest source of sugar in a small child's diet. It should be limited to a single 6 oz. bottle or cup a day (or less), but not toted around in the bottle. Watered-down juice is very popular, but is especially damaging to the teeth and appetite when consumed throughout the day (and night). Baby food companies cunningly promote juice by strategically placing rows of juice bottles above the desirable baby fruit and vegetable jars! *An infant has no nutritional need for juice.* Formula and breast milk provide an infant with enough water even in hot weather. Breast milk also contains lots of sugar (lactose or milk sugar). Infants that breastfeed past a year of age, especially as a calming agent, all day and throughout the night, often develop severely decayed teeth. This habit can lead to diseased permanent teeth.

INFANT

CHAPTER THREE

INFANT

MAKING YOUR OWN BABY FOODS

▲ ▲ ▲

If you have the time, making your baby food at home is a way to really be in charge of your infant's nutrition and to save money.

DO: Home preparation of baby foods requires special attention to cleanliness. Be sure to wash your hands with soap and water before handling food. Always use a clean cutting board and knife. Thoroughly wash, peel, and trim all fruit and vegetables to remove soil and unwanted food contaminants such as pesticides and chemical residues.* Although some authorities recommend using detergents to wash fruit and vegetables, I don't, because I'm concerned about adding residues to the foods from these detergents. Avoid using ceramic or glazed containers since they may contain lead. Lead poisoning may result if lead is leached out from these bowls and contaminate the food.

DON'T: Don't add salt or seasonings or use salted leftovers. Don't add sugar or honey. Don't add yeast or wheat germ. (Don't add any seasonings to commercially prepared food either!)

---

*The 1995 annual report of California's Department of Pesticide Regulations reports that more than 98 percent of the produce sampled by the state had "either no detectable residues or residues within legal limits." The benefits of eating ample amounts of fruits and vegetables far outweigh health risks posed by the low amounts of pesticide residues.

TOOLS YOU'LL NEED

Since you'll be pureeing most of the baby's food to a consistency he or she can swallow, you'll need a manual food mill or electric baby food grinder (available in most department stores), or a blender, or food processor, or a strainer with a wooden spoon. Babies' preferences for textures vary from fine to lumpy—this is true before and after their teeth come in. Your infant will let you know what consistency is preferred—don't feel you have to rush through purees to chunky foods.

STORING HOMEMADE FOODS

Refrigerate uneaten food promptly. Discard pureed foods after fifteen to twenty-four hours of refrigeration. It's safe to freeze most baby food for one to two months; but once a container is thawed or partially used, leftovers should be discarded. These rules also apply to commercially prepared baby foods.

Some people store pureed foods in Zip-Loc or baby bottle type bags and freeze them; others pour the puree into ice cube trays, freeze it, and then slip the cubes into freezer bags to store. Later several frozen cubes can be heated in a pan or microwave oven. Label all bags including the date of preparation.

USE OF MICROWAVE OVENS

It is unsafe to microwave infant formula because the fluid continues to cook even after it is removed from the oven and can burn the baby's mouth. Most other baby foods can be warmed safely in a microwave oven by heating for only a few seconds. Baby foods should be *warmed* to room temperature and not made *hot*. Microwave heating is very uneven. The container may feel cool, but it may contain pockets of food at scalding temperature. Stir the food thoroughly after heating to even out the temperature and be sure to recheck the temperature before offering it to your baby.

Preparing Fruit

Infants are born with a "sweet tooth" even before their teeth come in (mother's milk contains a large amount of natural sugar), so most fruits are well received. But beware of allergic reactions—strawberries and other berries should be avoided during infancy. And be aware of possible side effects: some fruits, like orange or tomato, which have high concentrations of peel oil, can cause a rash to sensitive skin. Wipe the baby's mouth with warm water and a soft cloth after feeding such foods.

BANANA PUREE

▲   Wrap a peeled banana in foil.

▲   Bake at 400°F for 15 to 20 minutes or microwave a banana (without the foil) until it achieves a very soft mushy consistency. Experiment with the time it takes in your particular microwave. The microwave oven is safe to use in the preparation of foods. In fact, microwaving fruit and vegetables destroys fewer vitamins and other nutrients than boiling, steaming or baking. *In all the recipes that follow, the instructions may be modified for microwave preparation.*

▲   Mash or blend to desired consistency. Add a little formula or breast milk to improve texture and make it thinner if needed.

APPLES, PEACHES, APRICOTS, PEARS, AND PLUMS

▲   Wash fruit well.

▲   Peel* (except for plums and apricots), remove seeds, pit and slice fruit.

▲   Put fruit in boiling water. (Use 1–2 tablespoons of water per cup of peaches or plums, 2–3 tablespoons

---

*If you peel and discard fruit skins such as apple or pear, remember that there is a trade-off: you may reduce pesticide residue somewhat, but lose dietary fiber.

of water per cup of apples, apricots, and pears.)

▲ Simmer apples, pears, and peaches for 15 to 20 minutes. Cook plums and apricots for 35 to 40 minutes. Remove plum skins.

▲ When fruit is soft, blend for about 30 seconds, or mash until smooth.

You can store these fruits in the freezer for up to two months.

Preparing Veggies

Most babies enjoy carrots, squash, broccoli, cauliflower, peas, and yams, and all these make nutritious first foods. Buy certified organic foods when they are available. This will decrease the probability of pesticides or chemical residues.

The general rules for cooking vegetables for adults also applies to infants: wash all vegetables thoroughly to remove soil and any trace of pesticide. Don't use too much water when you steam the vegetables— about one third of a cup of water per pound of vegetables is enough.

Add vegetables after the water is boiling, then cover and cook over medium-low heat until vegetables are tender. Don't overcook so that vegetables are mushy. Set aside the cooking water, now rich in vitamins, to mix with your mashed or blended or pureed vegetables to thin to the desired consistency.

Pour into an ice-cube tray and freeze. Then slip out the cubes and store them in a freezer bag.

CARROTS

▲ Peel, slice, and boil in a covered pot for 10 to 20 minutes. Grind or blend to desired consistency.

SQUASH

▲ Slice and boil summer squash for 5 to 15 minutes, winter squash for 15 to 20 minutes in a covered pot. Puree.

BROCCOLI AND CAULIFLOWER

▲　　Boil 15 to 20 minutes in a covered pot. Puree to desired consistency.

PEAS

▲　　Boil for 10 to 15 minutes in a covered pot. Puree.

YAMS, POTATOES, SWEET POTATOES

▲　　Peel and quarter.

▲　　Boil in a covered pot (add a little more water than for the vegetables above) for 15 to 20 minutes, then puree.

▲　　In the case of yams and potatoes, discard the cooking water and add formula, or breast milk to thin your puree.

BEANS

Garbonzo beans, baby lima beans, navy, pinto, red kidney beans, and lentils are all popular with babies, but some parents postpone their introduction until the infant is twelve to fifteen months old because of beans' association with gassiness. But most of my Latin American patients offer them earlier with no problems. One cup of dry beans make two-and-a-half cups of cooked beans.

▲　　Wash beans well.

▲　　Boil 1 cup of dried beans in 4 cups of water for 2 or 3 hours, depending on the variety of bean.*

---

*Most of my Latin American (especially Central American and Mexican) parents *do not soak beans overnight*. The practice decreases cooking time, but a busy parent may omit this step. Other parents find it easier to soak the beans overnight rather than watching them an additional two hours to prevent scorching.

▲   Blend or puree using the cooking water to thin.

▲   Or the beans may be mashed in a non-stick pan with chopped onion and cilantro, then "refried."

Strained Meats and Poultry

Begin these foods after the baby has learned to enjoy a variety of vegetables. A blender isn't really sufficient for preparing meat and poultry for your baby. You'll need a food processor, electric baby food grinder, or manual grinder.

Strained meats and poultry may be kept frozen for about two months.

CHICKEN OR TURKEY

▲   Boil or bake chicken or turkey as usual.

▲   Remove cooked chicken or turkey from bones; discard skin.

▲   Grind or blend meat in processor, adding some of the liquid in which you boiled or baked the meat to achieve the consistency your baby likes.

BEEF OR VEAL

▲   Use only lean beef or veal, and remove all visible fat.

▲   Boil veal for about 40 minutes, beef for 2½ hours.

▲   Grind or blend cooked meat in food processor, using cooking liquid for combining to the right consistency.

INFANT

General Principles in the Creation of Soups

Although most of my parents do not introduce soups until their children are two years old or older, Latin and Asian children are often given soup before age one.

▲   Start with a non-salt broth (canned or home made).

▲   There are hundreds of broth recipes available, so I have not included one here.

▲   To boiling broth add any or all of the following: Peas, carrots, potato, broccoli, choyote, chopped tomato, small pieces of chicken, cut up pieces of meat and an onion, cilantro or parsley if desired. *Do not be afraid to be creative.*

▲   Mash or blend the added vegetables and meats and return them to the soup. Younger children enjoy the nutritious broth and as they get older, begin eating the more textured ingredients. *Do not add salt!*

CHAPTER FOUR

FEEDING YOUR TODDLER OR PRESCHOOLER

▲ ▲ ▲

Toddlers' Table Foods

Most children begin to eat table foods at between one and two years, which gives you one or two years from the baby's birth to clean up your nutritional act. Because even though you think you won't feed your toddler the kind of junk food you indulge in, he's almost certain to have other ideas. Babies especially desire the foods they see their parent eating. In no time at all, your valiant efforts—the careful nursing, homemade baby foods, conscientious avoidance of salt and extra sugars, reading all those labels—can come to nothing when your baby gets into your bag of potato chips.

Not only must you watch what you eat, you must watch what you don't eat. If you turn up your nose at broccoli or fish, your child is likely to do the same. Interestingly, for some reason children seem to emulate their fathers' food habits in particular. So fathers beware: you're the role model!

Babies at the toddler stage love finger foods. Get ready for spilled food, cereal mushed in the baby's hair and slathered all over his face, clothes and your furniture. It's one big sticky mess for the next year or two!

Save the carpet by putting a plastic sheet under the high chair, or enlist a pet dog. But save your energy trying to teach table manners until the baby has developed better fine-motor coordination at about two-and-a-half to three years of age. When eating dissolves into playing, consider ending the meal promptly and allowing the child to leave the table. Some toddlers are not yet ready for exclusive self-feeding. These children need help if they do not eat enough alone. There are children at this age who won't eat at all unless they are fed. Don't become upset, children vary in their readiness. In addition, some children are slow or poky eaters. When they are rushed, they may leave the table before they're full, and go away hungry. I see this behavior often in kindergarten children who eat slowly. They feel they're missing all the fun playing outside with the children who wolfed down their lunch in a few moments. If your preschooler has this problem, discuss it with the teacher, who should allow your child more time to eat. Toddlers who wait too long for meals often lose their appetites altogether, so don't hold a hungry child off until the rest of the family is ready to eat. Since most children thrive on regularity, try to serve your toddler his or her meals and snacks at roughly the same time each day. Nutritional snacking or better timed meals may be the answer.

Consistency, color, and texture of foods become increasingly important to the toddler, but just as important is not giving up feeding a particular food after a rejection. Some babies adapt slowly to new situations throughout life, and children with this inborn temperament often reject anything new, including new foods. This behavior fortunately can be modified once you understand that you have such a child. Keep re-introducing these rejected foods daily for about twenty days in a row. As familiarity develops, more often than not, your child with accept the food. *The single biggest error a parent makes in food introduction is giving up after a few tries.* On the other hand, it is important not to force the baby to eat a particular food. Just keep presenting the food daily until it is accepted. Keep feeding time happy and relaxed. Good nutrition can easily break down at this point if the parent gives up and offers the child a special diet of crackers, grapes, raisins, peanut butter, and juice. A parent may believe that this diet is "better than nothing." What follows is a fight of wills, and the persistent child rules! Instead, keep eating time a happy time. If your child is not interested in the nutritious foods you prepare, allow him to leave the table to play. Save his dish of uneaten food for the time when he might be hungrier, but don't give him any other food. There are a few other "don'ts" as well. Don't bargain with your child or promise a dessert after she finishes her plate. Many studies have confirmed that this method often makes things worse. The slow to adapt, persistent child subsequently remembers the treat and a negative pattern of behavior quickly develops. Remember that the baby is rejecting the food and not your love. This confusion can easily creep into your feelings and cause frustration and anger. Your child may have the persistence, but not the *judgment* to make adult decisions. Never forget who the adult is! *If you judge that a particular food is not good for your child, don't offer it as a bribe or reward and certainly not as standard fare.*

Don't forget the effect of stress on your child's appetite. Stress of all kinds may have an effect on appetite: parental pressure to eat, a divorce, a separation, an illness within the family, a job loss, a new baby, new child-care arrangement, a new school, a new home, or even an overly ambitious schedule can interfere with a child's appetite. Of course when a child is ill, one of the first things that happens is a decreased appetite. Unless it is a chronic illness, the appetite usually returns in about a week.

Try soups with peas, carrots, small pieces of meat or chicken, rice, potato or noodles. Children who get introduced to soups at eight or nine months of age continue to like it when textures change from smooth to lumpy. Some babies gag on lumpy food until they are older and this is normal. Don't be in a hurry to advance textures too early. Avoid putting high-salt food such as ham or sausage into the soup. The child will not miss it, but if the baby already is used to salt, the soup might be rejected at first. As stated above, don't give up. Remember the twenty times rule! Appear indifferent to any and don't make a fuss over rejected foods. It usually makes things worse.

Do not serve Ramen noodles. They are extremely unhealthy because they are made by frying the noodles in fat before drying. Ramen, along with most instant cup-of-soups should be avoided at any age. Their high salt and fat content make these easy-to-prepare items a poor choice for snack or lunch.

Here are a few other suggestions for easy to prepare, nutritious finger foods, that make excellent snacks:

▲   Soft sweet peas

▲   Soft cooked carrot cubes

TODDLER

▲ Small pieces of very ripe banana

▲ Firm pieces of egg white or scrambled eggs

▲ Rice or small pieces of boiled potato (no french fries)

▲ Small pieces of poached or baked salmon or white fish

▲ Small pieces of boiled or baked chicken

More on Picky Eaters

Parents love "good eaters." They give back so much pleasure and that wonderful feeling of successful parenting. Mothers dream of the baby whose mouth is always ready for another morsel of "love." Then there is the nightmare baby who resists all initial attempts at being fed. These children can often be identified shortly after birth. As described above, they quickly undermine the confidence of the most secure parent! It is to the parent of such a child that I am addressing the following paragraph. *It's not too late to undo poor eating habits.*

Most toddlers eat less than they did the first year of life and sometimes refuse meals completely. A toddler is not growing as fast as he was in his first year, therefore his caloric needs are less. He or she still requires nutritious foods, but less. The slow to adapt, persistent toddler now seems to be living on air. Mothers panic and conclude, "Better to give the child something—anything—rather than nothing." So eventually the toddler's diet is reduced to several glasses of juice a day plus crackers, cookies, peanut butter, raisins and grapes. Most crackers and chips have an outrageous ratio of calories from fat and more salt than is healthy. About half the calories in Triscuits, Wheat Thins, Ritz Crackers, and Pepperidge Farms Goldfish come from fat. The result is a skinny and extremely cranky child. It's raisins in and raisins out (in the bowel movement), minus what sticks to the teeth, causing early decay. Juice is essentially pure sugar water which further destroys the child's appetite and decays the teeth. Add grapes and crackers and you have one of the worst possible diets for a child. Of course the child will hold out for these "foods"; however, the persistent, slow to adapt child will eventually respond to your efforts.

ADVICE ON HOW TO GENTLY BREAK THE BOTTLE AND PACIFIER HABIT

Many parenting books recommend that a child's bottle be removed at one year to prevent tooth decay when the child totes a bottle filled with juice (which is essentially sugar water) or milk all day and night. For those parents who feel the baby "needs" the bottle, it would be wise for them to put only water (never diluted juice) in the bottle and all "good" things in a cup. This will make it easier for you to remove the bottle in the future when you feel you *can handle the change. Here is one method of change to a cup that I have employed successfully over many years. It is virtually painless to the child and parent.*

When the child is between fifteen to eighteen months old, put only water in the bottle as described above. After a week or two, tell your child that the "Bottle Man" is coming on Saturday to get all the bottles and pacifiers to give to the little babies. Even if you think the baby will not understand what you are saying, it is important that you repeat this message with a happy and enthusiastic voice. Saturday morning, before breakfast, collect all the bottles, nipples, caps and pacifiers with your child and have him put them in a large paper shopping bag. Together, place the bag contents outside your front door and remind him in a happy and enthusiastic voice *that the Bottle Man will be there to get these items for the little babies. Next, eat breakfast together.* After breakfast *remind your child about the bag and investigate to see whether the Bottle Man came. The bag should be empty of the bottles, but inside he should find a new teddy bear or similar stuffed animal. Toy cars, trucks, or other items do not work as well as a stuffed animal. Explain that this is a present from the Bottle Man. Now the child can* substitute this stuffed animal for the bottle *as a security item and also cuddle it at bedtime. Instead of giving him a bottle at bedtime, cuddle your child in your lap and continue your bedtime ritual using a cup.* Once you make the conversion it is extremely important not to return to the bottle. *If he asks for the bottle or pacifier, remind him that the Bottle Man gave them to the little babies, and give him the stuffed doll that the Bottle Man left for him! Do not attempt the conversion when your child is ill. Using this method, weekends are an ideal time to convert to a cup. The most common comment I get from parents is,* "Had I known it would be so easy I'd have done it sooner!"

TODDLER

Here's the cure. Immediately stop all *juice, raisins, crackers, cookies, peanut butter and grapes!* In two to three days your child will be eating and drinking milk and wholesome foods again—as long as there are no other choices. The traditional advice found in most parenting books just doesn't work on children with this temperament. Try your best not to show frustration. *Be gentle, but firm* in not returning to the old diet. After your toddler is back on track, limit juice to only once a day and in a cup rather than in a bottle. If the child is thirsty offer plain water (unsweetened). The rule of thumb is, "all favorite liquids in a cup and only water in the bottle."

My daughter called me recently, concerned that her two-year-old was too skinny. She asked if there were some vitamin, mineral supplement, or magic tonic that would boost his appetite. She was sure I would know what it was. Fortunately, I had kept her health records from the time she was a baby, and I faxed her the pertinent information. Her height-weight proportions were almost exactly the same as her son's at the same age. He was doing just fine. Inappropriate expectations can cause much anxiety in a parent. Remember that genetic factors and matters of temperament will also have something to do with how robust an eater your child will become.

Eating disorders often begin with the too-skinny two-year-old child whose parents make food the center of his existence. If your child refuses to eat as much as usual for more than a few days, don't be alarmed. This is often normal. The most common cause of a decrease in appetite is illness or a cold. Once the cold is over the appetite returns. Consult with your doctor if your child's appetite remains poor. But if your toddler looks well proportioned in spite of his poor appetite, perhaps your expectations of how much food he needs is in error.

Several years ago a foster parent called me because she believed her two-and-a-half-year-old had emotional problems. She thought the cause might be the family's forthcoming move to a new community. The child was no doubt insecure, she said, though he needn't be. The problem was his stealing food—from their plates at mealtime, and by slipping out of bed to raid the refrigerator in the middle of the night. The child was bloated from overeating, the foster mother told me, even though she had cut back on his regular meals in order to compensate for the extra food he was sneaking.

Your guess is correct. The little boy was starving. By the time I saw him he was emaciated, too weak even to walk.

Although this is an extreme case, it demonstrates how errors in nutritional assessment can be made—even by educated, well-meaning people. These foster parents were both college graduates; the father was a minister. I'm convinced that neither of them would have purposefully done harm to the child they were raising. But our perceptions are clouded by personal bias as well as inexperience. For this reason it's important to check in with your child's physician periodically to ensure that the child's weight and development are within normal ranges.

Well-child checks are designed to spot early problems and provide guidance—both important facets of preventive health care. It's a myth that left to their own choices, children will naturally select the food they need over a period of time. Most children in our culture gravitate toward the worst junk foods and some of the most potentially harmful nonnutritious snacks.

We can't really expect our kids, especially the very young ones, to resist fast food advertising propaganda, peer pressure, and vending machines. *We* haven't resisted.

But we must. Now's the time to get our nutritional house in order, even in the face of the most convincing pleas. Trust me. As the father of five, I've heard some pretty compelling reasons for buying Sugar Frosted Flakes, potato chips, and beef jerky.

As stated earlier, don't use food as a reward, and don't withhold food as a punishment. Give a toy, watch a video together, make a trip to the zoo as recognition for your child's achievement—for having put away his toys, for doing well in school. Avoid making "treat" synonymous with food.

Keep mealtimes pleasant and relaxed. Traditionally, the family gathers together at mealtime. In our culture we usually meet at the end of the day. This is a time to share our day's experience; but what was nice about the day, is often preempted by a disaster at school or frustration at work. Work on accentuating the positive when food is served, and turn off the TV during mealtimes!

You will be getting much advice on what type of milk to give to your child. A fuss is being made over giving whole milk to your child until he or she is over two years old and then going to nonfat milk. The truth of the matter is that low-fat milk (2 percent) contains adequate fat and is the preferred type of milk for children between one and two. When children eat whole grains, vegetables, and meat too, they get a more than sufficient amount for optimal growth and nutrition. One-percent low-fat milk is probably also fine for most children as well, but I usually reserve this for children approaching two. The transition to nonfat milk is gradually made by two years of age. I'm not aware of a single case of nutritional problems due to too little fat in children over a year old that followed this advice. If you have a child who is exceptionally thin, it is important that you consult your pediatrician or health care provider to reevaluate your child's diet and health. A complete history and physical examination is needed. Don't attempt to "fatten the child up" with high fat foods.

COOKING TIP: Try the recipe for CREAMY POTATO SOUP on page 213.

FOOD FACT: Eggs may safely be introduced to a child over age one. Check out the section on eggs in Chapter 4, and try a BASIC OMELET, LOUIS'S DRENCH TOAST, and SCRAMBLED EGGS WRAPPED IN A TORTILLA on pages 197-198.

Snacks

When my son was born he quickly adapted to an every-two-hours eating schedule. My wife kept asking me when this demanding schedule would change. Twenty-five years later she notes that it never has changed: he has breakfast, a mid-morning snack, lunch, and afternoon snack, dinner, and a snack before bed. His "grazing" six meals a day did not make him overweight. *Calories do count*, but his total calorie intake over twenty-four hours was sufficient to cover what he burned from activity plus his growth needs.

Eating between meals gets bad press, but I think this is more about *what we eat* than *when we eat*. The human digestive tract is especially well adapted to snack-type eating rather than three major meals a day. As long as what we're eating is low in percentage of calories from fat, low in salt, and not totally without fiber as a result of ultra refining, nibbling throughout the day is no problem.

The problem is that many nibble-type foods are high in fat, high in salt, and low in fiber. Potato chips, corn chips (even "health food store" chips), granola bars, trail mix, crackers, cookies, doughnuts, cupcakes, Twinkies, ice cream, peanut butter and jelly, soda, Kool Aid, Hi-C, milk shakes, salted nuts, and a variety of candy bars, are examples. *Health food stores sell snack bars that are just as bad as any other candy bar, made with too much sea salt, honey, fructose, and cold-pressed oil.*

Snack foods that are high in fat and simple sugars contribute to obesity and tooth decay.* But healthy, low-fat snacks don't ruin the appetite for dinner as high-fat, high-simple-carbohydrate ones do. The "staying power" of the "instant energy" sports or chocolate bars is a platitude invented by copy writers.

Snacking is good. Don't change the habit, change the choice of your snack.

SNACKS FOR PRESCHOOLERS

Children like simple snacks. Frozen bananas are a favorite treat for the two-year-old and older. Peel any overripe bananas, those with dark skins that you usually discard. Cut them in half, then place each half in a plastic Zip-Loc bag and freeze. Once frozen, simply serve— no preparation is required.

A bagel and nonfat cream cheese is another favorite.† Don't forget cut-up fruit, corn kernels, peas, or garbanzo beans. Hummus is made by blending chick peas (garbanzos), adding a few drops of lemon, and blending in favorite non-salt spices that the child likes. This is a more nutritious substitute for peanut butter. Another favorite is low-fat, low-salt vegetarian chili beans, prepared from scratch or from a can. Health Valley makes delicious, wholesome chili. Matzo and water crackers are good choices with string cheese. An English muffin with low-salt tomato sauce and a slice of mozzarella cheese, microwaved, makes an instant pizza snack. Small cut-up pieces of chicken breast, or for the older child, a baked chicken leg, sprinkled with paprika and served over a bowl or rice make an excellent school lunch, trans-

---

*Life is a compromise. Baked goods need not be high in fat. Sunsweet's Lighter Bake is a fat-free, fruit-based replacement for butter or oil in recipes. Baked goods made with Lighter Bake instead of regular high-trans-fat shortening have 10 to 30 percent fewer calories and 50 to 90 percent less fat. For each cup of oil, substitute ½ cup of Lighter Bake.

†Buddy's Bagels Whipped Non-Fat Cream Cheese, especially the herbal variety, is one of the better-tasting brands. Millbrae, CA 94030, (415)652-9700.

ported in a Tupperware-like container. Air popped pop-corn is an excellent choice for children over five years old. *Younger children should avoid popcorn because it is easy to choke on.* Small bay shrimp or crab on whole wheat toast or water crackers make an excellent low-fat and high-protein snack. Smoothies, especially on warm days, made with nonfat milk and seasonal fruit are nutritious and loved by most children.

The Truth About Peanut Butter

Peanuts are one of the most allergenic foods. Peanut butter can act like a plaster patch on the back of a very young child's throat to block the airway. My dentist used to say that peanut butter was the plaster that attaches sugar to teeth (jelly being 100 percent sugar).

Peanut butter has a reputation for being a super source of protein. Four level tablespoons of peanut butter can provide your seven- to ten-year-old with 16 grams of protein, or half the protein she needs in a day. (The RDA for protein for a child seven to ten years old is 28 grams.) But those four tablespoons contain a whopping 32 grams of fat and 400 calories.* Seventy-five percent of those calories come from fat! Commercial peanut butter like Skippy or Jif uses additional hydrogenated fat—usually hydrogenated cottonseed oil to improve spreading and prevent the peanut oil from separating out. Cottonseed oil originates from the cotton plant, which has probably been sprayed with pesticide, thus endowing the oil with trace pesticidal properties. Salt and sugar are also added to commercial peanut butter to prevent mold growth and separation of the oil.

And that's not all. Peanuts contain aflatoxin, a naturally occurring carcinogen and liver toxin that is produced by mold on damp peanuts. Roasting does not destroy this heavy-duty toxin. The U.S. Department of Agriculture has a good program in place to minimize aflatoxin contamination of peanuts in commercially processed peanut butters, and it seems to be keeping contamination down to acceptably

*Peanut butter is high in total fat, but monounsaturated fat is the predominant type of fat. Nutritionists argue that monounsaturated fats may actually be good for you. That is why peanut oil is preferred over saturated fats such as butter or fats high in trans-fat ("hydrogenated" fats). But peanut butter contains many other ingredients, as noted above, to make it less of an ideal food for children and adults. For more information on fats, read Chapter 12.

low levels. But "real" peanut butter, made from ground peanuts in a home processor or at the health food store is believed to have ten times the amount of aflatoxin as the Skippy- or Jif-type brands.

But the main strike against peanut butter must be its fat content. Don't be fooled by a label that claims "No-Cholesterol Food!" Remember that cholesterol isn't found in *any* vegetable fat. But vegetable fat is atherogenic (clogs arteries with plaques of fatty-like tissue) and possibly carcinogenic when eaten in excess. Also be aware that "reduced fat" peanut butter is still not low-fat, though it may contain a fourth less fat. To produce the "reduced fat" peanut butter, the manufacturer replaces about a quarter of the peanuts with soy protein. But then the product can't be called "peanut butter" anymore. It becomes a "spread."

Peanut butter, like bacon and other extremely high fat foods, can be eaten occasionally, perhaps once a month in conservative amounts, but the daily peanut butter and jelly sandwich has got to go.

When you make a peanut butter sandwich, here are a few hints on how to lower fat:

▲   Reduce the peanut butter to 1 tablespoon.

▲   Substitute a thinly sliced or mashed ripe medium banana for the jelly.

This will produce a sandwich with 248 calories and 10 grams of fat, or 32 percent of calories coming from fat.

Study the following statistics before preparing your child's next peanut butter sandwich!*

▲   The odds of winning California's SuperLotto jackpot are 1 in 18 million. The odds of some other events:

▲   1 in 1 million (18 times more likely) to die from flesh-eating bacteria.

▲   1 in 650,000 (nearly 28 times more likely) to be killed by terrorists while traveling abroad.

---

*James Walsh, *True Odds*, Merritt Publishing. 1996.

▲ 1 in nearly 650,000 to be dealt a royal flush on the opening hand in a poker game.

▲ 1 in 48,000 (375 times more likely) to die of heart disease from eating a broiled steak a week.

▲ 1 in 5000 (3,600 times more likely) to die of cancer from eating a peanut butter sandwich a day.

COOKING TIP: Use the recipe for HUMMUS on page 199 as a healthful alternative to peanut butter.

CHESTNUTS

A forgotten snack food is the chestnut. Chestnuts are high in complex carbohydrates, and contain a mere trace of fat—two large chestnuts have less than 30 calories and only 0.2 mg of fat.

I have fond memories of street vendors roasting chestnuts over charcoal fires on cold winter afternoons and evenings. This was in Innsbruck, Austria, in the 1950s, where I attended the University of Innsbruck (when I wasn't skiing!). The smell of roasted chestnuts sold them. We bought them in small bags, and the process of peeling away the shell and inner skin warmed frozen fingers.

Chestnuts are also good boiled and served with brussels sprouts, or mashed and seasoned alongside small portions of lean roast meats. Introduce your family to chestnuts. It's a great snack food.

COOKING TIP: Try the recipe for CHESTNUT STUFFING on page 199.

Basic Foods

When your child is between the ages of one and two, introduce (and reintroduce, if necessary) some basic foods: potato, corn, wheat and other grains, legumes and cruciferous vegetables, such as broccoli or Brussels sprouts. Be sure to include these on your plate which will make them appear more enticing to your youngster.

Potatoes, corn, wheat, grains, legumes and vegetables are important complex carbohydrates. Most contain significant protein and little fat (as long as they're not doused with butter, margarine, oil, or cream), as well as starch and fiber. These basic foods should be at the heart of your toddler's expanding diet. (See Chapter 10 for more on carbohydrates.)

COOKING TIP: A great way to introduce vegetables to young children is the recipe for LENTIL SOUP on page 200.

FOOD FACT: Beans, Grains, and Vegetables are Basic Foods for children over age one. Tofu is also good to try. Read Chapter 4, and try the recipes for LENTIL SOUP, BEAN CUISINE'S "THICK AS FOG SPLIT PEA SOUP," BLACK-EYED PEAS, BEAN DIP, BEAN, TURKEY, AND BROCCOLI DINNER, FRIJOLES, BASIC MASHED POTATOES, BAKED POTATO, NEW POTATO WITH DILL SAUCE, POTATO LATKES (PANCAKES), MEAT, RICE, AND KETCHUP, POLENTA, VERACRUZANA SAUCE, SPECIAL CREAM OF WHEAT, BUCKWHEAT PANCAKES, QUICK OATMEAL, KASHA VARNISHKAS, MILLET PILAF, BASIC BARLEY, BROCCOLI, COLESLAW, STEAMED VEGETABLES, STIR-FRIED VEGETABLES, VEGETABLE SOUP, VEGETABLE SAUTÉ, GREEN SALAD WITH VEGETABLES, HUNGARIAN BUTTER LETTUCE SALAD, HUNGARIAN CUCUMBERS, CAROL'S BANANA-STRAWBERRY SMOOTHIE, BAKED APPLE, APPLE SAUCE, PEACH SHERBET, and BAKED PEARS FRENCH STYLE on pages 179-196, 200-203, 205.

TODDLER

CHAPTER FIVE

THE FOODS CHILDREN NEED, PART 1

▲ ▲ ▲

Eggs

Unless your child has eczema or has already shown an allergy to eggs, this food may safely be introduced to a child over age one.

The egg is composed of egg white, one of the purest and best proteins available, and the egg yolk, a repository for cholesterol. Interestingly, people with already high cholesterol levels (over 200 mg) don't experience much of an increase in their blood cholesterol level by eating eggs, whereas people with normal blood cholesterol (125–165 mg) show a dramatic increase in cholesterol when they eat eggs.

Infants may need diets higher in cholesterol and fats than adults, but this should not be interpreted to mean that you must go out of your way to introduce high fat or high cholesterol foods.

Egg yolk has traditionally been introduced to children early because it had the reputation of being a great source of iron. But now we know that the iron in egg yolk is poorly absorbed by the body. I'm especially wary of large amounts of egg yolk because environmental poisons such as pesticide residues, which contaminate animal feeds, may show up in concentrated amounts in animal organs such as liver, eggs, and chicken skin.

On the other hand, egg *white* is an excellent nonfat uncontaminated source of protein. Boil an egg. Pop out the yolk and discard it.

Chop up the white to garnish the salads of the older child. One to three eggs a week for a young child are nutritionally wholesome as long as they are not fried or prepared with butter, margarine, or oil.

FERTILE AND UNGRADED EGGS

A belief in "vitalism" prompts some people to buy fertilized eggs. From a nutritional point of view, fertilized and unfertilized eggs are identical. *The more important issue is that raw fertile eggs are a dangerous threat to health.* Graded eggs are sanitized using an antiseptic wash. Fecal germs on egg shells that haven't been through the antiseptic process cause hundreds of cases of food poisoning a year in the United States. Symptoms of salmonella food poisoning, which include nausea, vomiting, diarrhea, abdominal cramps, chills, fever, and achy muscles, usually begin twelve to twenty-four hours after eating contaminated food. Children, the elderly, and anyone with a compromised immune system are especially vulnerable to food poisoning.

Cartons of eggs sold in most supermarkets generally meet USDA Grade-A requirements. To be certain *never use raw or uncooked eggs.* Even graded eggs are often contaminated. *It is dangerous to put any raw egg in a milkshake. Unpasteurized eggnog or Caesar salad dressing are extremely risky and should be avoided.*

COOKING TIP: Try the recipes for BASIC OMELETS, LOUIS'S DRENCH TOAST, and SCRAMBLED EGGS WRAPPED IN A TORTILLA on pages 197-198.

Tofu

Tofu is a non-meat, non-dairy source of protein that is relatively high in calcium and low in price. It has been an important part of the Asian diet for more than 2000 years. Today most supermarkets and health food stores carry it. It's prepared from soybeans that have been soaked overnight, ground, boiled, strained, made into curd, cut into blocks, and kept refrigerated. Three-and-a-half ounces—about half a cup—contains about 145 calories and 8–10 grams of protein. Furthermore, soybean is a complete protein, that is, it contains all the essential amino acids. Although 3½ oz. of tofu contains 9 grams of fat, it is cholesterol free and the fat is mostly polyunsaturated.

Tofu can be added to soup and salads, or barbecued. It can be stir-fried, broiled, grilled, sautéed, or baked. It can be pureed to make dips, spreads, salad dressing and when mashed, it can be substituted for ricotta or cottage cheese.

There are two basic types of tofu, soft and firm. Soft tofu comes in thick, straight-edged blocks; the firm type has compressed edges. When you buy tofu, check the date for freshness. Rinse the tofu when you get it home, place it in a container of fresh cold water, and store it in the refrigerator. Change the water daily.

Miso is another soy product. It is a salty seasoning paste made from a combination of soybeans and a grain such as rice or barley. This product should be avoided because its sodium content can exceed 900 milligrams per tablespoon.

Potatoes

Along with rice, corn, and wheat, the potato is known worldwide as a staff of life. Spanish conquistadors carried it to Europe from the Andes in the sixteenth century, and it has become one of the most nutritious and versatile food staples.

It's a wonderful food, not at all fattening: a medium-size potato contains only 100 calories, is 99.9 percent fat free, and provides about half the vitamin C a person needs in a day. Potato skin is high in dietary fiber and contains most of the vitamin C. Although the potato isn't particularly rich in protein, its biological quality is as high or higher than the soybean protein.

People associate the Irish with potatoes, but I think of Eastern Europe. My mother prepared potato soup, boiled potatoes, baked potatoes, and mashed potatoes. Remembering her potato latkes, potato kugel, and potato knadel still makes my mouth water. By the time of her death at age ninety-four, she had supplied me with a generous variety of traditional Jewish potato recipes, some of which I've reprinted here, modified in the interest of less salt and fat.

Sadly, Americans have veered away from the wholesome use of potatoes. More than half of the potatoes we eat these days are in the form of potato chips, processed frozen french fries, fast-food french fries, and dehydrated potato preparations. In 1980, Americans ate five billion pounds of french fries, and one billion pounds of potato chips. While an 8-oz. potato has 140 calories, 8 oz. of potato chips contain 1200 calories, 28 teaspoonsful (133 grams) of which are pure fat!

While you still have some say in the matter, avoid starting your toddler on these foods. Stick to something wholesome like my mother's basic mashed potatoes.

COOKING TIP: Try the recipes for BASIC MASHED POTATOES, BAKED POTATO, NEW POTATO WITH DILL SAUCE, and POTATO LATKES (PANCAKES) on pages 179-181.

Rice

Rice is one of the most nutritious grains. It is the principal food for many millions of people throughout the world. Most children quickly learn to love rice. Although it doesn't contain an unusually high percentage of protein, it is of higher biological value than corn.* One half cup of rice contains about 3 grams of protein. Unpolished rice, such as brown rice, contains bran, a dietary fiber, in its husk. Rice bran lowers blood cholesterol as much as oat bran, but unlike oat bran, rice bran doesn't turn gummy when cooked. You can buy rice bran which is packaged like wheat germ and is used is similar ways. Sprinkle it on cereal, salad, and nonfat yogurt, or add it to baked goods. An ounce contains 8 grams of dietary fiber, 4 grams of protein, and lots of niacin, thiamin, magnesium, and iron.

FORMS OF RICE

Short and medium grain rice are wetter than long rice and their kernels stick together. You can overcome the stickiness by adding oil to the water in which you cook the rice, but by now you know I wouldn't

---

*Protein foods have been classified according to their ability to be digested and used by the body. The measurement is called biological value. Egg white is considered to have the protein of highest known biological value. Following egg white, in descending order, are fish, cow milk, and cheese, brown rice, red meat, and poultry (Garrison and Somer, *Nutrition Desk Reference,* Keats Publishing, 1985).

recommend any such thing. Don't add salt, either. If you don't like sticky rice, use long grain or parboiled rice.

Long grain rice is generally preferred for Chinese cooking and is good for curries, pilaf, or stews served over rice. The stickier rice is especially good for puddings or molded rice dishes, California roll sushi, and many Japanese dishes.

Kernels that break during the milling process are sold as *"broken rice,"* which is a little less expensive than other rice.

Whole grain rice, as opposed to *polished rice*, retains all the grain's nutrients, most notably vitamins and minerals otherwise lost in milling when the outermost husk is removed. *Brown whole grain rice* is a popular favorite. It has a nice nut-like flavor and is chewier than white rice. Short grain brown rice is even chewier than the long grain version.

Polishing or processing rice involves removing the outer layer. Polished rice has been discredited because it is deficient in B vitamins, but in fairness it should be noted that the proteins and amino acids of polished rice are biologically more available than those in unpolished rice. Polished rice has a lower fat content than brown rice, so it is less likely to become rancid. Supposedly polished rice also creates less gas in the bowels because it has less bran than the whole grain.

Enriched rice is polished rice to which iron, thiamine, and niacin have been returned in amounts approximately that of unmilled kernels. Uncle Ben's is a popular, easy to prepare "enriched" rice. You get the three B vitamins and iron that are added to all enriched grains, but you lose the fiber, magnesium, vitamins E and B-6, copper, zinc, and other nutrients such as the poorly understood phytochemicals (plant chemicals) that are in the whole grains, such as brown rice.

Parboiled or *converted white rice* has been specially treated to retain vitamins. It may contain two to four times as much thiamine and niacin as polished white rice. The term "parboiled" is slightly misleading; the rice is not precooked, but is actually somewhat harder than regular rice. It takes a little longer to cook than regular white rice, but the grains will be very fluffy and separate after they have been cooked. My personal favorites are long grain brown rice and converted rice.

Precooked rice has been fully cooked and dehydrated after milling. This is the "instant" or "minute rice" that needs no preparation beyond pouring boiling water over the rice according to the package directions, and letting stand for a few minutes before serving. This stuff is pretty tasteless and less nutritious than other rice. The newest addition to instant rice is precooked converted rice that has been vacuum-packed in a plastic bag. Simply immerse it in boiling water as directed on the package and in a few moments you have perfectly prepared rice.

Arborio is a starchy white rice with an almost round grain. This is the rice used to make the Italian dish risotto and it also works well for paella and rice pudding. Arborio absorbs up to five times its weight in liquid as it cooks, which results in grains of a creamy consistency.

Wild rice is botanically unrelated to rice. It is a native grain to North America. Like rice, it grows in marshy land. French explorers found it growing around the Great Lakes and called it "crazy oats," although it is no more related to oats than to rice. Because it is difficult to produce in large quantities, wild rice is extremely expensive. It has a distinct nutty flavor and chewiness.

COOKING TIP: Try the recipe for MEAT, RICE, AND KETCHUP on page 182.

Corn, Wheat, and Other Grains

CORN

Technically a grass, corn is the only cereal born and bred in America. It was the main food of the Indian civilizations of the Americas from the Canadian border to the Andes. The Pilgrims from England who settled here learned from the natives how to use corn.

The dried corn kernel is strong and hard on the outside, while its germ, or inside, is soft and almost floury. Indians showed the Southern Colonists how to pound, grind, and boil whole kernels in lye or lime water to make hominy, which remains a staple in the Southern diet. "Grits" refers to the flint-like, grainy, textured part of the kernel. (Unless cornmeal is soaked in water to soften it, the corn bread made from it is gritty.)

Toddlers tend to love corn bread, corn muffins, hominy grits, and corn flakes—all high in nutrients. Popcorn is one of the few popular snack foods that tastes good and provides solid food value, when not doused with butter, oil, or salt. *But I don't recommend it for children under five* because it's too easy to choke on.

My favorite form of corn is on the cob. A few years ago I planted eight rows of Eastern white corn in our big backyard garden, but because I planted them all at the same time, we had five or six dozen ears of corn ready to be eaten all at the same time. Some farmer I turned out to be!

Our solution was a neighborhood "Pick Your Own" party and feast that was a huge success. It was the first time I had ever tried corn without butter or salt. It was fantastic!

If you buy fresh corn from a farmer's market, take along a cooler. Warm temperatures quickly convert the corn's sugar to starch. Select corn with plump, juicy, well aligned kernels that are tightly packed. Buy those ears of corn with the husks still on, and discard ears with rusty looking tips or shriveled kernels.

To steam sweet corn, heat it through for about two to five minutes. To grill, cut off tassels, remove the silk, leave the husks on and soak in ice water for five minutes. Place over the coals, a few inches from the fire's center. Turn every five minutes. In fifteen minutes, the husk should be blackened and the corn ready to eat.

COOKING TIP: Try the recipes for POLENTA and VERACRUZANA SAUCE on pages 183-184.

WHEAT

The most widely grown of all cereal grains, wheat is a kind of berry that consists of an outer covering, the bran, which is high in minerals, B vitamins, and some protein; and the inner part, or endosperm, which consists mainly of starch and protein. The wheat germ resides in the endosperm. The germ is comparatively high in fat and vitamin E.

Wheat is made into white flour and whole wheat flour: white flour consists of ground endosperm only. Whole wheat or graham flour contains the bran and the entire endosperm. Because it contains the germ, which contains fat, whole wheat flour can spoil, whereas white flour can be stored fresh for much longer. On the other hand, whole wheat flour contains more fiber, minerals, vitamins, and slightly more protein than even enriched white flour (white flour to which thiamine, riboflavin, niacin, and iron have been added). Your toddler will enjoy whole wheat pasta, pilaf, and breads of many kinds. Bulgur wheat, very high in fiber, is made from several varieties of wheat. It is used as a cereal, in soups or salads, as a side dish or main meal. Too much can cause gassiness.

If your children have grown used to white bread, help them switch to whole wheat by preparing sandwiches with one slice of white and one slice of whole wheat bread. Another way to introduce whole wheat bread is to switch to a bread that looks like whole wheat but has the texture of white, like Roman Meal. This will let your child adapt to the color of whole wheat over a couple of weeks or even a month. Then switch to a mild whole wheat bread. The older the child, the more slowly the transition, especially with the slow to adapt, persistent child. Be patient and persistent—the long term gains are worth it.

COOKING TIP: Try the recipes for SPECIAL CREAM OF WHEAT and BUCKWHEAT PANCAKES on pages 185.

RYE

Rye has a stronger, heartier flavor than wheat, and is typically used to make rye bread. Today's American rye bread is usually one-third rye flour, two-thirds whole wheat flour. When I was growing up it was the real thing, a traditional Jewish rye with caraway seeds and a crunchy crust. Onion and corn rye breads were my favorites. Authentic black pumpernickel, and German or Russian rye breads are also delicious, and you can find them in small local bakeries. They're worth hunting for.

Generally speaking, food from grains such as corn, wheat, or rye are among the most nutritious foods we eat (as long as we don't add butter or margarine).

For the five-year-old, try low or nonfat cheese, lettuce and ripe tomato sandwiches on rye, but hold the mayo.* Many children do not develop a taste for lettuce until four years of age, so don't be too upset

---

*Some nonfat mayonnaise has such poor taste, you may want to return to your favorite high fat brand. Shop around and don't give up. There are improved and more tasty nonfat mayo-substitutes arriving weekly at your market.

if your toddler rejects salads. Keep trying, and be sure to make a salad a daily part of the adult diet. Remember, you're the role model!

OATS

Oats are an ancient grain, probably cultivated since the first century A.D. They are used most frequently as cattle food, humans consume only about 5 percent of the world oat crop. In America, oats are used mostly for hot cereal and more recently for muffins, cookies breads. Oats are an excellent source of complex carbohydrate and contain about 50 percent more protein than and bulgur wheat, and twice as much as brown rice. They are rich in vitamin E and the B vitamin folate, as well as the minerals iron, copper, zinc, and manganese. Oats are also a good source of dietary fiber, both soluble and insoluble. The soluble fiber is primarily responsible for lowering blood cholesterol. Two ounces of dry oats (1⅓ cups cooked) contain 5 grams of fiber and only 1 gram of fat.

Granola is made from oats, but commercial brands are extremely high in fat. Often highly saturated tropical oil, such as palm or coconut oil, are added to the oats before they are toasted. You can buy low-fat granola or you can make your own. Toast quick or old-fashioned rolled oats on a baking sheet in a 300°F oven and stir frequently. If you wish, stir in honey* to taste before toasting. Be careful not to scorch. After toasting, mix in your choice of wheat germ, bran, and chopped dried fruits. Let cool in a plastic bag or refrigerator.

Muesli is a cold cereal, very popular in Switzerland, Germany, and Austria. Like granola, mass-market muesli is often high in fat and calories, but you can prepare your own fairly easily. Mix uncooked rolled oats with rolled wheat flakes, bite-sized shredded wheat, wheat nuggets, 100-percent bran shreds, oat or wheat bran, or wheat germ. Stir in any of your favorite dried fruits and a small amount of unsalted, coarsely chopped nuts or seeds. If you prefer sweet muesli, add a little brown sugar, maple syrup, or molasses. Serve only to children over three or four, because younger children may choke on the seeds. Store in an airtight container in the refrigerator. If muesli is mixed with skim milk and refrigerated overnight, it will have the consistency of cooked cereal. If you prefer it crunchy, stir in nonfat milk or nonfat yogurt just before serving.

---

*Do not give honey to infants under one year of age. Refer to earlier warnings concerning the danger of infant botulism from honey. It is safe to use honey after the baby is over one year old.

COOKING TIP: Try the recipe for QUICK OATMEAL on page 186.

ETHNIC GRAINS

BUCKWHEAT isn't related to wheat, and isn't even a cereal. Technically or botanically, it's a fruit. In any case, it's another wonderful complex carbohydrate around which to build a meal. In middle European countries, buckwheat groats, or kernels, are prepared similarly to rice and called *kasha*. It is necessary to roast the kasha before boiling as roasting keeps it from developing a sticky, porridge-like consistency. Kasha and yogurt is an ethnic favorite among Eastern European Jews, as is kasha varnishkas—kasha with bow-tie noodles. The kernels can also be processed into flour for pancakes or waffles.

BARLEY, sold whole or pearled (with the tough though nutritious bran covering removed), is another delicious complex carbohydrate that not many Americans know about. In this country barley is used more as a source of malt for beer production; but cooked with raisins and grated lemon peel, it makes a nutritious and delicious cereal high in fiber, iron and other nutrients. It's also good in casseroles and soups. Aside from the flavor, I love the chewy texture of this grain.

MILLET is a term applied to a variety of small seeds used mainly for birdseed in this country, but in Africa, India, and China, millet is a staple grain. The most popular millets are sorghum, the premier cereal in Africa, used in the U.S. mostly for sorghum syrup; or pearl millet, which you can usually find in health food stores for use as a cereal, or in meal form. Millet is used to make porridge in North Africa and roti (a flat bread) in India.

COUSCOUS is a tiny grain made from semolina wheat. It may surprise you, but couscous is not enriched, and so contains fewer B vitamins and iron than macaroni or noodles. Nutritionally, it's white bread. Still, it may be a pleasant change from rice or pasta, couscous which has gained popularity, is now packaged in almost instant, ready-to-prepare boxes. Read the labels carefully for sodium content, because many of these mixes contain too much salt.

COOKING TIP: Try the recipes for KASHA VARNISHKAS, MILLET PILAF, and BASIC BARLEY on pages 187-188.

Beans, Peas, Lentils, and Other Legumes

Legumes are vegetables that come in pods. They include all beans, often named for their shape or color: kidney, black, pink, red, or white; peas, which are usually round but also grow elongated and multicolored like black-eyed peas; and lentils, flat, disk-like legumes that are green or pink or orange, and are sold whole or split. The peanut is also a legume, not a nut.

White beans, red beans, kidney beans, black-eyed peas, lentils, and garbanzos are all similar in content—they are outstanding complex carbohydrates, low in fats and salt, and high in fiber. They are also very economical, and among the most nourishing of vegetables. Use them in casseroles and soups, in salads or as a side dish. They're also a good source of water-soluble vitamins, especially thiamine, riboflavin, niacin, and folate.

Red, white, and kidney beans, black-eyed peas, lentils, and garbanzos are generally packaged dried, and most are available canned or frozen. Dried peas and beans lose their nutritional value after about a year of storage. Frozen and canned beans usually contain too much salt, but canned no-salt added legumes are now showing up in most grocery stores.

Aside from highest grades for nutritional and economic value, beans are rich in anticarcinogenic substances that may prevent or control certain cancers. Soybeans contain a particular type of anticarcinogen that may reduce the risk of some hormone-dependent cancers, such as breast or prostate.*

Beano is sold in most grocery and health food stores as an aid to reduce gassiness. It is a digestive aid. When a couple of drops of this digestive enzyme is added to your first spoonful of beans or lentils, the result are like magic! It is very effective, practically tasteless, and

---

*The once lowly soybean was considered, until recently, to be good for nothing but animal feed. Now soybeans prepared as textured soy protein burgers and tofu has gone mainstream. The chemical, genistein, found in soybeans, first identified in 1987, is believed to be effective in preventing prostate cancer or slowing progression of early stage prostate cancer when combined with a high fiber, low animal fat diet. Because the phytoestrogens found in soy mimics real estrogen, some of the discomfort of menopause may be alleviated by women who consume soy products. That's the theory as to why a lot of Asian women experience fewer symptoms and hot flashes. They get a tremendous amount of soy and have all their lives.

safe. For those of you unable to tolerate legumes because of gassiness, I highly recommend this additive. It is also safe for toddlers. Follow the directions on the label.

COOKING TIP: Try the recipes for LENTIL SOUP, BEAN CUISINE'S "THICK AS FOG SPLIT PEA SOUP," BLACK-EYED PEAS, BEAN DIP, BEAN, TURKEY, AND BROCCOLI DINNER, and FRIJOLES on pages 200-203.

Yellow Vegetables

Yellow vegetables are rich in beta-carotenes, which convert to vitamin A when eaten. Carrots, squash, yams, and sweet potatoes are examples of vegetables loaded with carotenes.* Yellow corn and cantaloupe are also rich in vitamin A or beta-carotene. If you are looking for foods high in vitamin A, think yellow.

Fortunately most children love carrots. The younger child should be given only steamed or cooked carrots because raw carrots may cause choking. For the older child, however, carrots make a wonderful snack. Supermarkets now sell ready prepared, peeled small carrots in bags. With the exception of beets, carrots contain more sugar than any other vegetable, which explains why children find it to be a satisfying snack eaten raw and a tasty addition to a variety of cooked dishes.

Tomatoes

Tomatoes complement many other foods such as poultry, meats, fish, pasta, pizza, and most other vegetables. Perhaps that is why it is one of the most popular vegetables among Americans. Botanically, the tomato is a fruit, but in 1893, the Supreme Court of the United States, in its wisdom, proclaimed it a vegetable! Whether tomatoes are a fruit

---

*Yams or sweet potatoes are rich in fiber, complex carbohydrates, calcium, potassium, and vitamins A and C. Despite the name, yams are related to the morning glory family and not the potato (from the Andes). When shopping for yams, choose smooth, hard tubers that are free of mushy spots, cuts or bruises. They should seem heavy for their size. Store yams in a cool, dry place, suspended in a wire basket or in an open paper (not plastic) bag. Do not refrigerate, which hardens the yam flesh and degrades its taste. Baked yams are delicious and easy to prepare.

or vegetable doesn't really matter; they are a delicious food.

At one time fresh ripe tomatoes were my favorite food. They were grown for flavor and I'd enjoy tomato sandwiches, tomato marinated with vinegar and onion, or tomato salad. Anything with tomato made a meal more delicious. Much of this has changed with the selection and cultivation of tomato varieties designed for shelf life, machine harvesting, size and shape for canning, with flavor being last on the scientist's plant design list. The university's plant science department has become an extension of agribusiness. These ubiquitous "cardboard" tomatoes should be avoided, and then industry might get the message that consumers desire flavor along with appearance. Greenhouse tomatoes are distinguished by the part of the stem and leaves still attached when they are sold. These are somewhat more tasty than those artificially ripened with ethylene gas. Try growing your own with your child this spring. The taste of a home-grown tomato is a revelation! Next best: tomatoes at the farmers' market. Children love to garden, and those who do are likely to taste and enjoy the fruits of their labor.

Tomatoes that are refrigerated or exposed to temperatures below 55°F lose their ripening potential. If you buy tomatoes slightly under-ripe, place them in a paper bag with an apple or banana and let them ripen at room temperature for a few days. This will enhance their flavor and texture.

When you buy canned tomato products such as tomato sauce, tomato puree, tomato paste, or stewed tomatoes, it is best to choose the "no salt added" brands. *The regular cans contain as much as twelve times the sodium of unsalted brands.* Avoid tomato juice and V-8 type juices, which also contain an enormous amount of salt.

Many children develop a rash around the mouth from the peel oils found under the skin of tomatoes. This is due to irritation and is not allergy. To prevent rash, wash your child's face with warm water and a mild soap, such as Dove, to remove peel oil.

Tomatoes are rich in vitamin C, beta-carotene, and potassium. They also contain some zinc, iron, folate, and the phytochemical lycopene.* Lycopene, a carotenoid, and other tomato nutrients may reduce the risk of prostate cancer. Every vegetable, every fruit, has

---

*Phytochemicals are substances isolated from fruit and vegetables that have medicinal power. They are considered to be nonnutritive because they aren't necessary for human growth, as are vitamins and minerals.

hundreds of phytochemicals. This is one more reason to increase fruit and vegetable consumption.

Greens

Green vegetables range in color from light to dark. They can be used raw in salads, or cooked into interesting side dishes. They are high in vitamin A (they contain beta-carotene like yellow vegetables), vitamin C, and folic acid or folate, and they contain significant amounts of calcium and iron. Along with other complex carbohydrates, they are an important component to the healthy diet.

Greens generally used in salads are the crispy iceberg and Romaine lettuces, and softer leaf lettuces, such as butter leaf, red leaf, oak leaf and others. The darker the greens, the more nutrition and fiber. Although iceberg lettuce is the number one best seller in the United States, it's the least nutritious variety of lettuce. Romaine and loose-leaf lettuces, for example red leaf, contain more vitamin A and calcium than iceberg. Butterhead varieties have more iron. Aside from lettuce, other delicious greens to add to a salad are endive, watercress, dandelion, spinach, Swiss chard, and mustard greens.

Greens good for cooking are mustard and beet greens, collard, kale, chard, and spinach. These also add tasty, colorful, textural interest to some casseroles.

Experiment with all these greens. Try the ones you've never tasted. You may discover you've been missing out on some delicious vegetables.

Green vegetables are the most common rejects of young children. If you keep preparing and eating them yourself, your youngsters will gradually accept them as part of the normal fare. Hopefully, the habit will continue into the teenage years, when the independent-minded child divorces himself from anything green and goes on a pizza, soda, potato chip, corn dog, and M&M diet. If your family seldom eats green vegetables, it's never too late to correct poor eating choices and habits.

Cruciferous Vegetables

The name, cruciferous comes from the Latin word meaning "cross," because these vegetables bear cross-shaped flowers. Family members include cabbage, cauliflower, brussels sprouts, watercress, broccoli, horseradish, kale, kohlrabi, mustard, radishes, rutabagas, turnips, and Asian and collard greens. These vegetables contain cancer fighting compounds called *indoles*. Cruciferous vegetables seem to help protect against cancer of the stomach and large intestine. Studies strongly suggest that these vegetables stimulate the release of anti-cancer enzymes. These enzymes and the antioxidant nutrients, such as carotenoid (beta-carotene and vitamin A) and vitamin C, help remove free radicals, unstable oxygen molecules that promote cancer. As a bonus, most cruciferous vegetables are good sources of dietary fiber. Kale, collard greens, and turnip greens also supply calcium, while others such as brussels sprouts provide iron. Fortunately most children enjoy broccoli. Experiment with this group of vegetables and introduce them early so your child will develop a taste for these wholesome foods.*

COOKING TIP: Try the recipes for BROCCOLI, COLESLAW, STEAMED VEGETABLES, STIR-FRIED VEGETABLES, VEGETABLE SOUP, VEGETABLE SAUTÉ, GREEN SALAD WITH VEGETABLES, HUNGARIAN BUTTER LETTUCE SALAD, and HUNGARIAN CUCUMBERS on pages 189-193.

Onions

Onions rank sixth among the world's leading vegetable crops. They are cousins to garlic, leeks, chives, and shallots. Americans eat 50 percent more onions today than we did ten years ago. The bulbs now rank just behind potatoes and lettuce as our most popular vegetable. Many onions, like Maui Sweet or red Bermudas, are quite juicy because of their high sugar content. Spanish onions are the largest and range in color from yellow to purple and have a mild flavor. White onions tend to be more pungent than yellows or reds. There are no nutritional differences among these types. Select onions that feel dry and solid all over, with no soft spots or sprouts. Avoid onions with green areas or a strong odor, which are signs of decay. Cut raw onions produce volatile compounds that irritate the eyes. To lessen

---

*Offer these vegetables daily in a soup, in salad, as a snack with a dip, raw, steamed, stir fried, mixed with pasta, in tomato sauce or in a Spanish omelet.

eye irritation, hold onions under cold running water as you peel. Chilling onions beforehand also helps.

Cooking onions produces a chemical change that makes them much milder. The heat convert's some compounds found in onions into a substance that is fifty to seventy times sweeter than table sugar! Although onions are not loaded with vitamins, they contain antioxidants called phytochemicals, (plant chemicals), that in laboratory tests have blocked the earliest changes in cells that enable tumors to grow. These are mostly sulfur-containing compounds, or organosulfurs, the same ones that irritate your eyes and give onions their sharp taste. Onions also are reported to lower blood pressure and cholesterol levels and may protect against stomach and esophageal cancers. They are a low-fat food and a great flavor enhancer for potatoes, rice, fish, ground meat, sandwiches, and soup. Virtually every cooking method has been used with onions; however avoid recipes that call for added fats. Also avoid fried onion rings which are extremely high in fat, as well as high-fat onion cheese dips and French onion soup.

Garlic

Garlic is a close relative of the onion. There is much hype about the medicinal powers of garlic, and health food stores continue to make claims that it protects the heart and is an anti-cancer food. To date, few trustworthy studies substantiate these claims. The National Cancer Institute and other universities are currently studying garlic and onion for such effects, but take heart, though: garlic wards off vampires!*

Many Latin American children are introduced to garlic at an early age. It is an excellent taste enhancer; you might want to experiment with it by making salad dressing with garlic vinegar. Place several peeled cloves in a bottle of wine vinegar and let stand for two to three days, covered, and then remove the garlic. Garlic or onion bread is another favorite. Heat the bread in the oven or microwave and then slice the loaf open. Rub the inside with a halved garlic clove or spread with baked garlic and then toast it under the broiler. If you want to use a mild olive oil or Parmesan cheese on the bread, use sparingly. Avoid butter or margarine.

Dracula: Bram Stoker, 1897. "There are things that so afflict him that he has no power, as the garlic that we know of. . . ."

Fruit

The most wonderful thing about fruit is that children adore its sweetness, yet it is extremely healthy. Of course too much of any good thing isn't a good idea, so beware of the *fruitaholic*, the child who is on a total fruit diet, such as grapes, raisins, and juice! It is not the purpose of this book to review in depth all fruit, but I do want to give you an overview to help you understand why fruit is nutritionally important and should be a part of your child's daily diet.

With a few exceptions, such as avocado, fruit is nearly fat-free. Many fruits, especially apples, are high in cholesterol-lowering and blood-sugar stabilizing fiber and also supply some minerals. Three of the most popular fruits, bananas, pears, and oranges, are loaded with potassium, while berries and dried fruit are rich in iron. Citrus fruits, berries, kiwi and papaya are rich in vitamin C. Yellow and orange fruits such as apricots, cantaloupes, peaches, nectarines, and mangoes, are the best sources of beta-carotene (vitamin A) and other carotenoids.*

Although grapes are usually not thought of as being especially nutritious, recently a cancer-preventing substance has been found in high concentrations in grapes. This suggests that there may be even more powerful compounds in other natural foods. This finding does not mean that people should eat a lot of grapes to prevent cancer. The overall message is that fruits and vegetables are very useful against disease.

Another health benefit of grapes,* *for adults,* comes from drinking wine, which can protect against heart attacks. In particular, red wine may protect against heart disease by preventing the formation of blood clots that can block arteries.

Don't forget that the whole grape is a common choking food and should not be given to toddlers under two.

---

*Read more about carotenoids in Chapter 13, under vitamin A.
*Red grape juice appears to slow the activity of blood platelets, making them less likely to clot and cause heart attacks in middle aged and older adults. *Eight to ten ounces of juice seems to be effective,* according to Dr. John D. Folts of the University of Wisconsin Medical School. His research has been funded by the Nutricia Research Foundation of the Netherlands and the Oscar Rennebohm Foundation of Madison, Wisconsin, and more recently by Welch's, which makes grape juice.

COOKING TIP: Try the recipes for CAROL'S BANANA-STRAW-BERRY SMOOTHIE, BAKED APPLE, APPLE SAUCE, PEACH SHERBET, and BAKED PEARS FRENCH STYLE on pages 194-196.

There are few short cuts to good nutrition. Each week a new herbal, vitamin, or mineral is featured at the health food store promising the consumer greater longevity, and a clearer, more facile mind. This approach is specifically derived from soft evidence suggesting some benefits from an amino acid, vitamin, mineral or herb and sold as a panacea. These products are very iffy at best. As an example, beta-carotene taken as a supplement by smokers actually increased morbidity and mortality due to lung cancer instead of giving the assumed protection. I am not saying that supplements are not important. They definitely are. Especially vitamin D, vitamin C, folic acid, vitamin E, vitamin B-12, (especially in the elderly and vegan vegetarians), B-6 in certain select groups, calcium, and selenium. But there is little evidence that these nutrients help very much if the consumer consumes a balanced diet high in fiber, low in sodium and saturated fats.

To get the protective effect of these nutrients, you must eat adequate amounts of fruits and vegetables every day. Foods work together in concert. Isolating any of the many nutritional compounds and putting them in a pill form unfortunately causes them to lose most of their effectiveness for reasons that are not totally clear. Save your money and buy the real thing! All those "nutrients" and antioxidants won't make up for a fatty, salty diet that is low in fruits and vegetables.

A sixteen-year-old who is anxious to "bulk-up" should avoid all those supplements and protein powders and instead work out with weights and eat my recommended diet. The main beneficiaries of supplements sold to teens in heath food stores and gyms are the pocket books of the purveyors of these pills and powders.

In the U.S., fresh fruit is usually available year round, but frozen and canned fruit are also nutritious. Although fruit loses some vitamins during the canning process, the loss is less than found in canned vegetables. This is because fruits are processed at lower temperatures, which destroys fewer nutrients. Try to avoid fruit canned in heavy syrup since it contains fewer vitamins and more sugar calories. Select water-packed canned fruit or canned fruit in unsweetened juice. Frozen strawberries, blueberries, cherries, and peaches are processed without cooking, and therefore there is little nutrient loss.

Dried fruits are an excellent source of vitamins, mineral, and fiber. Dried prunes, raisins, apricots, peaches and apples are available in all markets.* If possible, purchase the no-sulfite-added variety. Mild sulfite sensitivity or allergy may cause a slight tickling of the throat, while severe reactions can result in asthma or breathing difficulty. Check the health food stores for sulfite-free dried fruit. If you're not sulfite sensitive, variety packs that contain sulfites are available in most supermarkets.†

BEWARE OF SULFITES

Although the incidence of sulfite sensitivity is small in the general population, it can cause airway obstruction, cough, hives, and nasal congestion. The FDA banned the use of sulfites in fresh and raw fruit and vegetables in 1986. Commercial baby foods do not contain sulfites, but I do not recommend sulfite-containing foods at any age, if it can be avoided. Certainly it should not be given to children with a history of hives or asthma. Sulfites are also commonly found in avocado dip, shrimp, shellfish, bacon, and cold cuts. Federal law requires food manufacturers to list the sulfite content of any product containing more than ten parts per million. The FDA has a "generally recognized as safe" list (GRAS) that can give further information on sulfites.

---

*Mariani Premium Mixed Fruit is a blend of dehydrated sliced apple, pitted prunes, apricots, freestone peaches, and Bartlett pears. Mariani Packing Co. Inc. 320 Jackson Street, San Jose, CA, 95112.
†Sulfites are used widely by the food industry as a preservative and are found in processed potatoes, dried and packaged fruits, and beverages, shrimp and seafood, beer and wine, avocadoes, guacamole, cider and vinegar, pickled vegetables, some albacore tuna, white grapes, maraschino cherries, fresh mushrooms, beet sugar, wet-milled corn and conditioned dough. Symptoms of sulfite allergy include mild tickling sensation of the throat to more severe reactions including tissue swelling, hives, cough, asthma, and, rarely, allergic shock. Researchers speculate that asthmatic sulfite reactions may be related to a deficiency of the enzyme sulfite oxidase, which is required to break down sulfites in the body. For more information: Asthma and Allergy Foundation of America, 1125 15th St. N.W., Suite 502, Washington, DC, 20005; Tel: 202-466-7643.

Prunes are a variety of dried plums. As with other dried fruit, the drying process concentrates the nutrients. First and foremost, prunes are a high-fiber food, containing ounce for ounce, more fiber than dried beans and most other fruits and vegetables. Over half this fiber is of the soluble blood cholesterol-lowering type. Prunes are also rich in beta-carotene and are a good source of B vitamins, iron, and potassium.

Like other dried fruit, raisins are a concentrated source of sticky-sugar calories, and supply 2 mg of iron per ⅔ cup. That's 20 percent of the adult RDA for men and 13 percent of the adult RDA for women. That's as much iron, by weight, as cooked dried beans or ground beef. For the older child or adolescent raisins is a wholesome snack food. For the younger child, a diet of raisins along with excessive juice and crackers, often causes a skinny child with lots of tooth decay. So save this snack for the older child and don't forget to brush teeth afterwards.

To make a healthy low-fat trail mix, combine raisins with other dried fruit, puffed or shredded wheat cereal, popcorn, and sunflower seeds. Add spiced raisin into nonfat yogurt or add raisins and cinnamon to low-fat or nonfat cottage cheese. Or pack plumped spicy raisins along with cinnamon into a pita bread pocket for a low-fat "danish."

Real fruit juice is healthy, especially orange juice, but should be consumed in moderate amounts. Juices contain most of the fruit nutrients *except for the very important fiber.* Beverages labeled "juice" must be 100 percent juice. Read the labels carefully! *"Juice blends," fruit "punches," "drinks," and "juice cocktails," usually contain little juice, the rest being sugar water.* Avoid Hi-C, Tang, Hawaiian Punch, Capri Sun, Gatorade, fruit soda and the like. And don't get your child into the soda habit. *Soda is a poor choice because it destroys teeth, and its high phosphate content promotes calcium elimination from your body.* There are 10 teaspoons of sugar in one can of Coke! A growing body needs calcium for strong bone development. *Diet sodas are a special hazard and should not be a part of your child's diet.* Many parents mistakenly choose diet soda over regular soda because they believe sugar is a "poison." As described earlier in the book, sugar has received an undeserved reputation. It remains one of the healthier sweeteners. *The important thing to remember about sugar is to consume only a little of it.* When sugar becomes a major part of the diet, then it is harmful, like any nutrient consumed in excess. The *long term effect* of artificial sweeteners has not been adequately studied, in my opinion, and therefore should be avoided by children and teenagers. Let's protect our children from nutritional experimentation!

A juice often overlooked is prune juice. This nutritious juice contains 3 mg of iron or 30 percent of the RDA for adult men, and 20 percent for women. A cup of prune juice contains 473 mg of potassium, about the same amount as eight pitted prunes. It contains a few more calories than orange juice, 182 calories per cup compared to 110 calories in a cup of orange juice. Don't purchase brands with added sugar.

When buying fruit, remember that fresh fruit tastes the best. If you are buying fruit to eat today, buy ripe—especially apples, cherries, grapefruit, grapes, oranges, pineapple, strawberries, tangerines, and watermelon. For tomorrow or the next day, look for fruit that needs just a little ripening. To hasten the ripening of pears and peaches, put them in a loosely closed paper bag at room temperature. Apricots, bananas, cantaloupe, kiwi, nectarines, and plums can also be ripened in this way.

CHAPTER SIX

THE OLDER CHILD'S DIET

▲ ▲ ▲

During elementary school years, children spend far more time away from home. School and outside activities consume a large part of each day. Peers, older children, baby-sitters, and teachers influence your child's development. From these role models children pick up behaviors and habits—eating habits, as well as others. Sometimes parents begin to feel uneasy as they realize they have less control over what their children are doing and eating. With diet, as well as behavior in general, your chances of affecting the outcome will improve if you set a good example at home instead of resorting to criticism and threats.

One area that parents often question me about is school lunches. "What can I prepare for my child to take to school? It must be something convenient and transportable," they often ask. How can parents also make lunches nutritious and appealing? The latter is essential if you want to make sure your child won't trade the lunch you prepared for a bag of chips and cupcakes!

In my family we have dealt with the problem of school lunches for years. We have developed some good, nutritious recipes which have passed the test of time as well as the criteria for convenience. "Good food" need not be boring. Children need not feel deprived of life's goodies. Besides fresh fruits and fresh fruit juices, there are lots of nutritious low-salt, low-fat snacks easily prepared and commercially available. I will share them with you in the upcoming pages.

As a parent, you can become an activist whenever you see lots of junk food in a public or private school lunch program or at a PTA and after-school activities. Insisting that fresh fruit be offered along-side the snow cones, candy bars, chips, hot dogs, etc., won't make many inroads. These junk foods are too tempting for most children to resist, and the fruit will be left to rot. Your opponents will then remind you that your idealism is, "not practical." Don't accept such negativism. Armed with this book, you can explain why wholesome foods are practical, and when properly prepared and presented, are welcomed by children. Most parents realize their obligation to protect their children against the hazards of life. It is time to realize that junk foods are some of these hazards. In order to protect a child from falling into the habit of consuming large quantities of harmful foods, it is best not to have them available except for special occasions.

It is time I told you what I believe junk food is, if you haven't already guessed. To me junk food is one that contains an excess of calories from fat and sugar. In addition, salt is often a major ingredient, and fiber is usually absent or extremely low. It is untrue that "junk foods" are void of nutrients. They often contain many nutrients, including protein, minerals, and vitamins. *What makes them undesirable is the imbalance they bring to our diets.* Crackers, chips, hot dogs, salami, pepperoni pizza, ice cream, french fries, granola bars, Milky Ways, Lunchables, Hot Pockets,* and Top Ramen are a few examples of disaster foods, loaded with salt and fats and depleted of fiber. If you don't believe that these foods have become the mainstay of our children's diet, look at a typical week's menu from an elementary or high school, public or private, in your community. I'm not suggesting that these foods never be consumed. They can be enjoyed as party or holiday foods. Daily consumption is what makes junk foods dangerous.

When I first began cooking for myself as a graduate student in Philadelphia during the 1950s, the supermarket visit was an adventure in gastrochemistry. What were the food technologists coming out with today? I examined the shelves with the same glee I felt going to debut new cars.

Instant rice and instant mashed potatoes. One-minute oatmeal and wheat cereal. Chocolate cake and bake mix in a jiffy. Instant chocolate pudding. All my favorites now at my fingertips! Frozen turkey pot pie, ice cream, and canned peaches for a high-living dinner.

Now I'm talking like a traitor about these foods. They did carry

---

*Frozen sandwiches such as Hot Pockets Ham and Cheese are a 4½ ounce, 340-calorie indulgence with 15 grams of fat and 840 milligrams of sodium.

me through hard times. The nutritional ravages against my body by my chosen diet was not visible, so who knew? What I didn't realize then is that it isn't significantly more time consuming or difficult to eat healthy foods. It takes only moments to wash a fresh ripe peach or peel an orange.

Like other physicians of my generation, we smoked cigarettes and over-consumed most of the foods I am now condemning. We were completely ignorant of the connection between diet and what we called degenerative diseases of adulthood, which we believed were inevitable. It wasn't until I completed my formal medical training that I learned about the lipid hypothesis.* *This gradually changed my approach to nutrition from a biochemical concept to actual food choices.* It is clear that with all the new nutritional information, our children have an opportunity to enjoy the rewards of improved health and vigor throughout adulthood. As parents, we have the obligation to provide the best we can for our children. One does not have to be wealthy to provide the best nutrition. In fact, healthy foods often cost less than many of the expensive processed meals passed off as food.

Breakfast

Many families face a time crunch getting to work or school in the morning. Children often try to capture that last moment of sleep before getting up for school, or teenagers may be more interested in hair or makeup, so there is seldom time for breakfast. It is estimated that 50 to 70 percent of students go to school without breakfast and that an adequate breakfast is consumed in no more than 20 percent of American households. Some youngsters have grown so accustomed to not eating breakfast that they don't feel hungry until midmorning.

So the question comes up—just how important is breakfast? My answer is an unequivocal *very!* Studies on school children show a strong link between a nutritious breakfast and improved school per-formance. Furthermore, the studies reveal that school performance

---

*Research has expanded our understanding of the atherosclerotic process. It has validated the lipid hypothesis and has discovered additional factors contributing to the development of atherosclerosis. A diet high in saturated fat is a major cause of clogged blood vessels and often leads to heart attack and stroke. See Chapter 11 for more information on the lipid hypothesis.

is adversely affected by omitting breakfast. Children who skip breakfast seem to be more jumpy, have a harder time relating to peers and teachers, and have difficulty concentrating. The physiological reasons for these behavioral changes are poorly understood to date, but repeated observations have made them impossible to dismiss.

It's logical to assume that similar behavior and performance changes occur in adults who do not take the time to eat an adequate breakfast. For most people the time span between dinner and breakfast is anywhere from eleven to thirteen hours. Omitting breakfast adds another three hours to that fast. Fasting for this length of time puts a stress on the body and causes the formation of fatty acids which are released into the bloodstream. Free fatty acids contribute to the atherosclerotic process that damages and rapidly ages our blood vessels. Fasting also strains the gallbladder, which may lead an adolescent or adult to become more susceptible to a gallbladder attack. It is not my wish to deny the spiritual benefits of fasting to anyone whose religion recommends it for "cleansing the spirit," but there is no scientific evidence to recommend fasting from the nutritional point of view.

BREAKFAST ON THE RUN is one way of dealing with late starters, short of complete behavior modification. By that I mean a glass of 1-percent or nonfat milk, a banana and a bagel! Peel and eat the banana on the way to school. The bagel can be used as a midmorning snack if there is no time to consume it before class. Another alternative is a smoothie—a 4-oz. glass of real orange juice blended with a banana, strawberries, or ripe pears, plus 3 oz. of 1-percent or nonfat milk.

Instant cooked cereal such as Cream of Rice, Quick Cream of Wheat, Pillsbury Farina and instant oatmeal are popular cereals that may work if one has a little more time. Add hot water or milk and serve! The protein content of an average serving made with 4 oz. of nonfat milk is a respectable 8 grams. These cereals are low in fat and high in complex carbohydrates, with no sugar added. One drawback: because these cereals are so highly processed, the fiber has been milled out, unlike regular oatmeal which contains an appreciable amount of fiber. Replace the fiber by adding fresh fruit to the cereal.

Such cereals as Quaker 100% Natural, Heartland, and Granola are extremely high in fat and sugar. These cereals boast "naturalness," but oils and sugars have been added—a not so natural occurrence. Since a high-fat diet is more responsible for malnutrition in America than dietary deficiency, any high-fat cereal should be avoided. *Read the labels on the boxes and select cereals with no more than 3 grams of fat per serving.*

Dry cereals have won a place in the traditional American breakfast. Some observers have stated the nutritional value of dry cereal is proportional to the amount of milk used with each serving. In many instances this is true. However, some of the dry cereals offer better nutrition than others. It is important to read labels on dry cereals since most overuse simple carbohydrates such as sucrose, corn syrup, honey or molasses. Froot Loops, Cocoa Puffs, Sugar Pops, Cap'n Crunch, and Honey Combs are but a few of the cereals to avoid. Of the dry cereals, Shredded Wheat, Grapenuts, Special K, Nutrigrain cereals, and some of the Healthy Choice cereals rate favorably because most are low in fat and simple sugar and have some fiber. Select a cereal that has at least 3 grams of fiber.

Instant breakfast bars are really candy bars masquerading as food. Sports bars contain large amounts of sugar in the form of fructose, honey, molasses, corn syrup, dextrose, maltose, sorbital, corn solids and lactose. Most of these products are 40 to 70 percent simple carbohydrate when totaled. Not only do these sticky carbohydrates promote tooth decay, but they provide a high degree of calories without the natural nutrients of real food.* Many of these bars are low in fiber, compared with the usual amount of fiber accompanying equivalent calories found in complex carbohydrates. Their sodium content is often excessive as well. Check nutrition labels for sugars, fat content and fiber. The Nutrition Facts and ingredients label may be more revealing than the hype on the wrapping. It's true that a child may be eager to eat these breakfast bars, while hot cereal causes a lengthy debate; but the result is instant poor dietary habit. The next time you're shopping, check the ingredients on the Pop Tarts package. The first nine ingredients are sugars and then comes the trace of "dried apples." Even the low-fat variety is an expensive jelly sandwich on toast.

As for pancake mixes, most contain too much salt and fat. It is estimated that three pancakes, about four inches in diameter with a patty of melted butter on each, provides 37 grams of fat and well over 1000 mg of sodium. Pancakes are a favorite for children and adolescents alike. Fortunately it is not hard to prepare a nutritious pancake. Select a low-fat, low or reduced salt mix. Many new ones arrive on

CHILD

*To learn more about carbohydrates, read Chapter 9 for a quick refresher course.

the shelves monthly. If the recipe calls for milk, use nonfat milk. Reduce the suggested oil by a third, and if directions call for an egg to be added, substitute two egg whites and discard the yolk. Use a nonstick ungreased frying pan or griddle.

To make good pancakes, the nonstick pan must be sufficiently heated. If it is not hot enough, the pancakes will be tough, since pancakes must be cooked rapidly; however, be careful to avoid making the pan hot enough to burn them. Test the temperature by dropping a few drops of water in the pan—it should sizzle immediately.

A breakfast favorite of mine is *palatschincken*, an Austrian crepe or pancake. It's easy to make. Prepare a low-fat, low salt pancake mix but add more liquid to thin the mix. Pour about one tablespoon into a hot nonstick pan. Allow it to spread very thinly over an area about five inches in diameter. Turn it over and cook briefly. Remove the thin crepe from the pan and place on a dish. Put a tablespoon of your favorite fresh berries or jam in the middle and roll it up like a blintz or tortilla. Sprinkle with powdered sugar. Try it on a relaxed Sunday morning. It's especially delicious when it's raining or snowing outside!

Pizza

Pizza is probably the most popular main dish in America, so I won't suggest that you give it up. This gooey cheese and tomato sauce topping fast food is the mainstay of many school lunch programs. It is promoted heavily as a high source of protein, vitamins, minerals and complex carbohydrates, but what is omitted is that one portion of pizza often contains over 1000 mg of sodium and loads of artery clogging fat. Although every pizza is different, depending on the pizza parlor's recipe, many pizzas provide over 25–30 grams or 50 percent of its calories from fat. If it's a double-cheese pizza with pepperoni or ground beef, there's even more fat and salt. In general, pizza is also very low in fiber unless it is loaded with vegetable toppings. Defenders of the school pizza remind us of all that calcium and protein pizza provides. You draw your own conclusions. In the meantime, there are alternatives. Tasty lower-fat and lower-sodium pizza is available.

Lower-fat frozen pizzas can now be found at most supermarkets. Wolfgang Puck's Mushroom & Spinach has 11 grams of total fat and 520 mg of sodium per portion, while McCain Ellio's Healthy Slices

Pizza has only 6 grams of fat and 700 mg of sodium per serving. This basic pizza is a kids' favorite. Explore the Nutrition Facts label before buying your next frozen pizza, and the next time you're at the pizza parlor ask for a pizza with less cheese and a vegetarian topping instead of sausage or pepperoni.

Chicken Nuggets and Fish Sticks

Another high-fat, high-sodium favorite is the chicken nugget, now becoming a mainstay in the school lunch. Kids love these dishes and there is no need to give them up. What must be done is to prepare

---

MAKING YOUNG FISH FANS

Two of our most nutritious foods, fish and seafood, are most often greeted with a "yuk!" unless it is fried "fish & chips," fried "Filet o' Fish" dipped in a high-fat tartar sauce, or the heart-deadly seafoods such as heavily creamed New England clam chowder, lobster bisque, fried crab cakes, and fried shrimp. What is it about wholesomely prepared fish and shellfish that makes it so unappetizing to children and adolescents? My feeling is that it's because fish is not introduced early enough into a child's diet. In my private pediatric practice I see many first-generation Asian children, who are introduced to fish soups after or shortly before their first birthday. They seem to love fish. I have not seen an increase in food allergy in these children, but children with eczema probably should avoid fish until they are much older and not before consulting with their pediatrician, dermatologist, or allergist.

While many adults seem to be eating more fish, children need to be encouraged to sample foods such as broiled, grilled, or baked salmon, bass, swordfish, ahi tuna, or sautéed shrimp and scallops.

Introduce fish soups to your children when they are young. Tastes are developed early. When I worked in Vietnam I noticed that children and adults ate fish soup for breakfast! My first reaction was, "How could they?" By the end of my first week of work at the Children's Hospital #1 in Ho Chi Minh City, I was enjoying the traditional breakfasts of pho (a chicken soup with rice noodles) or fish soup.

---

them using tasty low-fat, low-sodium recipes. For example, Banquet Fat Free Breast Tenders are baked instead of deep fried and they are delicious, although too high in sodium. Compare this with Louis Rich's greasy Turkey Nuggets. Mrs. Paul's Low Fat and Low Sodium fish sticks are a great improvement over regular fish sticks and is another example of how innovative cooking can change a poorly conceived food into a wholesome dish. Keep checking the Nutrition Facts label and be sure to read Parts II and III of this book for more information on how to interpret the label.

COOKING TIP: Try the recipe for "FRIED" FILLET OF FISH on page 204.

Ideas for Snacks and Lunches at Home or School

CHILD

▲　　　Grilled cheese sandwich using nonfat sliced Swiss cheese. Use nonstick skillet or microwave on toasted bread briefly to melt cheese. Nonfat cheese tastes better if it is melted.

▲　　　Meat, rice, and ketchup mix packed in Tupperware-like container for transportation (see recipe on page 182).

▲　　　Baked apple, plain or with yogurt (see recipe on page 194).

▲　　　Tuna salad sandwich made with 50-percent-less-salt tuna and nonfat mayonnaise or nonfat yogurt. Make with one slice of whole wheat bread and one slice of white bread.

▲　　　Fresh fruit salad.

▲　　　Bowl of chili—vegetarian or with very lean meat.

▲　　　Chicken sandwich using low-salt ketchup or nonfat mayonnaise as a spread. Corn on the cob. When not in season, a bowl of corn kernels mixed with green peas. A Zip-loc type bag makes this mixture transportable.

▲   Boca Burger (vegetarian "hamburger" found in most health food stores' frozen section) grilled and served on a toasted bun with low-salt ketchup, slice of butter lettuce and slice of *ripe* tomato. Use sliced cherry tomatoes when vine ripened tomatoes are not available.

▲   Extra-lean roast beef sandwich with favorite roll. Use mustard as a spread. Serve with a banana or slice of melon. Have a side dish mixture of rice, broccoli, and sliced steamed carrots.

▲   Hamburger made with *extra*-lean ground beef. Add some rice and chicken broth to the meat mixture to keep it moist and enhance its flavor. For variety try mixing in a little mustard or barbeque sauce. Serve with low-salt brand of chicken rice or noodle soup (Healthy Choice or Health Valley). Add an apple or seasonal fruit.

▲   Meatloaf sandwich. Raw carrots and cherry tomatoes. Mixed dehydrated fruit (Mariani Premium Mixed Fruit is a blend of dehydrated sliced apple, pitted prunes, apricots, freestone peaches, and Bartlett pears. Mariani Packing Co. Inc. 320 Jackson Street, San Jose, CA, 95112)

▲   Cup of pea soup using one of the many low-salt, low-fat brands (such as Healthy Choice). Baked skinless drumettes of chicken, sprinkled with sweet paprika over rice. Slice or cubes of cantaloupe in a bowl with blueberries when in season.

▲   Boiled, steamed, or microwaved corn on the cob, without any salt, but a little butter substitute if desired. Broiled skinless chicken breast, plain or sliced thin on a bun with fresh salsa as a topping. Fresh orange, peeled.

CHILD

▲ Small bowl of macaroni with grated nonfat cheese, such as Kraft shredded nonfat mozzarella, sprinkled over it and microwaved until the cheese melts. Low salt vegetable soup. A fruit smoothie.

▲ Ravioli (Soy Boy) Plain, Ravioli Rosa, Ravioli Verde (Northern Soy, Inc. 545 West Ave., Rochester, New York 14611, (716) 235-8970). A great snack as well as a lunch! Serve with a small salad. Haagen-Daz Peach Frozen Yogurt Bar.

▲ Nachos. Bowl of low-fat, low salt-beans. (Don't forget the Beano—two or three drops with the first bite!) Strawberry-banana smoothie.

▲ Fresh toasted bagel with hummus or nonfat cream cheese. One tablespoon of cooked bay shrimp stirred into a cup of minestrone soup (low-salt brand). Raw celery and raw carrots. Nonfat Haagen Daz Frozen Sorbet Bar.

▲ Bowl of medium-sized shrimp and salsa. Baked potato with nonfat sour cream and chives. (Naturally Yours Fat Free Sour Cream* is especially delicious and has 67 percent fewer calories than regular sour cream.) Use salsa as topping for potato as well, if desired. Hungarian cucumber salad (see recipe on page 193).

▲ Leftover spaghetti with low-salt, low-fat tomato meat sauce. Serve heated or cold. Transportable in a Tupperware-like container. Fresh apple. Nonfat or 1-percent milk.

▲ Turkey sandwich made with unprocessed real turkey.* Use nonfat mayonnaise or cranberry sauce as a spread. Mashed potato, baked yam or sweet potato. Frookie Fat-Free Fruitins cookies.

---

*Naturally Yours Fat Free Sour Cream is distributed by M STAR Inc. 5956 Sherry Lane, Dallas, TX, 75225.
*Avoid the salted turkey roll or pre-wrapped processed chicken or turkey slices.

▲   Pita bread (pocket bread) stuffed with shredded lettuce, cooked ground lean hamburger meat or cooked ground turkey,* sprouts, and low-fat salad dressing on top. York Peppermint Pattie.

▲   Beef or turkey tacos with shredded lettuce, tomato, shredded nonfat or low-fat cheese. Glass of nonfat or 1-percent milk. Whole-wheat fig bars (Pride o' the Farm Fat Free).

▲   Cold leftover broiled salmon sandwich served with low-fat salad dressing as a spread, lettuce, and slice of ripe tomato. A salmon salad with medley of vegetables is another variation.

▲   Omelet made with two egg whites and one yolk. Cubed vegetable sauté, shredded mozzarella cheese, and lean low-salt ham, diced, for the inside. Served with salsa over the top when cooked. Serve with a toasted bagel and very small boiled new potatoes.

▲   Homemade pizza. Salad.

▲   Egg salad sandwich. Unsalted or low-salt whole-wheat pretzels.

▲   Chili dog (nonfat, reduced-salt hot dog on a toasted bun with nonfat chili beans spooned over it. Nonfat corn chips. Nonfat "ice cream" (such as Haagen-Daz Nonfat Yogurt Cherry Vanilla). This may be a reasonable compromise or substitute for the traditional PTA lunch, although most such hot dogs contain headache-producing nitrites.

▲   Waffles made with low-fat pancake mix or Buckwheat Pancakes using recipe on page 185. (Goldrush, San Francisco Style, Sour Dough reduced fat Pancake & Waffle Mix.† Recipe on box.)

CHILD

---

*The Turkey Store, Extra Lean Ground Breast or Butterball Fat Free.
†Goldrush Sour Dough Pancake & Waffle Mix. Cal-Gar, 383 Beach Road, Burlingame, CA, 94010.

▲   Gazpacho—especially on those warm days. Enchilada or taco.

▲   Banana bread, corn bread, or latkes with apple sauce.

▲   Wanda's spaghetti pie (see recipe on page 211).

▲   Sliced kiwi, dry cereal (Healthy Choice, Special K, Nutrigrain, or Shredded Wheat) and non-fat milk.

▲   Turkey hamburger. Haagen-Daz reduced-fat chocolate or vanilla ice cream (3 grams of fat per portion). Fresh orange slices or canned mandarin wedges over the ice cream.

▲   Teriyaki fish sandwich (see included recipe). Small bag of nonfat corn or potato chips. Grapes or seasonal melon.

▲   Bay Shrimp tacos with shredded lettuce, chopped onion, very ripe tomato, cilantro and tomatillo sauce topping.

▲   Low-fat bean burrito (see recipe on page 211), slice of watermelon if in season or Carol's banana shake.

▲   Salmon sandwich on rye or whole wheat bread. (Canned salmon mixed with nonfat mayo, chopped scallions, and sliced cherry tomatoes plus butter lettuce on top.)

▲   Spread 1 teaspoon of nonfat herbal cream cheese on a whole wheat tortilla. Place 1 or 2 slices of unsalted, sliced turkey on it and roll it up. This makes a great breakfast or snack.

▲   Substitute 100-percent orange juice for a Capri Sun drink. Avoid beverages that say "drink" or "punch," because most have little more nutrition than colored sugar water.

▲ Don't forget the ten super-foods: sweet potatoes, whole grain bread, broccoli, strawberries, beans,
cantaloupe, spinach and kale, oranges, oatmeal, nonfat (skim) or 1-percent fat milk.

CHILD

CHAPTER SEVEN

THE FOODS CHILDREN NEED, PART 2

▲   ▲   ▲

Fish and Shellfish

Tuna, pollack, cod, salmon, and flounder account for at least three-quarters of all the fish Americans eat. Other varieties such as bass, catfish, shark, trout, monkfish, orange roughy, swordfish, and mahi-mahi are growing in popularity. Although some fish are slightly high in fat, most fish are an excellent source of low cholesterol, low saturated fat, and high protein, and should be consumed more often by children, adolescents and adults. Some children enjoy fish from an early age while others seem to acquire a taste for fish a little later. This may be cultural, since most of my Asian and Hispanic patients seen to enjoy fish and shellfish by one year of age.

Unfortunately, fish sticks, "Fillet o' Fish," fish and chips, and other types of fried fish appeal to children too. Fish sticks are coated with crumbs or batter, fried, and frozen. Because they are easy to reheat in the microwave, they appear to be a simple and nutritious answer to preparing fish. Although fish sticks and these fried fish products are an excellent source of protein, they are made with pollock, an inexpensive fish very low in omega-3 fat,* and they are coated with

---

*Omega-3-fatty acids—also known as linolenic fatty acids—are found in cold-water fish and plant sources such as nuts, flaxseed and certain vegetable oils. Omega-6 and omega 3-fatty acids are special essential fats. See the next page and Chapter 11. Also see alpha-linolenic acid (ALA); docosahexanoic acid (DHA); and eicosapentenoic acid (EPA).

as much as 13 grams of fat or about 45 percent calories from fat. There's also a lot of added sodium-more than 900 mg per serving in some brands. Add salty ketchup, tartar sauce, or cocktail sauce and you're already exceeding the daily total Nutritional Guidelines recommendation for salt. If you do buy fish sticks, look for brands that say low-fat and low-salt. They should contain 4 grams of fat or less per serving and half the salt found in regular fish sticks. For example, Mrs. Paul's Low Fat Fish Sticks contains 4 grams of fat and 450 mg of salt per five-stick serving. This is a reasonable compromise if you're looking for something easy to prepare after an exhausting day. Check the Nutrition Facts label. I've included several fish recipes that most children love, such as Veracruzana Sauce (page 184)— great on broiled red snapper—and "Fried" Fillet of Fish—a "shake 'n' bake" preparation method for whitefish. My mock crab dipped in cocktail sauce recipe is another favorite of older children, teenagers, and young adults. Since crab is not a kosher food and therefore not eaten by many observant Jews, many Jewish cookbooks contain excellent tasty recipes for making imitation crab snacks or meals.

Fish provides more than relatively low-fat protein. It is high in docosahexaenoic acid (DHA), which is the fatty acid (a component of fat) that is needed for optimal brain growth and eye development. (Refer to the earlier chapter on nursing and breast milk.). EPA (eicosapentaenoic acid), another fatty acid found in fish lowers blood cholesterol and protects arterial walls against the harmful effect of LDL cholesterol. These compounds are referred to as omega-3 fatty acids (These "fats" are referred to as "fish oils.") and are also found in shellfish. Another or second variety of omega-3 fatty acid, *alpha-linolenic acid* (LNA) is found in plant foods and is especially high in oils like canola oil. This essential fatty acid (a fat that the body can't manufacture) is needed for the growth and maintenance of our cells, tissues, and entire body. Inside the body, a small amount of *alpha-linolenic acid* is converted to EPA and DHA. As described in chapter 12, there is another essential fatty acid. It is called *linoleic acid*. Foods high in linoleic acid are vegetable oils such as corn, safflower, soybean, and sunflower seed oils. Most of us eat ten times as much linoleic acid as alpha-linolenic acid. It is believed that the ratio should be closer to 1:1. When linoleic acid dominates too heavily over the omega-3s (alpha-linolenic acid, DHA, and EPA) we may be more prone to illness that cause inflamed muscles and joints, increased menstrual cramps, heart arrhythmias (irregular heart beats), and even post-partum depression. A 3-oz. serving of baked salmon provides almost 2 grams of EPA plus DHA. *That is ten times the calculated current intake found in the average American diet.* If you don't like fish, substitute your polyunsaturated salad oil, (corn, safflower, or soybean oil) with a plant omega-3 oil such as canola oil. Remember, though, it is important to keep total fat low, and if you follow my diet suggestions you will automatically consume sufficient essential fatty acids or fats. *And avoid fish oil supplements.* They may have unexpected and unwelcomed side effects, such as bleeding.

As much as I believe fish is an important part of the diet, pregnant women should avoid fatty fish such as sablefish, mackerel, bluefish, and striped bass because they contain pesticides, mercury, and cancer-causing PCBs. Eat swordfish, shark, or fresh tuna steaks no more than once a week due to the possibility of an elevated mercury content. A 1994 study of San Francisco Bay waters found unsafe methyl mercury levels in some fish caught in those waters, prompting warning that consumption of these fish be severely restricted. Pregnant women can avoid excess mercury by limiting consumption of canned tuna to seven ounces a week. Any freshwater fish caught in inland lakes, especially the Great Lakes, are more likely to be contaminated with PCBs and dioxin and should be completely avoided especially during pregnancy. PCBs also have been shown to contribute to learning problems in children.

COOKING TIP: Try the recipe for "FRIED" FILLET OF FISH on page 204.

Meats and Poultry

Americans love meat! Meat and poultry are the central focus of most of our meals. Meat is high in saturated fat and cholesterol, especially beef, pork, and lamb. In recent years consumers have become aware that a diet high in meat is associated with colon and prostate cancer and increased risk of an early heart attack, the number one cause of death for Americans. Does that mean you should not eat meat?

Children, adolescents, and adults can nutritionally benefit from a small amount of meat in their daily diet. The emphasis should be on small. For a teenager or adult, no more than 3½-oz. serving per day.

That portion amounts to the size of a deck of cards. Meats and poultry are exceptionally rich in iron, zinc, and vitamins B-6 and B-12. These nutrients are difficult to obtain in a meatless diet. The choice of meat or poultry should be low in fat—less than 10 grams of fat per 3½-oz. serving. I will list these foods below with their approximate fat content, so you will be able to make a nutritionally intelligent choice when selecting meats for your family meal, at home, your favorite fast food take-out, or restaurant.

COMPARING BEEF CUTS

GROUND BEEF: 3½ OZ. COOKED

	Calories	Fat (g)	Saturated fat (g)	Cholesterol (mg)
Regular ground beef	289	21	8	90
Lean ground beef	272	18	7	87
Extra lean ground beef	256	16	6	84

As you can see by the above table, cholesterol levels do not change very much between regular beef and extra lean ground beef. It is the fat content that does change, and fat is more atherogenic (more damaging to the blood vessels) than cholesterol. Therefore, concentrate on decreasing the total fat content of your food choices. When broiling or grilling hamburger, it is important to thoroughly cook the meat until there is no pink meat, and the juices should be brown. This will ensure that any harmful contaminating bacteria have been killed.

BEEF CUTS: 3½ OZ. COMPLETELY TRIMMED OF EXTERNAL FAT

	Calories	Fat (g)	Saturated fat (g)	Cholesterol (mg)
Eye of round, choice	175	6	2	69
Tip round, choice	180	6	2	81
Top round, choice	207	6	2	90
Sirloin, choice	200	8	3	89
Brisket	218	10	4	93
T-Bone steak, choice	214	10	4	80
Porterhouse steak, choice	218	11	4	80
Tenderloin,* choice	212	10	4	84
Ribs, whole, choice	237	14	6	77
Short ribs, choice	298	18	8	93

*Cuts of beef that end with the word, "loin,"as in tenderloin, is one of the leaner cuts.

When selecting beef, look for cuts that have little marbling and external fat. Ask the butcher to trim away all visible fat. At home, trim fat before cooking. This external fat is the biggest source of fat in beef. This fat trimming has no effect on tenderness, flavor or juiciness of the meat.

In low-fat cooking, beef can be served as a side dish rather than the main part of the meal.

COMPARING LAMB CUTS

Lamb is relatively high in fat. The best way to estimate the fat content is the cut. The information below assumes that all cuts have been trimmed of external fat.

Ground lamb is very high in fat. If you want to lower the content of fat in ground lamb, have the butcher trim lamb shoulder and grind it. This will reduce in half the fat content from approximately 20 grams of fat per 3½ oz. to 11 grams.

LAMB CUTS: 3½ OUNCES COOKED

	Calories	Fat (g)	Saturated fat (g)	Cholesterol (mg)
Shank	180	7	2	87
Leg	191	8	3	89
Loin	202	10	4	87
Shoulder	204	11	4	87
Blade	209	12	4	87
Rib	232	13	5	88

COMPARING PORK CUTS

Pork is not as lean as skinless chicken breast, turkey breast, or fish. However, if you eat small portions and pay attention to trimming away all visible fat, and stay with lean cuts, pork provides many important nutrients. Pork is an excellent source of thiamine, zinc, iron, and high quality protein. Bacon, sausage, spareribs, and hot dogs are extremely high in fat, salt and nitrites. Ham is also high in salt, and nitrites. These nitrites combine with protein during cooking and produce *nitrosamines,* which are linked to stomach cancer. These foods should be reserved for very special occasions and not be daily fare for your children or yourself.

PORK CUTS: 3½ OZ. TRIMMED AND COOKED

	Calories	Fat (g)	Saturated fat (g)	Cholesterol (mg)
Bacon*	576	49	17	85
Spareribs	395	30	11	121
Blade loin	247	15	5	93
Country style ribs	234	14	5	86
Loin	200	9	3	79
Tenderloin	164	5	2	79
Ham, canned†	155	5	2	30

COMPARING SAUSAGES

Sausages are very high in fats, salts, and stomach cancer producing nitrites and nitrates. Eat them sparingly and try to convince your misguided PTA to stop using these foods to raise money. Use sausages as a flavoring for foods, rather than the main course.

Gourmet sausages are appearing at many markets. Labels that brag "95-percent fat-free" may actually contain many fat grams, along with nitrites and a high sodium content. Before buying these tempting delicacies, read the Nutrition Facts plus Ingredients to get beyond the promotional hype. If you choose to eat them occasionally, be sure to decrease that day's fat allowance by preparing meals with high-fiber, low-fat, low-sodium foods.

SAUSAGES: 3½ OZ.

	Calories	Fat (g)	Sodium (mg)
Pepperoni, beef & pork	500	45	2000
Pork sausage, fresh, cooked	370	30	1300
Chorizo, beef & pork	450	38	1200
Kielbasa	310	27	1000
Liverwurst, pork	325	29	850
Hot dogs (2), beef & pork	320	29	1100
Hot dogs (2), chicken	255	19	1350
Salami, beef & pork	250	20	1000
Bologna, pork	245	20	1100
Bologna, turkey	200	15	675

*Three slices of bacon equals an ounce of cooked bacon, containing 110 calories—74 percent of which are from a full 9 grams of fat. Three and a half ounces of bacon contains a whopping 1000 mg of sodium!
†Canned ham, Canadian bacon, and cured ham all contain about 1000 mg of sodium.

COMPARING CHICKEN PARTS

Not all the chicken we eat is low in fat. Eating chicken *with the skin* will more than double the amount of fat. Chicken skin has 80 percent of its calories from fat, and over 20 percent is from saturated fat. Dark meat contains more fat that white meat and is slightly higher in cholesterol as well. Most children love chicken, and it is an extremely versatile meat. There are recipe books devoted entirely to chicken. Consult them and don't be afraid to alter the recipes by decreasing or eliminating any added cream, butter, margarine or oil.

A busy parent can buy skinless chicken breast fillets, fresh or frozen. Instant "gourmet" meals, such as Kim's Chicken, as well as low-fat nuggets can be prepared with minimum effort.

A chicken favorite among children is McDonald's Chicken McNuggets.* These Nuggets are loaded with 15 grams of fat, with 50 percent of calories from fat! Conscientious parents who want to give their child "the best of the worst" mistakenly choose McNuggets or the fried fish. A lower fat choice is a hamburger without cheese and a carton of milk instead of the soda. If you must buy the fries, which are loaded with the artery damaging trans-fats, settle for a small order to share.

Chicken liver is another favorite that should be avoided. Although it is relatively low in fat, 3½ oz. contains 630 mg of cholesterol, double the maximum daily amount of cholesterol recommended for adults. And that's not all. The liver is an organ that concentrates all toxins and therefore may contain higher levels of pesticides. Pesticides often contaminate the grains fed to the chickens or seeds eaten by "organic" or free range chickens, since DDT and other pesticides remain in the soil for years.

Eating less red meat does not mean your child should eat more chicken. The most important recommendation for healthy eating is to make vegetables, fruits, and grain products the largest part of your family's diet.

---

*If you buy the batter-dipped chicken breast and want to turn it into a healthier meal, remove all the skin. Taking off the skin removes about 8 grams of fat from a chicken breast. A deep-fried chicken thigh has 23 grams of artery clogging fat. Skip the onion rings (19 grams of fat) and the coleslaw (11 grams of fat in a ½ cup serving).

CHICKEN PARTS: 3½ OZ. COOKED

	Calories	Fat (g)	Saturated fat (g)	Cholesterol (mg)
Breast, with skin	197	8	2	84
Breast, without skin	165	4	1	85
Drumstick, with skin	253	16	4	91
Drumstick, without skin	172	6	1	93
Wing, with skin	290	20	5	84
Wing, without skin	203	8	2	85

Like beef, there is little difference between cuts and the cholesterol content of chicken. It is the high fat content of skinless verses skinned chicken that will make the major difference. Of course, fried chicken should be avoided, and if a recipe calls for sour cream, use a nonfat sour cream or nonfat yogurt.

COMPARING TURKEY PARTS

Turkey breast is the leanest of all meats with 7 percent of calories from fat. Even turkey breast with skin has only 18 percent of calories from fat. Almost all of the fat in turkey is found in the skin. Dark turkey meat is higher in fat, but is relatively lean if eaten without the skin. Roaster and hen turkeys are good choices for broiling, roasting, or grilling, as they are the most tender. Hens have a larger proportion of white to dark meat. Tom turkeys are larger and older than roasters or hens, and have a reputation for being tastier. Ground turkey is an excellent substitute for ground beef, but it usually needs more seasoning and moisture. Try fresh herbs to add both moisture and flavor. Egg white or tomato juice also enhances flavor and adds moisture to ground turkey. Packaged ground turkey often contains dark meat and may contain more fat, as much as 55 percent calories from fat. Be sure to check the Nutritional Guidelines on the label.

Avoid turkey rolls, and those turkey slices in convenient little bags. Instead choose sliced fresh turkey from your deli. "Lunchables" are to be avoided since they are loaded with salt, nitrites, and are high in fat. There are healthier convenience foods available for your children.

TURKEY PARTS: 3½ OZ. COOKED

	Calories	Fat (g)	Saturated fat (g)	Cholesterol (mg)
Breast, without skin	135	1	<1	83
Breast, with skin	153	3	1	90
Dark meat without skin	162	4	1	112
Dark meat with skin	182	7	2	117
Leg with skin	170	5	2	70
Wing with skin	207	10	3	115

COOKING TIP: Try the recipes for LOW-FAT TURKEY GRAVY and TURKEY MEATBALLS on page 206.

CHAPTER EIGHT

THE ADOLESCENT'S DIET*

▲ ▲ ▲

Adolescence may be defined as the teenage years between 12 and 20, but physical maturation and changes in nutrient requirements actually begin at younger ages and extend into young adulthood. The spurt of growth during adolescence is second only to the rate of growth during infancy, but less predictable. Every parent knows how important good nutrition is for their adolescent son or daughter and naturally turns to authorities such as physicians, dietitians, or "trainers," for guidance. Here is where more confusion begins since nutrient allowances, or Recommended Daily Allowances for adolescents (RDA's) are only estimates or educated guesses. Nutritionists took data on young children and adults, and applied it to adolescents without actually measuring their needs. The unusually tall teenager and the early maturer or late maturer will vary considerably in their needs. Their nutritional requirements (RDA's), therefore, should be looked upon more as guidelines and not embraced dogmatically. For

*The subjects of obesity and eating disorders such as anorexia nervosa and bulimia are extremely important since both often begin with the onset of puberty. However, it is beyond the scope of this book to discuss adequately these important problems. Rather I would refer you to your physician to direct you to one of the many excellent up-to-date books available. For older adolescents, a useful formula for calculation ideal body weight based on barefoot height is:

Males: 5 feet = 106 lbs. + 6 lbs. Per additional inch.
Females: 5 feet = 100 lbs. + 5 lbs. Per additional inch.

example, a fourteen-year-old boy may require 600–1200 mg of calcium a day, depending on absorption rates of 50 percent or 25 percent.* The RDA of 1200 mg of calcium per day, for example, is thus designed to meet the needs of the adolescent who is growing at the fastest rate. Levels less than that may be quite adequate for many teenagers. This explains the absence of problems in areas of the world where the daily intake is a minimal 200–300 mg of calcium per day.

The recommended dietary allowance of protein for fifteen-to-eighteen-year-old boys is 59 grams, but studies have shown that it is not unusual for intakes to be well over 100 grams of protein a day.† A high-protein diet stresses the kidneys and causes calcium to be removed from the body. Even the leading nutritional experts of the World Health Organization recommend progressively decreasing levels of protein. It is no wonder that nutritional deficiency of protein, simple carbohydrate, or fat is extremely rare among American teenagers. At highest risk for protein and calcium deficiency are teenagers on extreme weight-loss diets, teens from poor families, and those who eat no animal products.‡

Many nutritionists, in their preoccupation with deficiency states, continue to proclaim in the lay and medical literature that fast foods or junk foods allow the vast majority of adolescents to maintain an adequate nutritional status, despite their erratic eating patterns. These nutritionists state that despite skipped meals or choosing pie or fried chicken over lower-fat, high-complex-carbohydrate choices, teenagers will receive the necessary amounts of vitamins and minerals

TEEN

---

*Teenagers gain 50 percent of their bone mass during their pubertal growth spurt, and 90 percent of total body calcium is found in the skeleton (bones). Because most a girl's bone mass in the spine and upper femur (thigh bone) is reached at age sixteen years, anything that interferes with mineralization of bone during these critical growth years can have long-term consequences. This is the best age to prevent osteoporosis and future broken hips, especially since there are no good treatments for osteoporosis at the present time.
†The RDA of protein for fifteen-to-eighteen-year-old girls is 44 grams; the average consumption is estimated to be 63 grams.
‡It is between ages nine and twenty-four that most children store calcium in their bones. These are the years when many adolescent girls favor diet drinks and consume few calcium-rich dairy products. Osteoporosis is best prevented by maximizing calcium intake during these years. Encourage your teenager to drink nonfat milk or juice fortified with calcium to get the needed amount of calcium. A vitamin-D-fortified calcium supplement may be needed if your child has an aversion to dairy products.

because of the sheer quantity of food they consume.* I hope that by now the reader will appreciate the absurdity of such notions. These apologists for the food industry claim that the link between salt and hypertension, and the links between a high-fat diet and cardiovascular disease, gallbladder disease, and some cancers are not conclusive. To me they sound like the tobacco industry, which continues to make similar assertions about the link between smoking and disease. There are nutritionists who will tell you to consume all the salt you want, and this advice gets promoted on TV programs such as *20/20*. They would have you believe that the major nutritional issues confronting teenagers relate to calcium, iron, and protein, or vitamin A and C deficiency. This is a typical half-truth. No wonder parents are totally confused over what constitutes a nutritious diet. Experts, often aligned with the food industry, must share the responsibility for this confusion. Truth is the first victim when huge profits are at stake.†,‡

---

*Analysis of information from the Bogalusa Heart Study (as reported by Zive and colleagues in the *Journal of Adolescent Health*, 1996, pages 39–47) revealed that adolescents were most likely to be deficient in vitamins A, B-6, E, D, C, and folic acid. Mineral deficiencies were most common for iron, zinc, calcium, and magnesium. Adolescent girls were more likely than adolescent boys to have dietary deficiencies, due primarily to their decreased overall food consumption. Adolescents who were restricting their food intake to lose weight were at increased risk for vitamin and mineral deficiencies and might benefit from supplementation. This all may be true, but the overconsumption of artery-clogging fats, sodium, and highly refined, low-fiber foods must be revealed as the chief culprits of modern day malnutrition.

†In a 1998 Teen Eating Study by Channel One—the news and information cable channel that broadcasts in public, private, and parochial schools—1,500 teens were asked to chart all the food they consumed during a two-day period, including weekdays and weekends. Of the participants, 734 responses were complete and valid. The study was made up of 381 boys and 362 girls. It was found that one-third of all teen meals are eaten away from home, with teens estimated to be spending $12.7 billion a year at fast-food restaurants. Lunch is the meal most likely to be eaten away from home, with 58 percent buying it a school. Only 28 percent bring lunch from home. The after-school snack has become the "fourth meal," with the typical teen spending $1.25 a day, for an estimated nationwide total of $5.2 billion, to make it from lunch until dinner. Teens visit fast-food restaurants 2.13 times a week and spend an average of $5.72 per visit, for a nationwide estimated total of $13 billion a year, the study showed. Hamburgers are the most popular food (46 percent), followed by pizza (13 percent) and Tex-Mex (10 percent).

‡There is some evidence that dairy products may not be the ideal calcium source. A reanalysis of data from a National Dairy Council–supported study showed that girls taking extra calcium-rich dairy supplements for one year failed to do any better in bone mineralization than the control group. The dairy-supplemented group took 1437 mg of calcium a day while the control group only took 728 mg! *Nutr. Rev.* 1996; 54: 64–65.

Because of commercial hype and promotion, many adolescents incorrectly believe that the more protein in their diet the better. But excess protein is not converted to muscle, it's *converted into fat*! As pointed out earlier most teenagers need *less than* 60 grams of protein a day* (unless pregnant† or breast-feeding). While adolescent boys often overdose on protein, I'm concerned about those teenage girls who go in the other direction, under-consuming nutrients, while surviving on no-cal soda, chips, and candy or "sports bars."

Nutritional "science fiction books," like *The Zone*, by Barry Sears, Ph.D., were reviewed by Bonnie Liebman in the *Nutritional Newsletter*, July/August 1996.‡ This is one of many weight-loss diet books that explain such diets as the Scarsdale diet, the Rotation Diet, the Beverly Hills Diet, the Dr. Atkins Diet, or the Dr. Stillman Diet. All these fad diets *seem* to work—that is, weight is lost. The reason I'm taking time here to debunk the theories behind *The Zone* is because so many teenage athletes are being sold by their coaches many of the bogus concepts detailed in this book. Nutritional advice based on his low-complex-carbohydrate, high-protein diet should be dismissed as yet another fad diet soon to fade into history. Unfortunately, it will probably be replaced by another one filled with exaggerations based on half truths, pseudoscience, and convincing anecdotes.

Sears claims Americans are fatter because we're eating less fat. But according to data from the National Center for Health Statistics, fat intake has barely budged. The average American ate 81.4 grams of fat a day in the late 1970s and 82 grams a day in the late 1980s.§ Sears blames Americans' increased weight on the extra carbohydrates we're eating, but a much better explanation, according to Liebman, is that we're eating 100 to 300 more calories—and may be exercising less—than we were in the late '70s. Sears then says that

---

*Adolescent girls require approximately 0.36 grams of dietary protein daily per pound of body weight. Boys require about 0.45 grams of protein daily per pound of body weight. Most teens in this country meet or exceed this level, including teens on vegetarian diets.

†Pregnant teenagers have special nutritional needs because there are at least two growing bodies, the adolescent and the fetus. Protein requirements are increased by 10–15 grams per day, bringing the daily recommended protein intake to 60 grams per day. Most women in the United States, including those who might be at risk due to age or socioeconomic status, easily meet this level.

*Bonnie Liebman, M.S., is Director of Nutrition on the editorial staff of the Nutrition Action Health Letter from the Center For Science in the Public Interest (CSPI).

§*Morbidity and Mortality Weekly Report*, 43: 116, 1996.

carbohydrates are "the reason you're fat . . ." because, "when we eat too much carbohydrate, we're essentially sending a hormonal message, via insulin, to the body. . . . The message: Store fat."

Sears cites Stanford University endocrinologist Gerald Raven, but Raven "disagree(s) strongly with the notion that having high blood insulin, by itself, makes you gain more weight." When it comes to gaining—or losing—weight, what matters isn't insulin, but calories. "There are so many studies showing that if you decrease calories, people lose weight, and it doesn't matter if you do it by cutting fat, protein, or carbohydrate," says Raven. "A calorie is a calorie is a calorie." Again repeating Liebman's critic, "Sears is right when he says that—for some people—a very high carbohydrate, very low-fat diet can raise insulin levels—and that high insulin levels raises the risk of heart disease. But there's simply no good evidence that high insulin levels make you fat."*

Sears' next claim is that calories don't count . . . protein does and relates this to controlling, "eicosanoids." Eicosanoids are hormones that help regulate inflammation, the blood's tendency to clot, and the immune system. They may play a role in heart disease, stroke, and other diseases. Nutrition Actions review continues. "And what causes your body to make "bad" eicosanoids? You guessed it. Too much insulin caused by eating too much carbohydrate," says Sears.

Dr. Raven answers, "I am unaware of any evidence that changes in insulin have an effect on eicosanoids, and that eicosanoids cause everything from cancer to PMS." There is no evidence that eating equal amounts of protein and carbohydrate at every meal, as Sears suggests, lowers insulin levels. "Protein—when eaten alone—increases insulin secretion . . ." and "I see no reason in the world why it would be any different if the protein were eaten with carbohydrate," says Raven, but "no one has ever studied it."

Fortunately Sears recommends low-fat protein foods. But adolescents may easily miss that point. and "When they hear 'more protein,' they may go out to a ribs place or eat a few Big Macs without the buns."

Another myth is that beef is the best protein. It certainly is an excellent source of iron, but fish, egg white, breast of chicken, and turkey are equally good sources and considerably lower in fat and

---

*American Journal of Clinical Nutrition 63:174, 1996

TEEN

cholesterol. Also plant protein from rice, wheat, beans and corn are excellent sources of very low-fat proteins. Nonfat milk, although often thought of as a "calcium food" is extremely rich in nonfat protein, although low in iron.

It is sometimes argued that teenage athletes need extra protein or a higher amount of a specific amino acid, like "glutamine," and vitamins.* We've all seen the picture of the athlete sitting down to a big steak dinner during training. "Pure muscle building protein," in the form of supplements or meats does not increase strength or help build muscles. Muscle size and strength are developed by muscular work, not by eating meat or magical protein drinks. Extra complex carbohydrates, such as bread, rice, potato, cereals, pasta, vegetables, and fruit, are desirable to provide the extra energy for the muscular work and growth that go into muscle building. It is also rare for any healthy athlete to need salt tablets as a supplement to compensate for salt lost in perspiration. "Enzymes," DHEA (sold in many gyms alongside "High Performance" Ultra-whatever bars as a supplement) and "natural" multivitamin mixes promoted by coaches and trainers to the psychologically vulnerable teenager have as much nutritional value as a placebo. *"Power bars" are no substitute for real food.* The teenager may feel and say, "I took the protein vitamin drink and immediately felt that power surge." But vitamins and minerals do not work that way. What they are reporting is the powerful placebo effect of suggestion. Wishful or magical thinking is powerful and often clouds the intellect. Trainers and gyms often supplement their incomes with the concoctions they sell. Such conflict of interest may get in the way of their usual good judgment. They often give you what I call a "nutrition-biochemistry babble" sales pitch, which sounds very convincing to anyone with a casual understanding of clinical nutrition.

Adolescents are quick to accept the disinformation found is some health books, like *Fit For Life,* which claims—without any scientific evidence—that eating foods in certain combinations will render them

*Supplements are part of a multibillion-dollar business. So when you're asked to swallow, in addition to wholesome fruits and vegetables, some anticancer or fitness drink, remind the promoter what you've learned. So far there is no individual chemical, phytochemical, vitamin, mineral, or amino acid—despite the endless parade of headlines and promotions—that has been proven to improve upon your performance, that adds to or is a substitute for a good diet and exercise. These specialty foods, pills, or drinks are expensive "hope"-enriched potions.

indigestible or nonabsorbable, or that toxins will form if certain foods are eaten together at different times of the day or night.

When megadoses of a vitamin are recommended, beware of side effects. A vitamin given in doses so large that it is unlikely to have been obtained from one's natural diet may act more like a drug. By definition, a megavitamin is a vitamin given in a dose ten times the RDA or more. If there is a specific defect in a person's body chemistry limiting absorption of a vitamin or preventing normal amounts of vitamins from getting across cell walls into the body tissues, then megadose vitamins may be extremely helpful. Fortunately most of us do not have these problems.

If you still believe that a high-fat diet and cardiovascular disease is something that only adults should worry about, then listen to this: In the January 1997 issue of a prominent American medical journal it was shown how a high-fat diet is already at work causing artery blockage during early adolescence. Autopsies were performed on 1,079 men and 363 women between the ages of fifteen and thirty-four who died accidentally. The researchers found dramatic differences in the severity of fatty deposits and lesions on the arteries of young people, depending on whether they smoked or ate diets rich in fat.

What is the typical teenage lunch or snack? A Big Mac, French fries and a chocolate shake provide 1000 calories, with 31 grams of fat (50 percent of these calories come from fat!). In addition the Big Mac has 960 mg of sodium, and that doesn't include what is on the french fries. There is negligible fiber and excess sugar. Many school cafeteria lunches are often as bad, and worse.

A simple and valid assessment of the nutritional needs of teenagers is that they are similar to those of other ages except for a greater need for calories. If 65 to 70 percent of calories are provided by complex carbohydrates and 10 to 12 percent by protein, most likely the necessary mineral, fiber, and vitamins will be automatically provided.

There are special situations and needs during adolescence. No discussion on teenage nutrition is complete without some relevant information on iron.

Iron deficiency is one of the most widespread nutritional deficiency problems still seen in the United States. Although there is much written about other minerals and vitamins allegedly being in short supply in our diet, iron deficiency remains a real problem in infancy, adolescence, and especially pregnancy.

When one thinks of iron deficiency, anemia is the problem that often comes to mind. *But depletion of body stores of iron causes many problems in the body long before anemia or low hemoglobin occurs.* By the time anemia is present, many other bodily changes have occurred. Vital metalloenzymes are affected early, producing symptoms of irritability and poor appetite in children.* Other behavioral changes such as pica (eating dirt, soil, paint chips, etc.) and the craving for ice frequently occur. Treatment with oral iron supplements results in the disappearance of the ice craving, poor appetite, and irritability usually within a week or two, and long before the anemia itself is corrected. Chronic fatigue is believed to be a relatively late symptom in iron deficiency, but decreased work performance has been found in people with even mild iron deficiency.

A simple hemoglobin test might appear normal, while iron deficiency may exist without symptoms. This is especially so during periods of rapid growth as during infancy, adolescence, and throughout the childbearing period in women. During these times when demand for iron for hemoglobin formation and muscle is increased, additional iron is needed in the diet. Especially at risk are premature infants and children six months to three years of age.

Researchers from Johns Hopkins Medical School reported in the British medical journal *Lancet* their study in which 700 teenage girls in Baltimore high schools were screened for iron deficiency. Scientists were looking for girls with low iron levels, but not low enough to cause anemia. This study's screening method differed from how most physicians screen for low iron levels. Usually physicians check a simple hemoglobin or hematocrit. If anemia is not found, it is assumed that iron levels are adequate. But anemia reflects only severe iron deficiency. Moderately low iron levels can exist without anemia.

The researchers found 73 girls, roughly 10 percent, who had low iron levels, but who had not yet developed iron deficiency anemia. These girls were then screened with several standardized tests to measure verbal learning skills and memory. The group of girls was then divided into two groups, making sure that both groups had similar levels of iron deficiency and similar test scores.

---

*A *metalloenzyme* contains a metal as part of a protein catalyst. The role of trace minerals (metals) in enzymes and vitamins helps us understand the manner in which minerals participate in biologic processes and provides a fundamental basis in relating trace elements to health and disease.

Half the girls were then treated with iron pills and the other were given identical placebos containing no iron. After eight weeks the girls were re-tested. The half that were given iron had higher blood iron levels and higher blood counts. This result was expected, but in addition this group also did significantly better on the verbal learning and memory tests. Eight weeks of iron therapy was effective in improving scores on these important measures of brain function in iron-deficient high school girls.

For these reasons public health-minded nutritionists have promoted fortification. Rather than relying on people to remember to take extra iron every day in pill form, iron has been added to flour and cereal. For those who prefer to get their iron from more natural sources, good ones are whole wheat, fish, poultry, figs, beans, asparagus, black strap molasses, dark green vegetables, and extra lean meat. One cup of prune juice supplies 55 percent of an adult woman's RDA for iron. Cooking in iron pots and pans contributes a great deal of extra iron in the diet. The much fabled spinach,* Popeye's ready source, has many milligrams of iron but the bioavailability† of this iron is poor because it is in the form of poorly absorbable iron oxalate. The same is true of the iron in egg yolk. Broccoli has significantly more available iron (and calcium). Some foods decrease iron absorption. Bran and teas containing tannin‡ are two. (Coffee which contains no tannins, depresses absorption, but to a lesser degree). *More than a quart of milk* a day also contributes to iron deficiency.

Other foods increase iron absorption, particularly vitamin C rich foods, which counteract the effects of other iron inhibitors. Vitamin C, however, is not an important enhancer of medicinal iron absorption.§ This is important to remember, especially for pregnant women, who are often advised to take high doses of iron supplements. Taking a ferrous iron pill before breakfast insures excellent absorption.

---

*Spinach is good for you. It is exceptionally high in beta carotene and folic acid.
†"Bioavailability" is that amount of a nutrient which the body can utilize or absorb when consumed.
‡Tannin or tannic acid is what imparts the tan color to tea. This astringent vegetable compound also adds a constricting taste to your tongue and palate from strongly brewed tea.
§"Ferrous" iron is well absorbed. "Ferric" iron is the type of iron found in many vegetables. Vitamin C converts the poorly absorbed ferric iron to the more absorbable ferrous iron. Medicinal iron is "ferrous," that is, it's already in the "ferrous" state and therefore vitamin C will not further enhance its absorption.

It is extremely rare for older teenage boys or young adult men to be anemic due to lack of iron. Anemia in adult men should always be thoroughly investigated for its cause. Taking iron tablets could hide and postpone early diagnosis or recognition of blood loss in the stool from colitis, polyps, or intestinal cancer.

One word of warning. Poison Centers have become increasingly alarmed about the number of iron poisonings in young children. *Iron poisonings kill more children under age six than any other substance* and most of these poisonings occur as a result of children accidentally ingesting iron tablets or prenatal vitamins. As few as ten tablets of 325 mg. ferrous sulfate can be fatal to a child weighing less than 22 pounds. Treatment of iron poisoning should *not* be delayed. *If your child swallows iron pills, call your doctor and go to the emergency room right away!*

See page 153-156 for more information on iron, along with the RDA for elemental iron.

Vitamins Prevent Birth Defects

Now I wish to fill you in on some important information about vitamins that is of practical importance to all teenage girls and all women capable of becoming pregnant.

Many vitamins and their derivatives are currently being used in the mainstream of medicine as a medicine. For example, pregnant women who take vitamins containing the recommended 0.4 mg of folate (folic acid) a day are 50 percent less likely to give birth to a child with neural tube defects (anencephaly—a baby born without a brain—or spine defects such as spina bifida.) It has been suggested that at least 1 mg of folate be given daily to all teenagers and women of childbearing age. Cleft lip and cleft palate are two more congenital birth defects that may be preventable by taking daily doses of folate before and during pregnancy in the very safe range of between 1 mg and 10 mg.* It is important that this vitamin be taken daily *before* a woman knows she is pregnant, because by the time of a missed period, it is usually too late and the damage has occurred. Each year approximately 2,500 infants are born with neural tube defects in the America.

---

*Any dose of folic acid above 1 mg daily needs to be taken only under medical supervision because a high dose of folic acid may mask the neurological symptoms of undiagnosed pernicious anemia.

Folate is a water-soluble B vitamin that is excreted in the urine and is not significantly stored in the body. It is needed to make DNA. If there is insufficient folate available to make this DNA, cell division halts. When the fetus is first developing, cell division is so rapid that body folic acid is quickly depleted unless replenished daily with a high green vegetable diet, beans, orange juice, and/or with folate supplementation. Once the critical period of organ formation is passed, it is too late. Additional folate will not correct the problem once the facial, brain, or spinal cord defect has occurred. Most pregnancies are unplanned, and this is especially true with adolescents. That is why it is so important to give the daily supplements to all girls and women of childbearing ages and not to totally rely on dietary intake of folate.

Folic acid, by the way, has recently been found to protect the heart and it is now being used as a dietary medicine to help prevent the events that lead to heart attacks. Fortunately folic acid is an extremely safe vitamin. The required dosage of folate can be furnished by certain breakfast cereals and leafy green vegetables as well as fresh orange juice, but a supplement is recommended for those who are at high risk.

Although the water-soluble B vitamins are usually safe even when taken in excess of the RDA, beware of the possible side effects of large doses of any vitamins. There are times when more is not better, and it is the healthy teenager who is most vulnerable to the hype that "more is better." For example, *the fat soluble vitamin A is linked to birth defects when taken in amounts above the RDA*. Even as little as the amount contained in two or three multivitamin pills, or anything more than 10,000 international units a day of vitamin A may be dangerous to the developing fetus. One of every 57 babies born to women who had taken more than 10,000 IU of vitamin A will have a birth defect as a result. The problems involved malformations of the face, head, heart, and nervous system. Therefore, to be safe, check your vitamin bottles and be sure that the vitamin A levels do not exceed 5000 IU, the current recommended dietary allowance (RDA). I personally believe that the inclusion of vitamin A in over the counter multivitamins in the U.S. is not only unnecessary, but *a public health danger*. This vitamin is a well documented teratogen (a substance that causes malformations in the unborn child), and to have it incorporated with a prenatal vitamin seems to be poor a decision, especially in a country where vitamin A deficiency is, at worst, marginal (vitamin A deficiency is common in undeveloped countries because of poverty and ignorance). The less-toxic beta-carotene might be considered as a more logical replacement because beta-carotene is the safe, nontoxic form of vitamin A, even when ingested in large amounts.

PART II

▲ ▲ ▲

NUTRITION 101

CHAPTER NINE

THE CHEMICALS OF LIFE

▲ ▲ ▲

This primer offers the basics for understanding what infants, children and adolescents need nutritionally, and what foods will fulfill those needs. Without a basic understanding of the chemicals of nutrition (carbohydrates, protein, fats, fiber, vitamins and minerals), the important objective of ensuring nutritional well being could be easily clouded. A knowledge of how dietary chemicals are utilized by the body is important in determining how much of these foods are needed for health and for the restoration of body tissue in stress and disease. For this reason, these chapters on the chemicals of life are included. Readers should keep in mind that research is constantly adding to our knowledge of nutrition and therefore new information may alter some of the information presented in this book. We must always try to keep an open mind and be prepared to change our beliefs when new, scientifically-collected data warrant it.

The much abbreviated information that follows is a crash course in the basics of nutrition. It will help you read food labels and what's *between the lines* of these labels. It will make you much smarter about food; and if you act on what you learn here, it will help you and your family become healthier.

Energy

Our bodies require a certain amount of fuel to operate efficiently and the fuel we run on is energy derived from calories. *Many people don't know that a source of energy is nothing more than a source of calories.* The amount of energy we need—and therefore the number of calories we need—depends primarily upon our height, weight, age, and the type and amount of activity in which we normally engage. If you take in more calories than you can use, your remarkable body converts the excess into body fat and stores it for possible future use. It takes about 3500 to 4000 calories to produce a pound of body fat.

Calories are delivered to the body as sugars derived from carbo-hydrates, proteins, and fats. *Metabolism* is the means by which energy is made available to the body. The *basal metabolic rate* of a person is the amount of energy (calories) needed to run the body at rest (during sleep). Added to that is the amount of energy needed to fuel normal daily activity and the calories needed to maintain weight and growth. A sedentary person uses fewer calories (and less energy) than the one in perpetual motion. Infants and adolescents also need many extra calories because these ages are times of rapid growth. After age thir-ty-five or forty, many adults who do not exercise need fewer calories to maintain weight. In addition, many adults begin to move more slowly (or, as I keep telling myself, more efficiently) and, therefore, find themselves putting on excess weight while consuming the same number of calories they ate during their more youthful years. If an adult consumes a mere 25 calories a day in excess of need, in one year that would add up to about 9000 calories—or a two-pound weight gain. If this habit continues, in ten years that would translate to a 20-pound weight gain! This is the plight of many once-slender young adults, but it also helps to explain why slow-moving children gain weight so easily, when compared to the skinny child who is in constant motion and consumes twice the calories.

CHAPTER TEN

CARBOHYDRATES

▲ ▲ ▲

I hope that you endure with me through the following extremely important pages on the biochemistry of foods. It is necessary for you to understand these fundamental concepts in order to appreciate how fuzzy nutritional notions can direct you to poor nutritional and dietary choices.

The carbohydrates are a class of nutrients also called *saccharides* (compounds made up of sugar). The simplest are the *monosaccharides* which are also known as simple sugars. Examples of simple sugars are glucose (blood sugar), fructose (fruit sugar), and galactose (a simple milk sugar). *All sugars contain 4 calories per gram.*

When two monsaccharides or simple sugars combine chemically, they form a double sugar, called a *disaccharide*. Sucrose (table sugar), lactose (milk sugar), and maltose (malt sugar) are examples of the most common dietary disaccharides.

The more complex carbohydrates are known as *polysaccharides*. Their molecules are composed of combinations of monosaccharides and are very large. Examples are starch and cellulose. Starch is found chiefly in plants like corn, rice, potatoes, yams, and grains. Cellulose forms the cell walls of plants. Cellulose and starch are made up of simple sugars linked together. The linkages are different enough to make starch digestible but cellulose indigestible.

Another class of complex carbohydrates, consisting of polymers (repeating structural units) of monosaccharides, are the *oligosaccharides*. Oligosaccharides may prove useful as additives to nutritional products such as infant formulas and adult supplements because of their immune properties. Human breast milk, for example, contains twenty-five different oligosaccharides, which probably function as natural anti-infective agents.* There appears to be a correlation between the oligosaccharide content in breast milk and immunity at birth. These oligosaccharides may play an important role in protecting the newborn with an as yet underdeveloped immune system, and may be the newborns first line of defense against infections.

The simple sugars are absorbed very rapidly from the digestive tract while complex carbohydrates break down slowly during the digestive process, eventually being reduced to simple sugars. They are then absorbed into the blood stream in their simple form and converted into energy (calories) for the body to "burn" as fuel for activity or stored as fat for later use.

From this you can understand the theory of giving juices to provide "instant energy" or the before-game carbohydrate-loading meals of athletes as a source of "slow release" energy or fuel during major competitions.

Here is some practical information about sugar and carbohydrates. The sugar bowl on your kitchen counter is only the tip of the iceberg. There are hundreds of forms of sugar hidden in our diet.† Punch,‡ apple and orange juice, fresh fruit, ice cream, hot and dry cereals, pies, donuts, chili, pizza, Jello, hot dogs, bacon, ham, salami and cold cuts, stuffings, breads, soups, mayonnaise, catsup, salad dressing, flavored yogurt, canned vegetables, beans, and virtually all frozen foods to mention a few.

Besides refined cane and beet sugars (the common table sugar sucrose), there is refined fructose, which is similar to other table sugars. Advocates of fructose claim that because it is one-and-a-half times as sweet as sucrose, people will use less. Fructose, like all carbohy-

---

*"Oligosaccharide anti-infective agents." *Lancet*. April 13, 1996; 347.
†Average calorie counts of select beverages: soda-156 cal per 12 oz.; orange juice-109 cal per 8oz.; grape juice-155 cal per 8 oz.; whole milk-150 cal per 8 oz.; 2 percent milk-121 cal per 8oz.; skim milk-85.5 cal per 8oz.; water-0 cal per 8oz. International Dairy Foods Association.
‡Over the last three decades, average soft drink consumption among children and teens more than tripled, from 20.6 gallons in 1978 to 64.5 gallons in 1994, and the prevalence of childhood obesity has almost doubled in that same period of time: Curr. Concepts Perspect. Nutr. 8:1-8, 1996.

drates, provides 4 calories per gram. A widely used alternative sugar is corn syrup. Other sugars used commercially are molasses, maple syrup, honey, dextrose, lactose, levulose, and the "alcoholic sugars" mannitol, maltitol, and sorbitol.

Nutritious foods such as dried apples, apricots, and prunes, as well as fresh fruit are all high in sugars. These sugars are also sucrose and fructose, but they are combined with other nutrients such as minerals, vitamins, and fiber. Sucrose and fructose when in refined forms such as juice, or table sugar, whether white or brown, have been stripped of the fiber content and much of their mineral and vitamin content. In addition, these *refined* simple carbohydrates don't fill you up like the high fiber, low-fat complex carbohydrates. Because complex carbohydrates are bulky, you fill up before overeating.

Most of us have experienced the effect from drinking these simple sugars as a "pick-me-up" when we are tired or hungry. Because they are rapidly absorbed into the bloodstream, the body responds by pouring out insulin to lower this rise in blood sugar. This causes the blood sugar to quickly fall, often at a level below the original amount. Hunger returns along with "the shakes" as body adrenaline is released to counteract the insulin. Besides this rollercoaster effect, there is evidence that the increase in insulin promotes the dietary sugar to be converted into fat.

The average American consumes about 110 to 130 pounds of sugar per year. This represents 18 to 20 percent of calories consumed daily in a typical American diet, and that doesn't include the sugar calories from fresh fruit and fruit juices. My recommendation is that total carbohydrate calories should amount to about 65 percent of calories consumed, and most of these should be from complex carbohydrate. When 20 percent of calories are contributed by sugar, 30 percent by fat, 15 percent by protein what's left is a mere 35 percent of calories available from complex carbohydrates.* This high sugar

---

*To further clarify the above calculation here is the math: 20% (sugar) + 30% (fat) + 15% (protein) = 65% = total non-complex carbohydrate. 100% – 65% = 35%, which is the percentage of calories remaining for complex carbohydrates. In order to get complex carbohydrates increased to 65 percent of daily calories, one must decrease fat calories to 20 percent; decrease simple carbohydrate (sugars) to 5 percent and keep protein between 10 and 15 percent of calories (20% + 5% + 15% = 40% total non-complex carbohydrate calories). 100% – 40% = 60% complex carbohydrate calories. 60% + 5% (sugar) = 65% total carbohydrate calories.

consumption displaces minerals, vitamins, and fiber found in complex carbohydrates. The lost fiber content from these foods promotes constipation and indirectly contributes to other diseases such as diverticulitis* and obesity.

Sugar promotes tooth decay especially when consumed between meals as a sticky candy, in raisins or pastry. Behavior problems such as hyperactivity have been attributed to a high sugar diet, but most studies have not substantiated this association. The contagious enthusiasm of a birthday party or "free time" at school may be the real culprit rather than sugar. It has become much in vogue to blame misbehavior, learning problems, etc., on refined sugar. I suspect in many cases this may be an attractive escape from the responsibility of improving one's home and school structure. Class size and structure may have more to do with behaviors diagnosed as "hyperactivity" and "attentiveness problems" than diet.

Sugar, as a cause of cardiovascular disease, was reported by Dr. John Yudkin in *Lancet*, a respected British medical journal, in 1964. I'm including this information because I still see references to this invalid study in many health food stores. After Yudkin studied levels of dietary sucrose in patients with coronary atherosclerotic disease, he claimed that dietary sugar might be involved causally in coronary heart disease. In another study that followed, it was shown that the sugar intake of men with heart attacks or artery disease was twice that of others without cardiovascular disease. These findings stimulated more careful additional studies which did not confirm the original claims that sucrose was a major contributor to coronary heart disease risk.

Sugar should be limited in your diet, but it is not "a slow poison" nor does it produce cancer, diabetes, or heart disease. Its major harm comes from consuming it in excess, thus contributing to obesity and malnutrition by replacing more important nutrients, especially fiber.†

Like fats, sugar has an important place in nutrition when consumed in small amounts.

---

*Diverticulitis is an inflammation of a diverticulum (a tubular sac or out-pouching) of the colon.

†Refined sugar delivers no vitamins or minerals, and if not "burned" as energy, these extra calories can be turned to fat and stored in the body, often adding inches to undesirable places.

CARBOHYDRATES — EXAMPLES OF FOODS

EXAMPLES OF SIMPLE CARBOHYDRATES

Sucrose	Corn syrup
Glucose	Molasses
Fructose	Honey
Dextrose	Syrup
Invert sugar	Corn sweetener

EXAMPLES OF FOODS HIGH IN SIMPLE CARBOHYDRATES

Berries	Bananas
Oranges	Grapefruit
Apricots	Apples
Melons	Orange juice
Grapefruit juice	Apple juice
Apricot nectar	Peach nectar
Kool Aid	Lemonade
Hawaiian Punch	Hi-C
Tang	Hard candy
Coca-Cola	Soda

FOODS CONTAINING COMPLEX CARBOHYDRATES
(Starch and cellulose)

LEGUMES

Peas		Beans
Garbanzos	Peanuts	String Beans

TUBERS

Carrots	Yams	Potato

CRUCIFERS

Broccoli	Chard	Cauliflower
Cabbage	Bok Choy	Brussels Sprouts
	Broccolini*	

*Check out this new vegetable. It is a cross of broccoli and Chinese kale. This vegetable is also known as "Asparation." It looks like a streamlined broccoli with an asparagus-like stem and supposedly tastes like sweet broccoli. I am told it is lighter, sweeter, more tender and fresher tasting than broccoli. It is distributed by Mann Packing Company.

OTHER VEGETABLES

Lettuce	Celery	Asparagus
Eggplant	Cucumber	Onion
Garlic		Tomato

GRAINS

Rice	Wild Rice	Wheat
Buckwheat	Rye	Oats
Barley	Corn	Popcorn
Millet		Triticale

The foods containing complex carbohydrates have a small percentage of fat and protein in addition to starch and cellulose, the indigestible cell walls of plants. Remember that when you eat rice, corn, potato, or pasta, you are not eating pure starch. For example buckwheat (if you roast buckwheat before you boil it, you've got kasha) is fiber rich and high in copper and magnesium while wild rice has more zinc than any other grain. Barley is a good source of fiber and iron, while brown rice is the only rice that contains vitamin E. These foods contain significant protein with minimal fat, as long as you don't douse them with butter, margarine, oil, or cream. If you must use a "flavor enhancer" use an herbal nonfat sour cream or something similar to "I Can't Believe It's Not Butter" spray. Fresh salsa is another delicious and nutritious topping.

CHAPTER ELEVEN

PROTEIN

▲ ▲ ▲

Proteins differ from carbohydrates and fats chemically in that they contain nitrogen. The proteins of our bodies are composed of *twenty-two amino acids, in varying combinations*. Of these, eight can't be made by our bodies and are therefore called *essential amino acids*. These amino acids must be obtained in adequate amounts from the food we eat. They are tryptophan, leucine, isoleucine, lysine, valine, threonine, phenylalanine and methionine. All eight amino acids must be present in order for a protein to be nutritionally complete. Proteins that contain the essential amino acids in adequate quantities are called *complete proteins*. Examples are egg white, fish, meat, poultry, and certain vegetables, such as soybean and peanut.

Since 1983, I have worked several weeks a year as a pediatrician in many Central and South American countries as well as in Southeast Asia with two organizations, Interplast and Rotaplast International. My responsibility was to examine each child selected to have cleft lip or palate surgery,* to care for them in the recovery

---

*Cleft lip is a condition where a child is born with incomplete closure of the lip. This condition, called "harelip" in the past is usually repaired by plastic surgeons before the infant is six months old. Cleft palate, refers to incomplete closure of the palate, leaving a hole in the roof of the mouth. If this defect is not closed before the child is one year of age, difficult to correct, life-long speech problems often occur. The congenital defects may be genetic (run in families) or may be caused by environmental factors, such as insufficient folic acid in the diet. Taking folic acid *before* pregnancy occurs protects against many types of cleft lip and cleft palate.

room immediately after surgery and to be certain that each child received proper care during their convalescence.

I will never forget the first time I witnessed the devastating effects of protein deficiency. We just completed reconstructing this beautiful six month old infant's cleft lip. Because she was anemic, she needed extra oxygen, but her anemia was not severe. What I didn't realize was that the infant's poor and uneducated parents were feeding their daughter an infant formula they made with a little milk, but her diet consisted mostly of cooked corn meal. Corn is an incomplete protein because it does not contain the essential amino acid tryptophan. As a result, the child was protein deficient, and because I was unaware of her diet, I permitted the surgery to take place. When the baby's sutures were removed at the usual time healing had not occurred, and the beautiful repair fell apart. That moment was the beginning of my interest in nutrition.

Inadequate intake of essential amino acids over an extended period of time causes "protein starvation" and the protein deficiency disease, kwashiorkor results. *Kwashiorkor* is an African name that describes affected children with characteristic red hair, swollen bodies, and potbellies. I've seen kwashiorkor many times since that episode in Honduras where poor mothers feed their children formula made from corn. This is a third world disease and is extremely rare in the United States where overconsumption of protein is the rule.

If one is a vegetarian who does not eat any egg white, dairy or fish, the selection of foods must be more careful. Like carbohydrates, each gram of protein contains 4 calories.

Our bodies digest protein to form amino acids. Amino acids are necessary for growth, repair, and maintenance of our body tissues. We need a basic minimum of protein to remain in *positive nitrogen balance*. That is, we need to have enough protein intake to balance what our body wears out or excretes. If you are in *negative nitrogen balance*, it means that you are excreting more nitrogen (protein) than you are consuming. Your body must then obtain nitrogen by breaking down your muscles and the cells. This is extremely unhealthy and is called starvation!

How digestible a protein is, especially a plant protein, determines how much of its amino acids are actually available to our bodies. Whole proteins must be digested to amino acids before being absorbed into the bloodstream from the intestines. The term "biological value" is used to describe proteins as complete or incomplete. Complete proteins of high biological value are found in meats, egg white, fish, and poultry. The proteins that do not supply the essential amino acids, or else supply inadequate amounts, are known as incomplete or inadequate. They are usually of vegetable origin and that is why vegetarians should eat a greater quantity or variety of plant proteins. Having said this, I will reiterate that protein deficiency is not a nutritional problem in America. Nutritionists point out the need for increased protein intake during periods of the life cycle when rapid growth takes place. These are infancy, teenage years and pregnancy. However, protein from meat intake in America is in such excess that we see more of the toxic effects of too much animal protein (such as an increase in colon cancer) than protein deficiency.*

For example, infants are occasionally fed cow milk which has 20 percent protein, far in excess of the more nutritional 7 percent protein of human breast milk. Adolescents often take protein drinks believing that this will increase their muscle bulk and strength. This poor nutrition is not only unnecessary, but potentially dangerous. Too much protein also results in increased loss of minerals, such as calcium.

The RDA for protein for a growing male adolescent who is tall and well developed is 56 grams a day. For those nutritionists who refer to the RDA as a guide, use caution. *The National Research Council suggests that a diet should not be considered inadequate if it does not meet the recommended levels.*

For those individuals who are not in a rapid growth phase or pregnant, 10 percent of calories is sufficient protein. Pregnant and nursing mothers need extra protein, but not nearly as much as some nutritionists recommend. The RDA suggests 74 grams of protein for a pregnant woman and 64 grams for a nursing mother. Remember, this is a very high value and may be extremely inappropriate and excessive for a five-foot-tall 108-pound woman. For this reason it is more accurate to calculate protein needs using height and body build plus percent of total calories needed, as well as state of health. Few parents will tax their math skill to determine protein needs, and indeed, they shouldn't. In the real world, nobody does this. *I do not want to stress numbers,* since they will soon be forgotten and are irrele-

*Draser & Irving: *Br. J. Cancer*, 27, 167, 1973. Berg & Howell: *Cancer*, 34, 807, 1974.

vant to the shopper, who shops for food, and should *rely on principles*, such as buying fresh produce, grains, and low-fat protein foods. The at risk population for protein deficiency is the teenage girl on a diet soda and candy bar diet or the pregnant teenager. These children need special attention and nutritional counseling.

The RDA are "estimates of amounts of essential nutrients each person in a healthy population must consume in order to provide reasonable assurance that the physiologic needs of all will be met." This is a public health concept, according to Dr. Alfred E. Harper, past chairman of the committee on RDA. "The underlying premise," he states, "is that, since the requirements of individuals are not known, the recommendations must be high enough to meet the needs of those with the highest requirements. For essential nutrients, therefore, *the RDA must exceed the requirements of most members of the population*."

For infants the protein allowance is 2.2 grams of protein per kilogram of body weight per day.* This figure also contains the safeguards of being on the high side.

It might be fun for you to take out your hand calculator and calculate your daily intake of protein. Is it too high? If it is over the RDA it is probably in the danger zone.

RECOMMENDED DIETARY ALLOWANCES FOR PROTEIN

Sex & Age	RDA (grams)	Average Consumption (grams)†
INFANTS:		
0–6 months (13 lbs.)	13	
6–12 months (20 lbs.)	14	
CHILDREN:		
1–3 (29 lbs.)	16	
4–6 (44 lbs.)	24	
7–10 (62 lbs.)	28	
FEMALES:		
11–14 (101 lbs.)	46	66
15–18 (120 lbs.)	44	63
19–24 (128 lbs.)	46	65

* 2.2 grams of protein per kg is equal to about one gram of protein per pound.
†HHS. Nutrition Monitoring in the U.S. (1989).

Sex & Age	RDA (grams)	Average Consumption (grams)
FEMALES (continued):		
25–49 (138 lbs.)	50	65
50–69 (143 lbs.)	50	55
70+ (143 lbs.)	50	49
PREGNANCY:	60	
LACTATION:		
1st 6 months	65	
2nd 6 months	62	
MALES:		
11–14 (99 lbs.)	45	92
15–18 (145 lbs.)	59	122
19–24 (160 lbs.)	58	105
25–29 (174 lbs.)	63	105
30–59	63	93
60–69	63	79
70+	63	69

CHAPTER TWELVE

FATS
(LIPIDS)

▲ ▲ ▲

Although "fat" is the name often applied to all lipids, the broad category of chemicals with greasy properties—such as fat, fatty acids, and cholesterol—is more properly known as the *lipids*. The chemical composition of fats is similar to carbohydrates, but one gram of fat produces a hefty nine calories, over twice the calories obtained from one gram of protein or sugar. The fats in fatty tissue (adipose tissue) are called *triglycerides*. When we eat calories in excess, the chemical energy is stored as triglyceride molecules. This body fat (triglycerides) breaks down into glycerol and three fatty acids. *Glycerol* can then be converted into sugar and used as body fuel. The *fatty acids* come in many different lengths and levels of saturation. *Saturated fatty acids* are opaque at room temperature and are mainly derived from animal sources. Examples of foods that contain predominantly saturated fatty acids are whole milk and 2-percent milk, cream, ice cream, cheese, butter, beef, lamb, pork, coconut and coconut oil, and palm oil. Fatty acids (fats) that are liquid at room temperature are usually more "unsaturated." *Monounsaturated fats* (olive oil, canola oil, avocados) seem to be healthier than saturated fats. When monounsaturated fat replaces saturated fat in the diet, it may have a blood cholesterol lowering effect (lowering LDL cholesterol levels). But olive oil can't replace butter or shortening in baking, can it? Often, the surprising answer is yes, it can! Some olive oils, such as regular, highly processed olive oil, have a very mild flavor in contrast to extra-virgin and virgin varieties. Olive oil may be used in place of butter or other solid fats in the baking of cakes, cookies, muffins, and quick breads. It doesn't work well for pastries or crusts, because olive or any other oil saturates the flour and makes the finished product dense instead of light and flaky. *Polyunsaturated fats* (soybean oil, corn oil, safflower oil) appear to cause less damage to arterial walls than saturated fats, unless they are hydrogenated to make them solid—products such as stick margarine or Crisco. *Hydrogenated polyunsaturated fats* contain what is called "trans" fat and are about as atherogenic (artery damaging) as saturated animal fats such as bacon grease, butter, or cream. Trans fats are found in foods like french fries, Oreo cookies, pie crusts, chicken pot pie crust, potato chips, and many other foods that may be labeled, "cholesterol-free."* Fish fried in melted Crisco or stick margarine—along with Tater-Tots and chicken nuggets—are loaded with artery clogging trans fat.†

Oils are available in two forms: *combined oil* is in the seed or fruit (such as in the avocado)‡ as grown. *Free oil* can be expressed, bottled and sold. Corn oil, safflower oil, and sunflower seed oils are all free oils. Combined oil has the vitamins, minerals, fiber and other nutrients. To obtain free oil from corn, many kernels must be pressed to get one ounce.

Cholesterol is a lipid or fat-like substance found in all animal meat, whole and low-fat milk, cheese, butter, liver, sweetbreads, eggs, shrimp, crab, and shellfish. Cholesterol is not found in any vegetables. All those "cholesterol-free" advertisements stamped on vegetable oils and margarine are deceptive, in that they suggest "healthy," or that somehow the cholesterol was removed. As you will learn, trans fat and saturated fats are far more artery-clogging (atherogenic) than choles-

---

*Minimize the use of vegetable oils that have hydrogenated or processed to make them stable and solid at room temperature. The amount of trans fat does not appear on the "Nutritional Facts" food labels, so watch out for "partially-hydrogenated oils" in package ingredient lists.

†A new margarine marketed as Benecol contains a plant substance (a stanol ester) that prevents cholesterol absorption and can be used as a spread as well as for cooking. This margarine is being promoted as a natural cholesterol-lowering food. It may turn out to be the margarine of choice if all the early studies on this product prove to be true.

‡Avocados are high in monounsaturated fats, and are believed to be less harmful than saturated or trans fats. But beware of eating too much guacamole, because calories do count. Don't let "good" fat or the "low-fat" label give you a license to pig out. There is a trend toward overeating driven by the assumption that we can eat all we want as long as it's low in saturated fat.

terol. Fats in combination with cholesterol are especially atherogenic (bacon and eggs, or lobster dipped in butter or melted stick margarine). Boiled shrimp dipped in a nonfat cocktail sauce is a delicious low-fat dish and as long as the shrimp is not sautéed or fried, its small amount of cholesterol is of little nutritional consequence.

We have learned in recent years that there are various types of cholesterol, defined in terms of the types of protein they are associated with in the body. Since cholesterol, in pure form, is insoluble in water and blood, it tends to hook up with proteins forming what is called lipoprotein. *Lipoprotein* is a fat that has linked with a protein. This is the form in which cholesterol travels in the blood stream.

The body is able to make cholesterol, mainly in the liver, intestinal mucosa (lining), and various body tissues. Some ends up as *low-density lipoprotein* (LDL) and some as *high-density lipoprotein* (HDL). It is primarily the LDL cholesterol that is most artery-clogging (atherogenic) and leads to atherosclerotic vascular disease (heart attacks, strokes, blocked arteries). *That is why LDL is often referred to as the "bad cholesterol."* High-density lipoproteins (HDL) actually appear to protect against the buildup of artery-clogging plaques. HDL provides a mechanism for removal of excess cholesterol from the bloodstream. *HDL cholesterol is often referred to as the "good cholesterol."* Aerobic exercise and substitution of monounsaturated fats for saturated fats raises the good HDLs. (Use olive oil or canola oil instead of butter, margarine, shortening, lard, coconut oils, or hydrogenated polyunsaturated fats.)

Small amounts of fats in our diet are important because they contribute a necessary source of flavor. Dietary fat has essential physiologic roles. It delays emptying time of the stomach, thereby delaying the onset of hunger, stores energy, and is part of every cell membrane. In the gut certain vitamins are absorbed from fats. Cholesterol is important in bile formation (needed for digestion), adrenal, and sex hormones, and has many other important functions such as brain growth. The body can manufacture cholesterol and most fatty acids. Fatty acids not synthesized by our body must be obtained from our food. These are called *essential fatty acids*. The three fatty acids known to be essential for complete nutrition of infants, children, and adults are *linoleic acid*, (also referred to as an *omega-6* fatty acid), *linolenic acid*, (referred to as *omega-3* fatty acid) and *arachiodonic acid* (another omega-6 fatty acid). The reason essential fatty acid deficiency is so rare is that diets as low as 8 percent fat carry no risk of fat deficiency disease!

There are some fatty acids found in fish, such as salmon, called *DHA* (decosahexaenoic acid) and *EPA* (eicosapentaenoic acid) that may have a protective effect against the formation of artery-blocking cholesterol plaques, and seem to be especially important for brain development during infancy. DHA is found in breast milk, and efforts are being made to add this fatty acid to commercial baby formula because of its reported IQ-enhancing effect. My mother was correct when she referred to fish as "brain food."

It is common to hear supposedly well-informed individuals announce their "low cholesterol levels" as a badge of honor (normal healthy cholesterol levels range from 125 mg to 165 mg). How naive it is for adults or children to assume that they can consume all the fried eggs, ice cream, Tater-Tots, sausage or hot dogs, potato chips, and french fries they desire because they are thin or their cholesterol level is low. A diet high in total fats, salt, and highly refined carbohydrates—regardless of one's blood cholesterol level—will make one more likely to develop bowel cancer, hypertension, gallbladder disease, chronic constipation, and adult onset diabetes.*

Adult onset diabetes is often referred to as *noninsulin-dependent diabetes mellitus* or *type II diabetes*. People with diabetes have difficulty removing the sugar from their blood. After we digest a meal, glucose (blood sugar) is produced. In response, the pancreas then secretes insulin, a hormone that enables glucose to pass into the cells, where it is stored or burned as body fuel. In adult onset diabetes, insulin is produced, but it loses its effectiveness and is unable to adequately remove enough glucose from the bloodstream. Overweight and underactive people who have a familial history of diabetes seem to more readily develop this insulin resistance, or type II diabetes. Exercise and weight-loss help prevent the onset of this type of diabetes, which accounts for close to 95 percent of diabetes cases.

Type I diabetes is often referred to as *juvenile diabetes*. In type I diabetes there is little or no insulin because most of the insulin-producing pancreatic cells have been destroyed by something, perhaps a virus. It is unclear what this or these agents are, but the illness is fundamentally different from the more prevalent type II.

In insulin-resistant type II diabetes, a diet high in fat is especially dangerous, because these diabetics are at great risk for developing

---

*In spite of many wild claims found in bestselling nutrition books, no scientific cause and effect relationship has been established between diet and breast cancer.

atherosclerosis and heart attacks. In an effort to keep the body's blood sugar normal, lots of insulin is secreted. As a side effect, the body's triglyceride (blood fat) levels rise, LDL (bad cholesterol) levels rise and HDL (good cholesterol) levels fall. Heart disease begins along with risk of stroke, kidney failure, and blindness . . . all part of the disease. Most adults can prevent or delay the onset of these complications by following the dietary advice given in this book. By getting more exercise, eating less fat and protein, increasing complex carbohydrates and fiber, and avoiding most simple sugars, you will not only extend your life, you will improve life's quality and better enjoy your children and grandchildren.

The Lipid Hypothesis

In 1904, the German scientist Felix Marchaud proposed the name, "atherosclerosis" for an arterial disease characterized by obstructive patches, called *plaques*, within arteries. These atheromatous arteries* contained up to twenty times as much cholesterol as normal arteries. By 1912, Dr. James Herrick clearly identified and described how heart attacks are associated with atherosclerosis of the coronary arteries. That dietary saturated fats and cholesterol as found in animal protein could predictably increase a person's serum cholesterol was first established in the 1950s and 1960s. Much evidence now exists that an elevated serum concentration of cholesterol is a causal factor in the development of arterial atherosclerosis and coronary heart disease. *Even a modest elevation to as little as 200 mg can be significant in forming these obstructing plaques.* There are reputable scientists today who criticize this hypothesis because 100-percent evidence is not yet available. These nutritionists have not accepted the lipid hypothesis despite the growing body of evidence that supports it. Statements made publicly and widely disseminated by TV, radio, and the press have added to the confusion. The "cholesterol controversy," or more appropriately the "saturated fat controversy," is being kept alive by special-interest groups that are more concerned about the health of the beef, poultry, and dairy industries than the health of consumers. Similar "controversy" over salt as a major cause of high blood pressure is now being provoked by the primary users of salt—the processed- and frozen-food industry.

*Arteries that are filled with fatty cholesterol plaques.

Just as the tobacco industry has not succeeded in convincing intelligent adults that cigarettes are really harmless and non-addicting, those who suggest cholesterol, fats or high salt intake are not related to heart disease offer equally flimsy reasoning. Enough convincing evidence exists to strongly and safely recommend that for continued good health a diet should be low in fats, cholesterol, and salt. It should contain moderate amounts of protein and be high in complex carbohydrates and fiber-rich foods.

In addition to saturated fats, trans fats, and cholesterol, there are other players that contribute to the development of atherosclerosis. There are genetic or familial factors, insufficient dietary folic acid, antioxidants, and possibly infectious agents, like viruses or other microbes that may initially damage the lining of arterial walls, thus setting in motion the formation of cholesterol laden atherosclerotic plaques.* Particularly intriguing is the growing evidence pointing toward the role of germs or microorganisms—called *Chlamydia pneumoniae,* herpes virus, and mycoplasma—in the causation of atherosclerosis and coronary artery disease.†‡

A word of caution about a few popular, nutritious sources of fat. Avocados (guacamole!) are very fatty. They get between 75 and 85 percent of their calories from fat. That's some bundle of fat! They are an excellent source of folic acid, vitamin C, B-6, niacin, copper, magnesium and fiber. Although very little is saturated, it's still a lot of fat. So if you enjoy them, remember to eat only a moderate amount. A three ounce serving contains 15 grams of fat and 157 calories. Nuts are also very fatty (the chestnut, with only 8 percent of its calories from fat, is the exception), with an average of 84 percent of their calories coming from fat. An ounce of pistachios, for example (about 25 nuts), contains 16 grams of fat and 170 calories.

---

*Whether the origin or progression of a fatty plaque has an infectious component (viral or bacterial) is not clear. Periodontal (gum) disease and other dental infections are additional risk factors for the development of atherosclerotic heart disease.
†*Journal of the American College of Cardiology* 1997: 29; 1054–1059.
‡In a Johns Hopkins study reported in the August 18, 1998 issue of *Circulation*: 626–633, *C. pneumoniae* infection was linked to the development of atherosclerosis. The team studied coronary artery plaque samples from sixty Alaska Natives who died from nonheart-disease causes. In 75 percent of plaque samples, the bacterium was discovered within macrophage foam cells, which are known to be involved in early atherosclerosis. This finding further strengthens the link between *C. pneumoniae* infection and coronary heart disease.

CHAPTER THIRTEEN

FIBER

▲ ▲ ▲

What grandmother referred to as "roughage" is now called *fiber*. Until recently it was believed that fiber was of no nutritional value. In fact, food processors removed the fiber from grains such as wheat and rice to "improve" textures and color. They called this process "refining," and it has given flour the smooth white color and texture for our cakes, breads, and cereals.

Bran is often used synonymously, but incorrectly, with the term dietary fiber. Dietary fiber is that part of cereal grains and all vegetables not digested and absorbed by the intestines. Fiber can be divided into two broad categories, *soluble* (as found in oat bran, barley, beans, carrots, peas, sweet potatoes, yams, figs, berries, and fruit pectin such as apples and grapefruit,) and *insoluble* (as found in wheat bran, corn, black-eyed peas, figs, and berries). Most plants contain both types in varying amounts, but certain foods are particularly rich in one or the other. Whole grains are quite complex and contain substances we know little about nutritionally. Besides minerals such as selenium, copper, magnesium, vitamin E, phytic and phenolic acids, there are lignins, phytoestrogens (plant estrogens), antioxidants, and other unknown factors. The best way to get fiber plus these other nutrient is to eat a diet rich in complex carbohydrates. Seeds and nuts are also excellent sources, but they should be eaten very sparingly because of their high fat content.

Now we know that in addition to preventing constipation, insoluble fiber is believed inhibit the development of colon and rectal cancer,* reduce the likelihood of gallstones, and decrease the risk of diverticulosis.

Diverticulosis is a condition in which tiny pouches, called diverticula, form within the wall of the colon. When the pouches trap food, they may become painfully inflamed (diverticulitis) causing pain, bleeding, flatulence, diarrhea, or constipation. Experts estimate that in North America, a third of people over forty-five and two-thirds of those over eighty-five have it. By reducing constipation, the insoluble dietary fiber may help to prevent the development of diverticula and relieve the inflammation once it occurs. Soluble fiber improves blood sugar in adult onset diabetes and type I diabetes by slowing the absorption of sugar in the intestines, thus reducing the need for more insulin. Soluble fiber also reduces blood cholesterol by lowering LDL (bad cholesterol).

What isn't clear is whether it's the fiber alone that causes the benefits attributed to fiber. Those adults who consume 25–30 grams of fiber a day, in study after study have reduced the risk of cancer, heart attacks, diabetes, and the symptoms of diverticulosis. It is assumed that this is because of the fiber in the diet, but it may be the fiber plus the ingredients found in high-fiber foods (grains, vegetables, and fruit). Isolating a single ingredient, such as fiber or beta-carotene, and giving it as a supplement in the form of a capsule has yielded disappointing results. There is something about eating whole foods in the form of whole grains, fruits, and vegetables that scientists have not unraveled. That is one reason why I do not encourage the fad of sprinkling bran over your food. In fact, one of the more common causes of recurrent belly pain in childhood is caused by bran (branbellyache).

Look for cereals that are whole-grain and high in fiber. Avoid the sugar-added cereals. Not only do they rot your child's teeth, they also

---

*A diet rich in fiber may not protect you from colon cancer. The health and eating habit of 88,000 women were studied by Charles Fuchs and colleagues at Harvard University for over sixteen years. In contrast to some previous findings, they determined that women who consumed at least 25 grams of fiber a day were just as likely to get colon or rectal cancer as women who ate half that amount. More rersearch is needed to settle this issue, but this study illustrates how important it is to keep an open mind and continue to restudy (research) accepted "truths." Nevertheless, fiber should remain an important part of our daily diet.

replace the fiber and other nutrients found in whole grains. If you select granola or muesli, use the low-fat versions.

Although there is no RDA for fiber, the recommended intake is 0.2 grams of dietary fiber per pound to a maximum of 35 grams daily. (To calculate the recommended dietary fiber for a 25 pound child: $25 \times 0.2 = 5$ grams of dietary fiber.) Or for a more rapid calculation: for every 25 pounds of body weight, 5 grams of fiber is recommended. Thus a 75-pound child's recommended dietary fiber intake is 15 grams.

EXAMPLES OF CEREALS HIGH IN WHOLE GRAIN*

COLD CEREALS	HOT CEREALS
Cheerios	Oat bran
Grape-Nuts	Oatmeal
Nutri-Grain	Quaker Multigrain
Raisin Bran	Ralston High Fiber
Shredded Wheat	Roman Meal
Total	Wheatena

For granola lovers, choose the low-fat granola cereals such as Healthy Valley Fat-Free Granola, Kellogg's Low-Fat Granola, or Quaker 100% Natural Low-Fat Granola with Raisins.

The practical side of finding suitable high-fiber foods may be confusing unless you buy unprepared foods. For example, the label on bread may show a reasonable amount of fiber, but it may have been added from peas or other foods. This fiber may prevent constipation and diverticulosis, but it doesn't have all the ingredients of antioxidants and phytochemicals found in whole grain. Here are some hints to help you break through the utter confusion set before the average—and even the sophisticated—consumer.

▲ If the label says:
"whole grain" or "whole wheat"—it's a whole grain.

▲ If the label says:
"cracked wheat," "made with whole grain," "made

---

*One easy way to select a dry cereal for your children is to have them choose a cereal they like as long as it has at least 3 grams of fiber. Most cereals that have three or more grams of fiber are nutritious.

with whole wheat," "multi-grain," "oat bran," "oat-meal," "pumpernickel," "seven-grain," "seven-bran," "nine-grain," etc., "stoned wheat," "wheat," "wheat-berry," "whole bran"—it's mostly refined grain!

EXAMPLES OF HIGH-FIBER LOW-CALORIE FOODS*

Food	Serving size**	Fiber (grams)	Calories
Dried Figs	3	3.6	190
Apple††	1	3.5	81
Pear††	1/2 (large)	3.1	61
Carrots	2/3 cup	3.1	32
Strawberries	1 cup	3.0	45
Broccoli	2/3 cup	2.9	26
Spinach	2/3 cup	2.8	28
Orange	1	2.6	62
Zucchini	2/3 cup	2.4	15
Prunes	2	2.0	40
Blueberries	1/2 cup	2.0	39
Peach††	1	1.9	37

**All serving sizes are for cooked vegetables
††With skin

Juicers are very popular and they're fine as long as you use a juicer that doesn't discard the fiber pulp.† There are juicers that use all the fruit or vegetable.

*J. Am. Diet. Assoc. 86: 732, 1986
†Vita-Mixer 4000 Vita-Mix Corporation 8615 Usher Road, Cleveland, Ohio 44138. 1-800-848-2348.

CHAPTER FOURTEEN

VITAMINS

▲ ▲ ▲

Vitamins are organic compounds that *cannot by synthesized by our bodies* and are necessary *in minute quantities* in our diet to keep the body in good condition.

If our bodies were maintained by a diet containing only purified proteins, carbohydrates, fats, and the necessary minerals, it would not be possible to sustain life. Vitamins are necessary as an accessory food factor. They act as *biocatalysts* within the body. That is, they promote necessary chemical reactions in the body, without being consumed in the reactions. They function as *coenzymes* or parts of coenzymes. For the vitamin to work it must first enter a cell in the body and combine with a particular kind of protein called an apoenzyme. When a coenzyme attaches to an apoenzyme, a complete or holoenzyme is formed. Extremely small amounts of vitamins are needed. Once all the apoenzymes in the body are saturated to form complete enzymes, more vitamins will collect in the body fluids and be stored, or the excess will be excreted. The vitamins are generally divided into two major groups: fat-soluble and water-soluble. Fat-soluble vitamins are usually found associated with the lipids (fats) of natural foods. These include vitamins A, D, E, and K. The water-soluble group includes vitamin C and the vitamins of the B complex.

The RDA for a vitamin is enough to saturate our entire body with that vitamin. Unlike water-soluble vitamins, the fat-soluble vitamins

THE WATER-SOLUBLE VITAMINS

Vitamin levels for the water-soluble vitamins are measured in either milligrams (mg, thousandths of a gram) or micrograms (mcg, thousandths of a milligram).

The vitamins of the B complex and their synonyms are listed with the accepted current name first and the historical names in parenthesis:

1. *Thiamin (Vitamin B-1, antiberiberi substance, antineuritic vitamin, aneurine)*

2. *Riboflavin (Vitamin B-2, lactoflavin)*

3. *Niacin (Vitamin B-3, P-P factor of Goldberger, nicotinic acid)*

4. *Pantothenic acid (Vitamin B-5, filtrate factor, chick antidermatitis factor)*

5. *Pyridoxine (Vitamin B-6, rat antidermatitis factor)*

6. *Lipoic acid (thioctic acid, acetate replacement factor)**

7. *Biotin (Vitamin H, anti-egg white injury factor)*

8. *Folate (liver lactobacillus casei factor, Vitamin M, fermentation residue factor, pteroylglutamic acid, folic acid group)*

9. *Inositol (mouse anti-alopecia factor)*

10. *Para-aminobenzoic acid; PABA**

11. *Vitamin B-12 (cyanocobalamin, cobalmin, antipernicious anemia factor, extrinsic factor of Castle)*

Ascorbic Acid (Vitamin C) is the other water-soluble vitamin.

*These members of the B complex are not considered to be vitamins in humans.

THE FAT-SOLUBLE VITAMINS

Vitamin levels for the fat-soluble nutrients A, D, E, and K are measured in international units (IUs).

Vitamin A (retinol)

Vitamin D (calciferol)

Vitamin E (tocopherol)

Vitamin K

are stored in our body fat and can be toxic if large amounts build up.* So again, we are reminded that too much of a good thing can be harmful. Or, if not harmful, then wasteful, since in a normal person most of the water-soluble vitamin supplements wind up in the toilet.

Many diseases of humankind, including beriberi, scurvy, night blindness, and pellagra, are known to be caused by lack of these essential food factors. These vitamins were originally assigned letters of the alphabet. Now that we have been able to identify the chemical structures of vitamins, nutritionists prefer to use their chemical names rather than the letters. In some cases the letters formerly assigned to the vitamins have been dropped entirely. "Biotin" has replaced the term "vitamin H," and "folic acid" has been substituted for "vitamin M."

Vitamins act both independently and often together. Most vitamin deficiency disease is seen predominantly in areas of the world where war and famine exist, and the cases usually show mixed deficiency. It is more common for isolated deficiency to occur in specific circumstances, for example: vitamin K deficiency as an isolated event occurs in infancy. The infant most vulnerable is the breastfed newborn.

---

*Recent research has demonstrated that, while water-soluble vitamins from food cannot generally reach dangerous levels, supplements should still be used with caution. The latest recommendations from the National Academy of Sciences (NAS), for example, call for 1.3–1.7 mg of vitamin B-6. Although some people claim a very high intake of vitamin B-6 can produce valuable health benefits, doses greater than 100 mg have caused nerve damage and are listed as a health risk in the new NAS recommendations. The report also warns of toxic effects from excessive doses of niacin.

Normal adults rarely lack Vitamin K. In the newborn, however, the quantity of the vitamin derived from the mother is small. At birth the intestines do not contain the bacteria necessary to manufacture vitamin K and the breast milk does not supply it. Mild vitamin K deficiency in the newborn is common. Very low levels of vitamin K may cause hemorrhages in the newborn. This disaster can easily be prevented by giving the infant oral or intramuscular vitamin K once soon after birth.

Another situation is found in vitamin D, the "sunshine vitamin" deficiency. There is a saying in the Alps of Austria, "Fall baby—spring rickets!" Austrian winters are long and cold. Infants are wrapped and away from sunlight from October until late March. The result is that eight months after birth, the infant has the soft bones and extreme irritability that are the marks of rickets. Most of the infants who become deficient are fed cow milk that has no vitamin D. Human breast milk is also deficient in vitamin D, but the illness is more rare in breast fed infants. Strangely, the deficiency is also seen in the Caribbean, where it is common practice in some cultures to wrap infants completely to keep them protected from the sun.

Vitamin deficiency is very rare in the United States because fresh vegetables are readily available year round. In addition, bread, flour, cornmeal, grits, macaroni, and spaghetti products as well as infant cereals and dry cereals are vitamin enriched. In spite of this, there remains a vulnerable group that still exists in this country.

At risk is the person on a high-level macrobiotic diet whose diet is not varied but is mostly rice. Beware of bizarre fad diets, regardless of how eloquently they are presented.

Another at-risk group is the elderly bachelor or widower who may prepare his own foods. Both are particularly prone to the development of vitamin C deficiency, a syndrome termed "bachelor scurvy." They're not eating enough fruit. Food faddists who avoid raw foods, particularly fruits and vegetables, are at risk to develop vitamin C deficiencies. Deficiency malnutrition is common among alcoholics, the poor, the elderly, and the chronically ill. In contrast, vitamin excess is a disorder of the well-to-do.

A megavitamin is a vitamin given in a dose ten times the RDA or more. If there is a specific defect in a person's body chemistry limiting absorption of a vitamin or preventing normal amounts of vitamins from getting across cell walls into the body tissues, then megadose vitamins may be extremely helpful. There are, for example, infants born with defective apoenzymes or inborn errors of metabolism. By giving such a patient megadoses of a vitamin you can force the coenzyme (vitamin) reaction by mass action. Vitamin D–resistant rickets is one example where megavitamins can be used to good advantage. Folate or folic acid as a 1mg to 10mg (1000 micrograms to 10,000 micrograms) daily megadose supplementation before pregnancy may prevent certain types of cleft lips and palates and is currently under investigation.* This B-complex vitamin is also being recommended by many cardiologists, in large or megadoses as an aid in the prevention of coronary heart disease in certain susceptible patients in addition to the current recommendations of a low-fat diet, exercise, and avoiding tobacco.

Claims that niacin regulates blood sugar in hypoglycemia and is useful in the megavitamin treatment of schizophrenia or that it is of value in the prevention of heart problems have not been substantiated by adequate controlled studies. Instead, what we have mostly are testimonials by people, including physicians, that they "felt better" after taking megadoses of these vitamins. It is important to keep in mind that these feeling are based far more on faith and wishful thinking than on scientific fact. The same is true for megadose therapy of vitamins and minerals to correct mental retardation or autism. When faced with a situation believed to be "hopeless" most of us are tempted to try anything as long as it is not harmful. The usual feeling is, "What do I have to lose, anyway?" In such a case the decision must remain a personal one. But be careful. Some of these concoctions are not without danger. Hope should never be taken away from anyone in a desperate situation, but false hope can only lead to disillusionment. When someone realizes he has been "used" or "taken" by a professional opportunist during a vulnerable moment in his life, it magnifies the feelings of sorrow and loss.

Consumers are receiving an unprecedented flood of information,

---

*Folate or folacin is the natural form of the water-soluble B vitamin found in food. Folic acid is the synthetic form of the vitamin and is found in multivitamins, folic acid supplements, and foods fortified with folic acid. Folate is 30 to 50 percent less bioavailable than folic acid. This is because folate is a "polyglutamate" and the body must convert it to a "monoglutamate" before it can be absorbed. Folic acid, the synthetic form of the vitamin, is a "monoglutamate" and requires no conversion for absorption. This information is of practical value because to obtain the recommended daily 400 mcg of folic acid from foods, an individual must consume about 800 mcg of natural folate. It may be very difficult to obtain the needed

some of which is properly analyzed while some is widely publicized without proper scrutiny. This often misguided nutritional information is actively promoted by "health food" stores and by doctors who practice unconventional or "fringe" medicine. The Internet is loaded with these "nutritional" promotions. Caveat emptor—buyer beware!

The idea that "natural" vitamins provide special benefits for our bodies has been promoted by manufacturers and retailers of these vitamins. Vitamins have the same properties whether natural or synthetic. Many vitamins labeled natural or organic are not what you might imagine those terms to mean. Rose hips vitamin C tablets are made from natural rose hips, which have natural vitamin C combined with chemical ascorbic acid, the same vitamin C used in standard tablets. If no synthetic vitamin C were added to the tablet it would have to be as big as a golf ball. Makers of natural vitamin C often suggest that synthetic vitamins do not contain other hidden or not well-known micronutrients that are included in the natural forms. They point to the "associated factors," flavonoids, protopectins and minerals of the whole fruit, including the so-called "P factors." Although the rational conclusion is to eat the entire fruit or vegetable to obtain all the nutritional value, instead the consumer is told their diet needs a promoted supplement. "Natural" B-complex vitamins are mostly synthetic chemicals added to yeast and other bases. Vitamin E products are derived from vegetable oils, but in order to concentrate the vitamin in a capsule, various chemical solvents must be added. The vegetable material is grown with the usual pesticides and chemical fertilizers. Finally, the gelatin capsule must contain a preservative so that it won't turn rancid. Since the vitamins are identical, no one can tell them apart, neither in a test tube nor in an animal. The health food industry designs its advertisements to make you feel vulnerable and inadequate so you have a need to "play it safe" and purchase the magical nutrient. How far have we come since Ponce de Leon marched through Florida seeking the "Fountain of Youth?"

amount of folate from the diet alone since a considerable amount of folate may be destroyed when foods are cooked, processed, or stored. Women considering pregnancy should begin taking a daily folic acid supplement at least three months before and continue taking it for the entire pregnancy. Many public health advisors suggest that all women of child bearing age should begin taking daily folic acid supplements and continue until menopause. These authorities remind us that at least 50 percent of all pregnancies in the United States are unplanned. See page 000 for more information on folate and prevention of birth deformities such as neural tube defects, cleft lip and palate, and early miscarriage.

THE RECOMMENDED DIETARY ALLOWANCES (RDA)

	Vitamin A (mcg RE)*	Vitamin D (IU)	Vitamin E (IU)	Vitamin K (mcg)	Vitamin C (mg)
INFANTS:					
0–6 months	375	7.5	3	5	30
6–12 months	375	10	4	10	35
CHILDREN:					
1–3 years	400	10	6	15	40
4–6 years	500	10	7	20	45
7–10 years	700	10	7	30	45
MALES:					
11–14 years	1000	10	10	45	50
15–18 years	1000	10	10	65	60
19–24 years	1000	10	10	70	60
25–50 years	1000	5	10	80	60
51+ years	1000	5	10	80	60
FEMALES:					
11–14 years	800	10	8	45	50
15–18 years	800	10	8	55	60
19–24 years	800	10	8	60	60
25–50 years	800	5	8	65	60
51+ years	800	5	8	65	60
PREGNANCY:	800	10	10	65	70
LACTATION:					
1st 6 months	1300	10	12	65	95
2nd 6 months	1200	10	11	65	90

*RE = retinol equivalents. One retinol equivalent = 1 mcg retinol or 6 mcg beta-carotene. To calculate IU value: for fruits and vegetables, multiply the RE value by 10: for animal-source foods, multiply by 3.3.

RDA (continued)

	Thiamine (mg)	Riboflavin (mg)	Niacin (mg)	B-6 (mg)	Folate (mg)	B-12 (mg)
INFANTS:						
0–6 months	0.3	0.4	5	0.3	25	0.3
6–12 months	0.4	0.5	6	0.6	35	0.5
CHILDREN:						
1–3 years	0.7	0.8	9	1.0	50	0.7
4–6 years	0.9	1.1	12	1.1	75	1.0
7–10 years	1.0	1.2	13	1.4	100	1.4
MALES:						
11–14 years	1.3	1.5	17	1.7	150	2.0
15–18 years	1.5	1.8	20	2.0	200	2.0
19–24 years	1.5	1.7	19	2.0	200	2.0
25–50 years	1.5	1.7	19	2.0	200	2.0
51+ years	1.2	1.4	15	2.0	200	2.0
FEMALES:						
11–14 years	1.1	1.3	15	1.4	150	2.0
15–18 years	1.1	1.3	15	1.5	180	2.0
19–24 years	1.1	1.3	15	1.6	180	2.0
25–50 years	1.1	1.3	15	1.6	180	2.0
51+ years	1.0	1.2	13	1.6	180	2.0
PREGNANCY:	1.5	1.6	17	2.2	400	2.2
LACTATION:						
1st 6 months	1.6	1.8	20	2.1	280	2.6
2nd 6 months	1.6	1.7	20	2.1	260	2.6

The following additional information on selected vitamins is provided because there is currently special interest in these nutrients. For more in depth information on the vitamins I have omitted, visit your local bookstore or public library and refer to the most current texts.

Vitamin C
(Ascorbic acid)

Vitamin C is needed daily in the diet because our bodies cannot manufacture or store it. An adequate supply of vitamin C prevents scurvy. Scurvy is a disease found in persons with little or no vitamin C intake over a prolonged period. In scurvy there is bruising, infected gums with loose teeth, bleeding into the joints and muscles of the legs and arms. Finally, if not corrected, jaundice develops, followed by edema (swelling), fever, convulsions and finally death. This is the classic description of scurvy, and in all my years of practice, I have never seen a case in a child. So please do not think your bruises are due to vitamin C deficiency.

Cigarette smoking and birth control pills increase the need for vitamin C. But no case has yet been reported of any individual who ate one fruit or vegetable daily and developed scurvy because of smoking. Megadoses of vitamin C have been used to treat viral illnesses such as the common cold, hepatitis, influenza, infectious mononucleosis, and pneumonia. The most common side effects of such treatment have been stomach and intestinal upset, diarrhea, abdominal cramping, and flatulence. Lowering the dose of vitamin C usually eliminates these symptoms. The proponents of this type of vitamin therapy suggest that the dose should be increased to the amount needed to produce these symptoms, then the dose should be lowered slightly. Although there is no strong evidence that vitamin C prevents the common cold, there is some evidence that it may decrease the symptoms and shorten the duration of the illness. Many of my patients take vitamin C supplements and I see as many of these patients for illness as I see who do not take vitamin C. This, of course, is a noncontrolled observation! Of greater importance is the value of vitamin C in preventing the conversion of dietary nitrates into a potent carcinogen, nitrosamine. Vitamin C taken daily as a supplement, or even better, daily consumption of foods high in vitamin C, could decrease the risk of intestinal cancer by preventing nitrosamine formation. Vitamin C also blocks the bacteria *Hilocobacter pylori,* a major cause of stomach ulcer and, possibly, stomach cancer. Citrus fruits,* strawberries, melons, tomatoes, broccoli, spinach, potatoes, and green and red peppers, are all good sources of vitamin C, as are a number of tropical fruits, such as kiwi and papaya. At this time there is a flurry of interest in vitamin C by eye specialists because according to animal studies, high levels of vitamin C in the eye appear to protect against the cataract-inducing effects of ultraviolet radiation from the sun. Prolonged exposure to ultraviolet light is believed to contribute to cataract formation. Middle-aged people who took vitamin C supplements for many years lowered their risk of cataracts by as much as 80 percent.

Fortunately, most of the warnings about possible toxicity of vitamin C when it is used as a drug are exaggerated. Compared with the drugs we use daily in medical practice, over-the-counter, or socially, vitamin C is a remarkably safe substance.

The story behind discovering the cause of scurvy is fascinating. During the eighteenth and nineteenth century Great Britain needed a large navy to protect and service its colonial based economy. Scurvy became prevalent when sailors began to spend months at sea without fresh fruit or vegetables. It was of economic importance for Britain to find out what caused scurvy. In 1795, lime juice was given to all British sailors on the recommendation of the Scottish physician, James Lund, who knew that the Dutch had given citrus fruit to its sailors for several hundred years. Gradually, scurvy began to disappear from British sailing ships. That is why British sailors became known as "Limeys."

When I was a student I was told by one of my professors that the American naval medical community refused to believe the claim that limes prevented scurvy. To test the theory, so the story goes, Florida key limes where collected and given to American sailors who were at sea for months. The key limes did not protect the American sailors from scurvy, therefore the theory was rejected. We now know that Florida key limes are the only citrus not to contain vitamin C! It took many more years before citrus fruit was introduced to the American navy.

---

*The citrate in orange juice inhibits the formation of calcium stones in the kidney.

Vitamin A
(Retinol or beta-carotene)

As a child, the worst part of my day was preparing for bed. That was the time for *cod liver oil*. In those years water-soluble vitamins had not been made, thus the natural vitamin A was given to most children of my generation. The oil was so horrific, I can still taste and smell these vitamin drops. This experience must have been shared by other children because one major complication of giving cod liver oil was pneumonia. Small amounts of the oil would get into the lungs after a struggling child had a gagging or choking spell. This fat-soluble vitamin, found in its natural state, was so irritating to lung tissue that a severe chemical pneumonia developed when the vitamin drops were not totally swallowed but accidentally went down the wrong tube. Fortunately, we now have a water-soluble form and that's what's in children's polyvitamin drops.

Vitamin A is found in animal products like liver oils, liver, and egg yolk. Retinol is another name for it because it is needed for proper vision. Beta-carotene is a provitamin and the body can convert it to vitamin A in the liver.* A provitamin, or precursor, is a substance the body can make into a vitamin. It is the carotene that makes vegetables yellow. It is also in green vegetables, but the dark green chlorophyll color conceals it. About 90 percent of the storable vitamin A is in the liver. People with diabetes, low thyroid hormone and those who use a lot of polyunsaturated fatty acids without antioxidants (vitamin E) have a decreased ability to convert beta-carotene to vitamin A. This vitamin is needed to maintain normal vision in dim light, is involved in bone and tooth enamel growth, wound healing, and promotes healthy skin and mucous membranes (the linings of organs, such as the lungs, bladder, stomach and intestines). Vitamin A improves antibody response and other immune processes to help fight off infection and cancer cells.

---

*Beta-carotene and other members of the carotenoid family are more than vitamin A precursors, that is, substances that are converted into vitamin A in the body. Today we know of more than 500 different carotenoids. Two carotenoids, lutein and zeaxanthin, may protect the eyes against age-related macular degeneration, which afflicts one in three people over age seventy-five. Another carotenoid, lycopene, may help prevent or delay prostate cancer. There are no RDA's for the various carotenoids. Food composition tables currently used by nutritionists lump beta-carotene and its relatives together under the heading vitamin A, making it difficult to identify good sources of particular carotenoids.

Because of all the beneficial effects of vitamin A, there was overuse of this vitamin to prevent infection, to improve eyesight, and decrease acne. The complications of hypervitaminosis A—were encountered, such as terrible headache due to brain swelling, bone and joint pain, hair loss, itching, dry skin, tender bones, weakness, fatigue, and most disastrous, birth defects. Therefore, be sure to remain within the RDA for vitamin A. Too much beta-carotene can lead to orange-yellow skin, which was epidemic in the 1970s when drinking lots of carrot juice was the fad. Fortunately, carotenosis, as it is called, is of no real consequence and will clear when there is a reduction in carotene intake. Beta-carotene, one of more than forty carotenoids found in food, is one of the most potent antioxidants. The carotenoids are believed to work in concert with other antioxidants. Although beta-carotene vitamin pills are popular, they have not been shown to reduce the risk of cancer or heart disease. This is disappointing news, but no surprise since vegetables and fruits contain so many different chemicals in various combination. Our basic understanding of how foods protect us from cancer and heart disease is fragmentary. You would never guess how little we know by reading the exaggerated claims on products sold in gyms and "health food" stores. There will always be someone trying to sell you food supplements of dubious value in this multibillion dollar market. Below is a table highlighting good sources of four of the over forty known carotenoids. This underscores what people are missing when they rely on supplements alone. Get your carotene the old fashioned way. Eat carrots, broccoli, squash, spinach and green leafy vegetables, and cantaloupe and other deep yellow or orange fruits. The deeper the color, the higher the carotenoid content.

SOURCES OF COMMON CAROTENOIDS*

	Beta-Carotene (mcg)	Lutein & Zeaxanthin (mcg)	Lycopene (mcg)
½ cup cooked broccoli	1,014	1,404	0
½ cup Brussels sprouts	374	1,014	0
1 medium raw carrot	5,688	187	0
½ pink grapefruit	1,611	0	4,135
½ cup cooked kale	3,055	14,235	0

*Tuft University Diet & Nutrition Letter: Vol.14, No.1, March 1996.

SOURCES OF COMMON CAROTENOIDS (continued)

	Beta-Carotene (mcg)	Lutein & Zeaxanthin (mcg)	Lycopene (mcg)
½ pink grapefruit	1,611	0	4,135
½ cup cooked kale	3,055	14,235	0
1 medium peach	86	12	0
1 cup raw spinach	2,296	5,712	0
1 medium tomato	640	123	3,813
¾ cup tomato juice	1,638	0	15,616

Vitamin E
(Tocopherol)

Vitamin E is another favorite nutrient surrounded with a magical aura. It has been promoted as a substance that increases sexual prowess, fertility, and protects against heart attacks. It is also claimed that vitamin E applied to a healing wound will diminish the scar.

Pure vitamin E was first isolated from wheat germ oil in 1936. Although alpha tocopherol is the active compound most often designated as vitamin E, there are seven other naturally occurring tocopherols, designated as beta, gamma, delta, zeta, epsilon, eta, and 8-methyl-tocotrienol. Their biological activity varies greatly.

Vitamin E functions as an antioxidant and helps protect polyunsaturated fatty acids in cell membranes and elsewhere in the body. Outside the body it prevents rancidity of oil. Because vitamin E prevents a process called peroxidation within cells, it was hoped that megadoses of it would protect cells against the aging process and therefore prolong youth and prevent heart attacks. These reasonable ideas are still being studied. There is also some preliminary evidence suggesting that vitamin E has a protective effect against the formation of the artery-clogging disease called atherosclerosis. Many cardiologists are now recommending vitamin E supplements to adults who have risk factors for developing a heart attack. A study published in the *Proceedings of the National Academy of Sciences,* April, 1997 suggests that (dl)alpha-tocopherol, the form of vitamin E found in pills, does an incomplete job of as an antioxidant. To get full benefit from the vitamin, people also need gamma-tocopherol. This may be a "test tube" observation with little practical importance. Time and more studies will determine whether this antioxidant is truly beneficial in pill form. I'm certain that vitamin pill companies will quickly jump on the bandwagon and add the second form of the vitamin to their formula.

Very preliminary studies suggest that vitamin E may delay the onset of Alzheimer's disease; however, it is too early to tell whether vitamin E is protective. Other investigators must see whether these results can be duplicated. Meanwhile, the answer is to eat foods containing the more complete form of vitamin E. Fruits and vegetables are the best source of antioxidants because they also provide thousands of phytochemicals that enhance the effects of antioxidants. Rich natural sources of vitamin E are whole grains, breads and cereals, soybeans, wheat germ oil, safflower oil, lettuce, and most green leafy vegetables.

Laboratory rat experiments demonstrated a heightened sexual potency from vitamin E, but unfortunately, in humans large doses can reduce sexual organ function.

Vitamin E deficiency occurs rarely and produces few symptoms, while excesses can cause headaches, tiredness, giddiness, inflammation of the mouth, chapped lips, muscle weakness, low blood sugar and bleeding tendency. By antagonizing the action of vitamin A, large doses of vitamin E can also cause blurred vision.

Some of the worst rashes I've seen came from vitamin E oil repeatedly rubbed on scars. The oil is a potent skin sensitizer. Why then do people use vitamin E on scars and claim benefits? The answer is relatively simple. There's nothing that heals better than a newly healing scar! In addition, any oil is soothing. Yet most experiments show that anything placed on or in a wound slows healing. My advice is to use a pure vegetable oil if you enjoy the soothing effect, but avoid Vaseline and vitamin oils unless you wish to invite red, bumpy, and irritated skin.

Vitamin D
(Calciferol)

As discussed earlier, vitamin D is the "sunshine" vitamin. Because vitamin D is needed for the normal calcification of bone and teeth, it is very important in the development of a healthy child. Vitamin D is actually more like a hormone than a vitamin.* It is produced in the skin and released into the blood to affect bone and other tissues. If the intake of vitamin D is low or if the child has inadequate sun exposure, even with sufficient dietary calcium and phosphorous, a child or adult will have poor calcification of bone. Menopausal women who take calcium supplements without vitamin D will not receive optimal benefits from taking calcium. Because most milk is fortified with vitamin D, deficiency of this vitamin in children is seldom a problem in this country.

Folic Acid
(Folate)

Folic acid deficiency may be one of the most common vitamin deficiencies in this country.† The word comes from the Latin *folium*, which means "foliage," because it is found in leafy vegetables such as spinach, kale, broccoli, asparagus, chard, sprouts, and other greens. Folic acid (folate) is available from fresh, *unprocessed foods*. Many fruits contain folic acid, such as oranges, cantaloupe, pineapple, banana, and many berries, including strawberries, loganberries, and boysenberries. Because so many parents and children live on a diet high in processed foods, they are at risk for folic acid deficiency. Folic acid is needed to make DNA, and DNA is needed for cell growth and division. When the body is actively producing cells, such as during early pregnancy, there is a tremendous need for extra folate. Since folate, a water soluble B-complex vitamin, is not stored well in the body, humans must consume a constant supply through foods or supplements. If deficiency is present in a pregnant woman, cell division stops, and if this is at a critical time in the development of a fetus (unborn infant), organ formation may be incomplete. Such deformities, (called neural tube defects), can result in spina bifida, in which

---

*The function of the hormonal form of vitamin D goes beyond calcium and bone. There is evidence that it can suppress or slow the growth of certain cancers.
†Beginning in 1998, the Food and Drug Administration will require that any grain product wishing to market itself as enriched be fortified with 140 mcg of folic acid per 100 grams of food. This is considered by experts to be too low to significantly prevent the birth defects caused by folic acid deficiency. It is estimated that only 25 percent of women of childbearing age are consuming the recommended 0.4 mg (400 micrograms) of folic acid every day. The new FDA rule will increase the number of women daily consuming 0.4 mg to only 28 percent.

the spinal cord resides outside the spinal column. Defects of the face, including cleft lip and palate, may also occur. Children with neural tube defects are more likely to have a variant gene that controls the conversion of the amino acid homocysteine* to methionine. This mutation may interfere with an intermediate step in the conversion, preventing the overall process from occurring. Researchers have speculated that too much homocysteine prevents the closure of the neural tube, leading to these defects. If the mother consumes adequate amounts of folic acid prior to conception, the conversion of homocysteine to methionine may still proceed, regardless of the child's genetics, and the neural tube may close. Since these problems occur early in pregnancy, it is especially important for all girls and women of childbearing age to consume a diet high in folate. I recommend that anyone of childbearing age take *at least a 0.4 mg supplement daily.*† Beginning folate after the critical first few weeks of pregnancy will be too late to correct or prevent the possible damage. When you consider that most women are not even aware of being pregnant until they miss a period, you can see how important it is to develop good dietary habits early. A diet rich in complex carbohydrates in the form of daily fresh vegetables and fruits is needed if you are to have healthy, normal children.

---

*Homocysteine becomes elevated when the body folic acid is low. It is an indirect measurement of folic acid. Recently it has been observed that men with high serum homocysteine levels have about a threefold higher rate of heart attack. It is unclear whether these men had high homocysteine levels because of a diet deficient in folic acid or for a genetic reason. When high doses of folic acid are given, (about 1–5 mg a day), the homocysteine level returns to normal. Cardiologists are now screening men for homocysteine along with cholesterol levels if there is a family history of early heart attacks. Studies are now underway to determine whether supplemental folate is of value in delaying or preventing heart attacks. There are other benefits of this B vitamin. Recent studies suggest that daily doses of 400 mcg of folic acid might prevent 30 to 40 percent of colon cancers.

†Folate reduces the blood levels of homocysteine. Homocysteine is also believed to contribute to heart disease by making artery walls sticky, thus blocking the flow of blood through the body. Since heart disease risk rises with age, folate becomes increasingly important for reducing homocysteine levels.

CHAPTER FIFTEEN

MINERALS

▲ ▲ ▲

There are a number of definitions of the word "mineral." In order to understand what the word means in nutrition, a quick review of some basic chemistry is necessary. Remember that all matter is composed of atoms. There are different types of atoms, such as oxygen, iron, and zinc atoms. These atoms are the basic building blocks of matter. Different types of atoms can combine to form *chemical compounds*. For example, the atoms hydrogen and oxygen are combined to form the chemical compound, *water*.

Nutritionists use the term "mineral" to refer to the various types of *atoms* needed by the body. A mineral is an atom or an *element* (not a compound like a vitamin), obtained from food, that is essential to health and is needed in small quantities, sometimes in tiny amounts called "trace elements." Ordinarily, minerals are not eaten in pure form but actually are obtained as part of various compounds in our foods. The body can separate minerals from the food compound in which they are found.

Sodium, calcium, magnesium, and phosphorous are examples of minerals or elements needed by the body, while the minerals, copper, zinc, iron, and iodine are examples of trace elements.

There are fifteen major elements of nutritional importance, and six are required in relatively large amounts. These include calcium, phosphorous, magnesium, potassium, chlorine, and sodium. The remaining nine are essential trace elements: iron, zinc, iodine, manganese, selenium, copper, fluoride, chromium, and molybdenum. These trace elements have specific metabolic roles in enzyme systems. Enzymes, as you may recall, are large protein molecules. Most metabolic processes of the body depend on the action of these enzymes.

Not all the minerals listed above will be discussed here. Sodium has already been discussed in Part I (see pages 24–27). Additional information on calcium and iron is included here, but more information is also provided in Part I (see pages 63–64 on calcium, pages 63–70 on iron) since these minerals are so important to normal growth and development.

Calcium

Calcium is the most abundant element or mineral in the body. Not only is it important for our skeleton and bones, but also for nerve conduction, blood clotting, skeletal and heart muscle contraction, and many other metabolic processes. Calcium metabolism is complicated and is just beginning to be understood. The amount of calcium consumed is only one part of a chemical chain of events that includes vitamin D, parathyroid hormones, intestinal absorption, bone mobilization and deposition, urinary excretion, magnesium, phosphates, dietary protein, gravity or weight-bearing exercise and other unknown factors.

Concerns about calcium absorption have arisen in regards to a diet high in phosphorous. This has been of some concern to nutritionists because the consumption of high phosphate foods can decrease absorption. Soft drinks, food additives, and meats are high in phosphates. The possible adverse effects of a continual high-phosphate (and high-protein) intake on calcium and bone loss should not be taken lightly. A high-salt diet also contributes heavily to calcium loss. A diet high in convenience foods such as canned or dehydrated soups, or ready-to-eat frozen dinners provides an excessive salt load to children and adults even if the salt shaker is never used. These long-term effects may be of greater consequence than a low-calcium diet.

The need for calcium varies in our life cycle. Needs increase during times of rapid growth of skeleton and muscles, such as pregnancy, lactation, infancy, and especially during adolescence. Not enough calcium in the diet is common in teenage girls on a high soda, candy bar or "sports bar" diet, but in this group there are multiple nutritional factors that need attention and a calcium supplement is only part of the answer. An unbalanced diet that has excessive salt, phosphorous, protein, and insufficient vitamin D (plus little weight bearing exercise) is a major contributor to calcium deficiency and osteoporosis later in life.

Children and young adults who are bedridden begin to lose calcium and continue to do so until exercise and walking are resumed. Although calcium from dairy products is more completely absorbed, supplementary calcium with vitamin D may be substituted in those who are unable to tolerate milk. If you take calcium supplements, take them at night because it helps reduce calcium loss into the urine which occurs during sleep,* but beware of taking too high a dose of calcium because the excessive amount may help form kidney stones or cause other toxic problems.† It is safest to first consult a physician before taking calcium supplements. *Another piece of sound advice is to cut down on salt, soda (phosphates), and excessive protein* because they can remove calcium from the body and counteract the effect of any calcium supplement. Women who cut the amount of salt in half, from the average of 3450 mg (about twenty times the amount the adult body needs!) to 1725 mg of sodium *protect their bones as though a 900 mg calcium supplement had been taken.* When you consider that one in two women over the age of fifty will fracture a bone due to osteoporosis, (a brittle bone condition), you can appreciate how much a high-salt diet promotes this condition. A cup of broth, a glass of V-8 juice, some cheese, and a salad with anchovies and olives contain enough salt to bump you into calcium-losing mode.

You may have read that phytates and oxalates in green vegetables make calcium less bioavailable, and this may be true, but as a practical consideration this is rarely an important problem. Besides the

---

*Some nutritionists and experts on osteoporosis disagree with the notion that it's better to take calcium supplements at bedtime. They believe that spreading out a calcium supplement during the day leads to more calcium absorption. Whether you favor one approach over the other should not be the major issue. What is important is that 1000–1200 mg of calcium from all sources (diet and supplement) be consumed daily by your teenager to prevent osteoporosis later in life.

†If you've had a calcium oxalate kidney stone (your doctor would know), then oxalate-rich foods can cause you trouble. It would be prudent to limit your intake of beans, beets, blueberries, celery, chocolate, grapes, nuts, rhubarb, and spinach. It appears very safe to take the 1200 mg RDA of calcium without worrying about kidney stones, as long as you don't take more as a supplement.

usual list of calcium rich foods, don't forget calcium-fortified orange juice or calcium-fortified apple juice (Gerber) as a convenient nonfat, nonprotein source of extra calcium. There is little difference in calcium absorption between sources of calcium as long as supplements are taken with food. If taken on an empty stomach, calcium citrate seems to be absorbed best. Calcium carbonate, although the least expensive, should be taken with food for maximum absorption.

Cheese provides substantial nourishment at the expense of over 50 percent of calories from fat as well as an enormous salt content. Vegetarians who avoid red meat often unwittingly substitute large amount of cheese daily. Three thin 1-oz. slices of cheese fulfill the RDA (age nineteen and over) for calcium without any help from milk, yogurt, or other calcium sources. Nutritionally speaking, cream cheese is considered a fat (like butter) and should not be classified with milk, yogurt, and other cheeses.* To get the same amount of calcium found in an 8-oz. glass of milk, you'd need to eat 13 oz. (more than a cup and a half) of regular cream cheese! Do not overconsume cheese or dairy products.

RECOMMENDED DAILY ALLOWANCE FOR CALCIUM

INFANTS:

0 to 6 months	360 mg
6 months to 1 year	540 mg

CHILDREN:

1 to 10	800 mg
11 to 18	1200 mg
19 & over	800 mg

PREGNANCY AND LACTATION:	1200 mg

Interpreting labels can be difficult, especially when it comes to understanding mineral needs. The above RDA for calcium is expressed in milligrams of "elemental" calcium. The elemental calcium is the same as usable calcium. For example, if a calcium supplement lists the contents as "calcium citrate = 950 mg," look carefully

---

*Cottage cheese has very little calcium. Low-fat or nonfat cheeses are an excellent compromise for the cheese lover, and should be substituted for regular cheese whenever possible.

at the label to see how many milligrams of "calcium" or "elemental calcium" are in the product. If the label says, "calcium (elemental) = 200 mg," that is the amount of calcium the supplement provides. This is true of all minerals. It is the elemental iron or elemental zinc that is usable.

Potassium

Potassium is an important nutrient found predominantly inside cells. This element, along with sodium, is necessary for electrical impulses to travel along cell membranes. Electrical impulses in body cells are affected by too little or too much potassium. Low potassium causes muscle weakness and heart disturbances while a high blood potassium level could be toxic to the heart. Potassium helps to lower blood pressure. A high-potassium, low-sodium diet is helpful in the control and prevention of hypertension. Although most Americans consume excessive sodium, the typical diet is low in potassium. Adults require about 3000 mg of dietary potassium daily.* While half a cantaloupe contains 1000 mgs of potassium, and some fruit juices are excellent sources, many children, adolescents, and adults consume drinks such as Kool Aid (containing only 1 mg of potassium), cola drinks (7 mg of potassium) coffee (40 mg of potassium), or beer (36 mg of potassium) instead. Simultaneously, the hundreds of milligrams of sodium contained in these drinks drives potassium out of balance. This combination of excess sodium and insufficient potassium contributes to the development of hypertension.

Hypertensive people who take diuretics lose potassium in their urine along with sodium. Fatigue is the most common symptom of chronic potassium deficiency. The resulting muscle weakness and fatigue may be gradual and the extent of weakness not fully appreciated until the problem has been corrected.

In childhood, the major causes of potassium deficiency are related to diarrhea and hormonal imbalances. Because potassium regulates

---

*There is no RDA or Estimated Safe and Adequate Daily Dietary Intake for potassium. The adult recommendation of 3000 mg of potassium per day is based on guidelines established by various health organizations and experts.

heartbeat, adolescents and young adults on a prolonged weight-losing diet consuming exclusively a low-potassium "liquid protein diet" or those with anorexia nervosa can have a very low heart rate and become gravely ill. Maintaining consistent levels of potassium in the blood and cells is vital to body function.

Potassium is found in a large range of foods, especially oranges and orange juice, bananas, potatoes (with skin), apricots, prunes, tomatoes, whole grains, legumes, meats, and fish.

Magnesium

Magnesium is an important mineral in human nutrition and shares many of the attributes of calcium. Its distribution in the body is much the same as potassium. Magnesium, calcium, and potassium control the body fluid and keep it from becoming too alkaline or acidic. Magnesium is an integral part of bone crystal, and it activates enzymes for hundreds of reactions including those that involve the expenditure of energy. It is a component of chlorophyll and is also found in animal protein. Good sources of magnesium are whole grains, legumes, dark leafy greens, vegetables, baked potatoes, beans, bananas, apricots, tuna, and salmon.

Because it is found in so many foods and is abundant in nature, magnesium deficiency is extremely rare in healthy people. Deficiencies are mostly seen in alcoholism. Average consumption from our food is around 300 mg a day.*

Young, weight-conscious women appear more susceptible to magnesium deficiency. This may be explained by the common use of diuretics, known to cause deficiency. Liquid protein diets are also associated with magnesium deficiency. Along with this loss is a loss of potassium, and a type of potassium deficiency that is difficult to correct.

Grand mal seizures, muscular weakness, heart muscle damage, and heart irregularities are some of the more severe consequences of magnesium deficiency.

---

*Researchers at the National Cardiovascular Center in Osaka, Japan, found that daily magnesium supplements of 480 mg decreased blood pressure in Japanese adults with high blood pressure.

Chlorine
(Chloride)

Chlorine is extremely important in electrolyte balance and is a necessary component of gastric juice. Salt is the main provider of chloride in the body. Chloride also aids in the conservation of potassium. While dietary deficiency states are rare, in childhood it can be caused by chronic vomiting and in adults by the overuse of diuretic drugs. Many years ago a soybean-based infant formula was removed from the market after it was discovered to contain excessively low amounts of chloride. Some infants, consuming this product early in infancy when no other foods were offered, developed symptoms ranging from marked irritability to severe growth failure. There was no outside source of chloride from solid foods for these infants to correct this deficiency. Catastrophes such as this demonstrate how dangerous it is to rely on a single food to provide all our nutrients and points to the danger of fad diets, like total milk, fruit, and high-protein or liquid protein diets.

In the late 1960s, Dr. Joseph M. Price published his hypothesis claiming chlorine to be the major cause of cardiovascular disease. He pointed to chlorination of water supplies as the origin of heart attacks. To support his argument he compared the lack of chlorination of water in China, Japan, and parts of Kenya to places where it was present. His figures pointed to a direct relationship between the amount of chlorine consumed and the rate of heart attacks. Advocates of this hypothesis have prepared graphs of "surveys" to support these contentions as reasonable.

The adage, "figures don't lie, but liars figure," comes to mind when data is presented regardless of the source. In spite of my skepticism I have been caught many times blindly accepting information on face value because a study was performed by a reputable investigator at a prestigious institution. *Careful measurements that are reproducible* come slowly and with difficulty but are extremely important if we are to avoid embracing every wild claim by both charlatan and scientist.

The chlorine theory has been studied and despite claims of conspiracy that chorine is a "sacred cow" of the establishment, there is no valid statistical evidence to support these claims. Careful statistical studies have not shown a significant relationship between chlorine intake and heart attack rates.

Our drinking water must be guarded against contamination from industrial waste at all costs, but chlorination of our water supply is not only safe, it protects us from waterborne disease capable of causing severe illness. There *is* a *theoretical* risk from drinking chlorinated water. Chlorine is known to react with organic material and other pollutants to form traces of chloroform. Chloroform is a carcinogen, and there has been a study linking the presence of chloroform in the water supply to a slightly higher incidence of certain cancers. According to a February 1998 study from the California Department of Health Services, published in the medical journal *Epidemiology*, a contaminant commonly found in chlorinated drinking water, trihalomethanes, may be linked to a higher risk of miscarriage among pregnant women who drink five or more glasses of tap water a day.* The study found that pregnant women in their first trimester who drank at least five glasses of tap water a day were roughly twice as likely to have a miscarriage as women who drank less water or whose water had lower concentrations of the contaminant. Health officials said they were taking the results seriously, but stressed that the findings are not definite and need to be confirmed by further research. Some health officials recommend that pregnant women find alternatives to unfiltered tap water, like bottled water.

I enjoy bottled water because of taste, but many people choose bottled water because of a fear of their municipal water supply. The water supply in the United States is probably one of the safest in the world, but to keep it so, constant vigilance and support are needed to safeguard our most precious resource. *If you use well water, be sure to have it tested for safety.*

Iron

Iron deficiency, paricularly among infants, adolescents, and pregnant women, is still a problem in the United States. Anemia is the most recognized effect of iron deficiency, but many other problems,

---

*Trihalomethanes are a family of chemicals formed during the chlorination process used in most municipal water systems nationwide. Trihalomethanes form when chlorine reacts with organic matter or with components of sea water. The EPA has been considering a stricter standard for trihalomethanes, because exposure to the contaminant has also been linked to an increased risk of cancer. The study was led by Waller and Shanna Swann, an epidemiologist with the state Department of Health Services. The EPA helped fund the study.

including irritability and poor appetite, can manifest due to depletion of body stores of iron long before anemia or low hemoglobin
occurs. Another sign of iron deficiency is a craving for dirt or ice
(pica). It has been suggested that ice craving can occasionally cause
alcoholism since it is socially acceptable for adults to drink ice with
alcoholic drinks. Allegedly the iron-deficient compulsive ice eater
gets habituated to the alcohol as well. Iron supplementation generally reverses these symptoms within a week, though the iron deficiency itself takes longer to correct. Iron deficiency, even in its mild form,
has been found to result in decreased work performance.

Doctors test for anemia with a simple hemoglobin test. The results
might appear normal, and a patient may have no obvious illness, but
iron deficiency may still exist, especially during infancy, adolescence,
and throughout a woman's childbearing years. During these times,
additional iron is needed in the diet. Regular aspirin users are also at
high risk for iron deficiency. For these reasons, nutritionists have
promoted iron fortification of flour and cereal. Iron supplement pills
are readily available, and iron-rich foods include whole wheat, fish,
poultry (especially the dark meat), figs, dates, prune juice, beans,
asparagus, black strap molasses, oatmeal, enriched bread, dark green
vegetables, and extra lean meat. Cooking in iron pots and pans can
also add iron to the diet. Some foods can interfere with the absorption of iron—phosphates found in sodas, bran, and teas containing
tannin, for example, should be avoided. Other foods increase iron
absorption, particularly vitamin C–rich foods. Taking a ferrous iron
pill before breakfast insures excellent absorption. Small amounts of
animal protein (nondairy) such as beef, poultry, or fish added to a
meal can increase iron absorption from food fourfold.

Many people wish to take iron supplements because of the fact
that the bioavailability of iron in foods varies so greatly.* In the ordi-
nary diet 10–20 mg of iron are consumed each day, but less than 10
percent of this is absorbed. The requirements for iron found in the

*Hemochromatosis, one of the most common hereditary diseases in the United
States, is a deadly genetic disease that causes the organs to store too much iron.
It can cause liver damage, diabetes, and sterility and is often a silent disease,
causing no symptoms. Men over fifty are five times more likely than women to
show symptoms of hemochromatosis. High iron levels have been found in young
men in their twenties and thirties. It can be detected by laboratory tests called
"ferritin" and "transferrin saturation" blood levels. Ask your doctor to test you
for hemochromatosis. Adult men should avoid iron supplements unless they
need iron and are certain they do not have hemochromatosis.

RDA take into account the low amount of iron actually absorbed from iron pills. I tell my patients that in recommended doses iron is safe, but to be careful not to consume too much iron as a supplement* because in large amounts it can be toxic and can cause abdominal discomfort. Ferrous sulfate is a good supplement to take if needed, as it is very well absorbed. Some "chelated iron" compounds, sold because of their less irritating effect on the gut, are often passed out in the stool without being absorbed.

Infant formulas should have 12–18 mg of iron per quart. Breast-fed infants get iron from breast milk in adequate amounts because of its extremely high bioavailability. Fortified infant cereals should not be feared. They are especially nutritious and contain the type of additives that are nutritionally desirable. Premature infants especially, if not breast fed, should be on an iron-fortified formula.

Heavy menstrual periods are a frequent contributor to iron deficiency, which is why women after puberty and during childbearing years are frequently iron deficient. It is very popular now for many men and women to totally avoid red meat. Women who avoid red meat are especially vulnerable to iron deficiency without obvious symptoms and might benefit from a small daily iron supplement. It is extremely rare for an adult man to be anemic due to lack of iron. Anemia in adult men should always be thoroughly investigated for its cause. Taking iron tablets could hide and postpone early diagnosis or recognition of blood loss in the stools from colitis, polyps, or intestinal cancer.

See Chapter 8 for more information on iron.

RECOMMENDED DAILY ALLOWANCES FOR IRON**

INFANTS:

0 to 6 months	10 mg
6 months to 3 years	15 mg

CHILDREN:

4 to 10	10 mg
11 to 18	18 mg

**Individual requirements vary greatly; increasing the dietary iron through fortification may be desirable, particularly during pregnancy.

---

*Be sure to put all pills or medicines locked or out of reach of climbing toddlers and young children. Iron poisoning remains one of the more common and often deadly poisonings in children.

RECOMMENDED DAILY ALLOWANCES FOR IRON (continued)

Males 19+	10 mg
Females 19–50	18 mg
Females 51+	10 mg
PREGNANCY:	36 mg
LACTATION:	18 mg

The above RDA for Iron is expressed in milligrams of "elemental" iron. The elemental iron is the same as usable iron.

Ferrous sulfate tablets that contain 325 mg of iron = 65 mg elemental or available iron.
Ferrous gluconate tablets that contain 325 mg of iron = 39 mg elemental or available iron.
Ferrous fumarate tablets that contain 200 mg of iron = 66 mg elemental or available iron.
Ferrous sulfate (1 teaspoon, liquid form), 220 mg of iron = 50 mg elemental or available iron.
Children's multivitamins with iron have very small amounts of elemental iron, typically 12–18 mg.

Zinc

In 1963, zinc was first recognized as an essential element for humans. A normal American diet easily supplies the RDA for zinc because most Americans eat animal protein and zinc is found in abundant amounts in all meats. Diets that exclude meat, fish, and other zinc-rich foods such as eggs, milk, and whole grains may produce symptoms of zinc deficiency. Deficiency is also a potential problem in alcoholics with liver disease and patients with chronic kidney disease, rheumatoid arthritis, inflammatory bowel disease, or malabsorption syndrome (nutrients poorly absorbed from the gut). The rash that is characteristic of zinc deficiency resembles eczema. It occurs on the face, hands, feet and ano-genital regions. Other signs of zinc deficiency are loss of appetite, loss of taste, and possibly slower wound healing. These symptoms can also appear in individuals following an unusual crash diet.

At the opposite end of the spectrum is zinc toxicity due to zinc over-dose (As with zinc deficiency, this is extremely rare, except in cases in which a person has been taking large zinc supplements and has a diet that is already high in zinc). Sometimes zinc poisoning (toxicity) is due to the ingesting of foods stored in galvanized containers. Water that flows through galvanized pipes does not pose a problem, however.

Symptoms of zinc toxicity are stomach upset, nausea, vomiting, bleeding in the stomach, and anemia secondary to this blood loss. Long term zinc overdose can also interfere with resistance to infection.*

Zinc deficiency in humans was first reported in the early 1960s in very short individuals found to be on a diet low in meat and fish, but very high in bread made from grains high in phytates. Phytates are known to bind zinc and thus inhibit its uptake in the body. Upon treatment with supplemental zinc these patients showed a striking response in growth and development of secondary sex characteristics. Immediate responses to zinc supplementation in *deficient* persons include personality changes and clearing of skin lesions as well as increased body growth, particularly in infants. Children with zinc deficiency are extremely irritable and difficult to manage. The first response to zinc supplementation in deficient young children is that they become more placid, usually within twenty-four hours after the first treatment.

Recently, intriguing studies have suggested that zinc lozenges, when started within twenty-four hours of symptoms, may be effective in reducing the symptoms and duration of the common cold by up to 42 percent. A study showed that if zinc lozenges were started within twenty-four hours of onset of cold symptoms, and administered no less than two hours apart (up to eight lozenges per day) cold symptoms lasted only 4.3 days versus the 9.2 days found in a matched placebo group.† Researchers aren't sure how zinc affects the common cold, but they do know that in a test tube, zinc stops many cold viruses from multiplying. To date more than 300 zinc-dependent enzymes have been identified, thus promoting multiple theories on how zinc might work in preventing the common cold. It may induce the production of interferon, or the effect may be due in part to correction of subclinical zinc deficiency in selected persons. There is no shortage of theories! Whatever the mechanism, these recent studies raise the intriguing possibility that zinc may be effective in reducing the duration and severity of the common cold. Unfortunately, zinc is not always well tolerated. Ninety percent of those taking zinc lozenges

*Large doses of zinc can interrupt the function of iron, aggravate a marginal copper deficiency and potentially contribute to calcium deficiency. Since all nutrients have the ability to influence the absorption of others, supplementation with any single vitamin or mineral, when taken in large amounts, is often not a good idea.

†*Ann Intern Med* 1996; 125 (2): 81–88.

(23 mg of elemental zinc, usually as zinc gluconate) reported mild to moderate side effects such as nausea and bad taste.

Carefully conducted studies are needed before this therapy can be recommended, especially to children. If zinc becomes a widely used remedy against the common cold, long-term surveillance will be necessary to verify its safety.*

THE RECOMMENDED DIETARY ALLOWANCE FOR ZINC

INFANTS:	
0–12 months	5 mg
CHILDREN:	
1–10 years old	10 mg
Males 11+	15 mg
Females 11+	12 mg
PREGNANCY:	15 mg
LACTATION:	
1st 6 months	19 mg
2nd 6 months	16 mg

Fluorine
(Fluoride)

When communities began to add fluoride to drinking water in the 1960s, rates of tooth decay fell by 50 to 60 percent. Fluoride strengthens tooth enamel, making it more resistant to acids formed in the mouth by sugar-fermenting bacteria. For those children living outside of water districts that fluoridate their water, fluoride drops or pills are almost as effective as drinking fluoridated water. But even the most motivated parent knows it is difficult to remember to give a child that daily fluoride pill for ten or more years. Parents often are more motivated to give a daily multivitamin to their child, so fluoride is often prescribed combined with a multivitamin and these preparations work as well as if they were given separately. Fluoride given on an empty stomach is 100 percent absorbed, but when given with milk or

*Zinc toxicity has been seen in people who took just ten times the RDA of 15 mg of zinc for several weeks.

a calcium-rich meal, it is incompletely absorbed. Fluoridated tooth-paste is very popular and is of value in reducing caries. Very little toothpaste is needed to brush teeth adequately, and since many young children swallow toothpaste, it is prudent to keep the amount of paste to a small bead. Too much fluoride can cause slight mottling of the tooth enamel. The risk of mottling can be reduced by carefully fol-lowing the current recommended supplementation dosages by the American Academy of Pediatrics Committee on Nutrition. Fluoride also favors the deposition of calcium, thereby strengthening bones, and may help prevent osteoporosis. The safety and nutrition advan-tages that result from fluoridation of the water supply have been demonstrated, but there are those who feel our water supply should not be tampered with. Although the argument for "freedom of choice" may be valid, the scare tactics used by antifluoridationists are unsupported by reputable studies. The amount added—one part flu-oride to one million parts of water—does not cause cancer, nor is fluoridation a foreign plot to weaken our children's bodies, as some claim.

Breast milk, cow milk, prepared infant foods, beverages, and sodas contain virtually no fluoride. Various food snacks have been graded for their cavity-producing capacity. Raisins are the worst, fol-lowed by cookies, sticky candy bars, doughnuts, and presweetened cereals; then nut butters, chips, and soda. While on the subject of tooth decay, I would be remiss not to mention fruit juice. Fruit juice is pure sugar. That's right—natural sugar, but nonetheless sugar. I frequently observe parents giving three bottles of juice a day to their infants and toddlers to use as a pacifier. This means that the child washes his or her teeth with sugar constantly, which leads to "apple juice teeth." It need not be apple juice, it can be any fruit juice or even cow or breast milk (they contain the milk sugar, lactose). In addition to tooth decay, the sugar in fruit juice often is responsible for a poor appetite and results in a very irritable child. Limit juice to once a day and if you must use the bottle as a pacifier, *fill it with pure water, and not dilute juice.*

Supplementation of the diet is no substitute for a wholesome diet. To achieve and maintain healthy teeth and gums throughout life, oral hygiene, optimal nutrition, and avoidance of sticky snacks are critical.

FLUORIDE SUPPLEMENTATION SCHEDULE

▲   No supplementation for water containing over 0.6 ppm fluoride
▲   No supplementation for infants under six months of age.
▲   No supplementation for children under three years of age where fluoride
    level is over 0.3 ppm.

AGE OF CHILD FLUORIDE CONTENT IN DRINKING WATER

	<0.3 ppm*	0.3–0 ppm	>0.6 ppm
Birth–6 months	None	None	None
6 months–3 years	0.25 mg**	None	None
3 years–6 years	0.5 mg	0.25 mg	None
6 years–16 years	1.0 mg	0.5 mg	None

*1.0 part per million (ppm) = 1 mg fluoride ion/liter

**2.2 mg sodium fluoride contains 1 mg. fluoride ion (dose given in fluoride ions)

Selenium

Recent studies suggest that selenium might be involved in a variety of important biological processes, including those of the immune system. Animal studies have demonstrated that selenium offers some protection against environmental carcinogens. Selenium is one of a group of minerals including zinc, copper, iron, and manganese, all of which help neutralize free radicals. That is, they help fight cell damage caused by oxygen-derived compounds, and thus they may protect against certain cancers. For these reasons it has been recommended that malnourished people take selenium as a supplement. There is no specific RDA for selenium, but the usual suggested amount is 50–200 mcg per day for adults and about 30–150 mcg per day for children.

In the general population, dietary selenium intake varies greatly, depending on the type of food consumed and the geographic location in which these foods are produced. Selenium is not distributed evenly in agricultural lands. As a result, many of our foods are grown in selenium-deficient soils. Since selenium is not essential for the growth of grains, fertilizers usually do not contain selenium. In the U.S. and Canada it has been reported that the more selenium found in the soil and farm crops, the lower the human cancer rate in those areas.

Keshan disease is a potentially fatal heart-muscle and muscle-weakness disease found in young children deficient in selenium. It is seen in China where selenium is deficient in the soil. It is occasionally seen in premature infants kept on intravenous fluids for weeks when the nutrient fluid has no added selenium. Selenium supplementation programs in China have eradicated this widespread problem.

Fortunately, seafood, especially oysters, halibut, swordfish, salmon, and tuna, is rich in selenium and is an excellent low-fat source of protein as well. Other foods rich in selenium include yeast, asparagus, garlic, whole grains, and cashews. Although kelp is rich in selenium, many other toxic metals such as arsenic and mercury may also be present.

Copper

Copper is an essential nutrient that the body stores in the liver. It is crucial to respiration, hemoglobin synthesis, bone and connective tissue growth, and normal function of the central nervous system. There are several extremely rare causes of copper deficiency at birth that have to do with genetic inborn errors of metabolism (Wilson's disease, Menke's disease). Copper deficiency due to inadequate intake of this mineral is primarily seen in patients fed for long periods on intravenous fluid deficient in this mineral. An early feature of nutritional copper deficiency is anemia unresponsive to iron therapy. Large quantities of supplemental zinc can also impair copper absorption. On a practical level, copper deficiency should not be a concern to parents.

Good dietary sources of copper are shellfish, (especially oysters),* beans, nuts, whole grains, and potatoes.

Iodine

Iodine is needed for normal cell metabolism and for the thyroid gland to make thyroid hormones. Insufficient intake of this trace element can lead to a goiter due to enlargement of the thyroid gland. Goiters were once common in parts of the world, called "goiter belts,"

---

*Raw or uncooked shellfish is dangerous at any age, but especially in the very young and old. It is safer and wiser to consume only cooked, steamed, barbecued, or baked shellfish and crustaceans.

where the soil was deficient in iodine. In the United States, the goiter belt included the Great Lakes region and the Plains states. In the 1930s about 40 percent of the people in Michigan had a goiter due mainly to iodine deficiency. As a public health measure, iodized salt was introduced, and although we still see goiters in America, they are rarely due to iodine deficiency.

Cretinism, a form of mental retardation, is found in infants born with little or no thyroid hormone and was once commonly caused by iodine deficiency. The mental retardation of cretinism can be prevented by giving these infants thyroid hormone immediately after birth. Most newborns in the United States are screened by a blood test to help obtain an early diagnosis of this preventable disaster.

The best sources of iodine are iodized salt, seafood, and dairy products and crops from iodine-rich areas. It is extremely unlikely that iodine deficiency would occur in children or adults on a low-salt diet, since only minuscule amounts are needed—micrograms—and therefore supplementation is rarely needed. Most multivitamin-mineral supplements contain 150 mcg.

RECOMMENDED DAILY ALLOWANCE FOR IODINE

0–12 months	40–50 mcg
1–3 years	70 mcg
4–6 years	90 mcg
7–10 years	120 mcg
11+ years	150 mcg
PREGNANCY:	175 mcg
LACTATION:	200 mcg

CHAPTER SIXTEEN

THE FOOD GUIDE PYRAMID

▲ ▲ ▲

A Guide to Daily Food Choices (for Adults)

The Food Pyramid is a visual model of what constitutes a healthy diet. It is divided into many sections, each representing a food group, with the largest section at its base. Foods in this section should make up the largest part of your adult diet. As you get to the top of the pyramid the sections become smaller, suggesting smaller portions of the daily diet should be consumed from this group. The smallest section at the top of the pyramid represents *Fats, Oils and Sweets*, and the advice is to use these foods sparingly, that is, 1–2 tablespoons of added fat a day and 2–6 tablespoons of added sugar a day. These guidelines are of limited value for children. The size of food servings recommended in the Food Pyramid is more appropriate for adults, and there is little to warn the parent against *hidden* fat or salt that may be lurking in the lower levels of the pyramid. After looking at the recommended portion size for vegetables, parents might correctly wonder, "What child would eat all of that?" Obviously, serving sizes must be scaled down for children, especially those under ten.

Each section contains pictures of foods, which affords quick identification of the healthy foods. A clever promoter could place a picture or icon of his food in the pyramid, suggesting its whole-someness. For example, the bottom section is for grains, primarily unprocessed—*Bread, Cereals, Rice, and Pasta*—instead, products like pizza with cheese, olives, and pepperoni toppings or a box of macaroni and cheese might be displayed.

The *Milk, Yogurt, and Cheese* section near the top of the pyramid does not stress nonfat dairy. If you follow the portion size of recommended servings within this group plus the adjacent *Meat, Poultry, Fish, Dry Beans, Eggs, and Nuts* group, you and your children most likely will be eating excessive amounts of protein and fat.

That two-thirds of the Food Pyramid is devoted to the complex carbohydrate should serve as a visual reminder that whole grains, fresh vegetables, and fresh fruit should be the most prominent part of each meal, while only one third or less of your plate should be covered with meat, poultry, fish, cheese, or eggs. This message redeems the other flaws, but clearly, this Pyramid needs work. I'm looking forward to a revision that will focus on educating parents to make better nutritional choices for themselves and their children. While we are waiting, here is my version of the pyramid.

The USDA Food Guide Pyramid

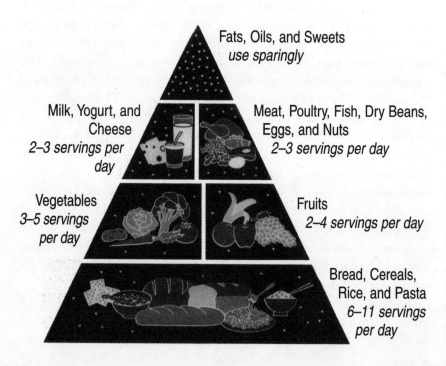

Fats, Oils, and Sweets
use sparingly

Milk, Yogurt, and
Cheese
2–3 servings per day

Meat, Poultry, Fish, Dry Beans,
Eggs, and Nuts
2–3 servings per day

Vegetables
*3–5 servings
per day*

Fruits
2–4 servings per day

Bread, Cereals,
Rice, and Pasta
*6–11 servings
per day*

A New Food Guide Pyramid for Children

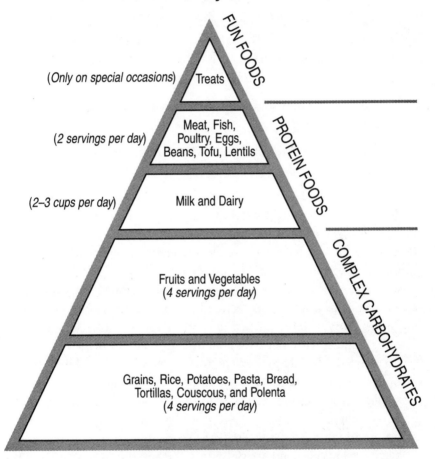

The serving size has been adjusted to accommodate the nutritional needs of children.

COMPLEX CARBOHYDRATES—
THE FOUNDATION OF THE PYRAMID

▲ Grains, rice, potatoes, pasta, bread, tortillas, couscous, polenta: 4 servings per day.

▲ A child's serving size is one-half to one-third the adult portion. An adult serving would be one slice of bread, five crackers, or half a cup of cereal, rice, couscous, polenta, potato, and pasta.

▲ ½ cup cooked spaghetti approximates the size of an adult fist

▲ ½ cup mashed potato approximates the size of half an apple

More examples of foods found in the category: High-fiber muffins; grits; cornbread; and corn, wheat, rye, or oat cereals should be easy to find. Select dry cereals and crackers with three or more grams of fiber per serving. More difficult to find might be high-fiber pasta or bagels. Combine any low-fiber grain foods with fiber-rich spreads such as hummus instead of high-fat cream cheese. Use a low-fat high-fiber vegetable sauce as a topping for macaroni or spaghetti. Use the highest fiber rice available to you—such as brown rice—and try to avoid the highly processed "instant rice." Eat the skin of baked or boiled potatoes to increase the fiber and mineral content.

Children love crackers. It's true that they are a grain, but most have had much of the nutrition removed and replaced with too much sodium and fat. Select crackers that are as high in fiber as possible.

Other grains to avoid are dehydrated Ramen soups. The fiber has been removed from the noodles, and to make things worse, the noodles are fried. These products also contain excess salt and MSG. Most boxed macaroni and cheese should not be listed as an acceptable grain for similar reasons.

Many foods—such as milk, pizza, soups, and sandwiches—are combinations of complex carbohydrates, fats, proteins and simple sugars. That's why we need the Nutritional Facts labels along with the Children's Pyramid.

MORE COMPLEX CARBOHYDRATES—
FRUITS AND VEGETABLES

▲   This portion of the pyramid contains fruit and vegetables. It should be a dominant portion of the meal. Vegetables and fruit for breakfast? Why not!

▲   Fresh fruits and vegetables: 4 servings per day.

▲   A child's serving size is one tablespoon per year of age or half the adult serving, whichever works best for a particular food. A two-year-old serving size would be half a banana or pear, while using the table-spoon method, it would be two tablespoons of fruit or vegetable.

Examples of this category—Vegetables: carrots, squash, yams, peas, broccoli, brussels sprouts, string-beans, spinach, Swiss chard, lettuce, celery, cucumbers, tomatoes, kale, and radishes. (Soups are an excellent delivery system for vegetables and most children love soups.) Fruit: apples, bananas, watermelon, kiwis, figs, oranges, peaches, pears, tangerines, grapefruit, plums, mangos, cantaloupe, strawberries, blueberries, and cherries. Fruit juice should be limited to once a day. Instead, eat the entire fruit, since it contains all that nutritional fiber and nutrients that are discarded during the juicing process.

PROTEIN FOODS

This section contains low-fat protein-rich food sources. Over the past sixty years, this group of foods has been over-consumed.

MILK* AND DAIRY

▲   Low-fat 1% (not 2%) milk or dairy: 2–3 cups per day.†

---

*One cup of milk is equal to 1 cup of yogurt or 1½ oz. of low-fat natural cheese.
†For mixed foods, estimate the food-group serving of the main ingredient. A slice of plain pizza would count in the grain group because of the crust, the milk group because of the cheese, and the vegetable group because of the tomato sauce.

▲ For a younger child, 2 cups of milk per day is adequate. A child who fills up on milk has little room left over for other important foods, such as fruits and vegetables.

▲ 1 oz. of low-fat shredded mozzarella cheese approximates the size of a ping-pong ball.

▲ 1 oz. of cubed low-fat Jack cheese approximates the size of 4 dice.

MEATS, FISH, POULTRY, EGGS, BEANS, TOFU, AND LENTILS

▲ These protein foods should be eaten for 2 servings per day.

▲ A child's serving size is about half an ounce. Since there are two servings a day, that would be one ounce per day. Keep in mind that the recommended adolescent or adult serving of meat is 2–3 oz. at a meal. A child under three years who takes 2 cups of milk plus one ounce of meat, beans, lentils, peas, fish or poultry, fulfills the RDA for protein. For children over three years, add one more ounce of a protein-rich food.

▲ 3 oz. of beef or turkey breast approximates the size of a deck of cards.

Examples found in the category: fish (not fried), shrimp, eggs (not fried), low-fat cheese, lean beef, turkey, lean pork, chicken (no skin and not fried), tofu, lentils, and beans (not cooked with lard!).

Remember that milk is a high-protein food in addition to being an excellent calcium source. But dairy is very low in iron. If your family avoids red meat, (an excellent source of iron), be sure to eat iron-fortified grains and cereals. Consider taking a daily iron supplement after consulting with your personal physician.

DO NOT OVERWHELM YOUR CHILD WITH A PLATE THAT IS TOO FULL OF FOOD.

THE TIP OF THE PYRAMID

This portion contains "fun foods" or "holiday foods" and may be consumed on special occasions. They are not truly "foods" but are treats that add joy to the life of a child (or adult)—if these foods are kept special. Historically, these foods were served on holidays, and when used in such a way they pose no long term nutritional problem. *But when packed daily in the school lunch bag they become a health hazard.*

Examples found in the category: ice cream; potato chips; french fries; fruit roll-ups; M & Ms and Snickers bars; fruit punches; pickles; hot dogs and other sausages; roast duck; liver paté; liverwurst and other lunch meats; chicken nuggets; smoked fish; butter or margarine; and Caesar, Roquefort, mayonnaise, or other high-fat dressings.

PART III

▲ ▲ ▲

RESOURCES FOR PARENTS

CHAPTER SEVENTEEN

RECIPES

▲ ▲ ▲

Stocking the Wholesome Kitchen

KITCHEN TOOLS FOR LOW-FAT COOKING

1. Set of non-stick cookware. This lets you sauté without butter, margarine, or oil. Also keep a can of nonstick spray on hand for baking pans or cookie sheets, if called for. Depending on how creative you want to get, nonstick muffin or cupcake pans and a nonstick wok can also come in handy.

2. Air popcorn popper.

3. Roasting rack so meat or poultry doesn't have to sit in its own fat while it cooks. Fat collects at the bottom of the pan and can be drained off after cooking.

4. Blender or food processor for making purees, smoothies, sorbets, soups, shakes, and other drinks; as well as grating carrots, shredding cabbage, and chopping celery, parsley, or cilantro. I like the Vita-Mixer-type juicers that don't remove the pulp.*

5. Electric mixer.

6. Steamer basket.

*Vita-Mixer 4000 Vita-Mix Corporation 8615 usher Road, Cleveland, Ohio 44138 Tel: 800-848-2348.

7. Plastic spatulas.

8. Thick plastic cutting board (better than wood because it retards bacterial growth).

9. Zipper-closing plastic bags.

10. Microwave oven. They're safe and very helpful in preparing low-fat meals at a moment's notice. Microwave cooking destroys fewer vitamins than other methods of cooking.

KITCHEN CONDIMENTS AND STAPLES FOR THE CUPBOARD AND REFRIGERATOR

1. Herbs, especially fresh herbs, enhance the flavor of foods and allow you to reduce or eliminate salt.

2. No-salt-added condiments (as in ketchup), herbal salt substitutes, salt-free seasonings, lemon juice, no-salt-added tomato juice (even if you add a little salt to "improve" the flavor, it will still be less sodium than the regular tomato juice), garlic cloves, onions, cocoa instead of chocolate, nonfat sour cream,* nonfat mayo, nonfat plain yogurt, vinegar, virgin olive oil, canola oil, a plastic bottle of I Can't Believe It's Not Butter Spray (great flavoring and only 2 grams of fat in 18 spritzes), fat-free low-sodium chicken broth.

3. Fat-free or low-fat muffin and pancake mixes. Fat-free fudge brownie or angel food cake mix. Whole grain breads.

4. Low-fat or nonfat salad dressings. Low-fat or nonfat mayonnaise. Fresh salsa.

5. Precut, prechopped, bagged greens and precut veggies, such as broccoli, cauliflower, and carrots,

*Some brands of nonfat sour cream have a poor taste, but many others are excellent. Check the different brands at your local market and don't stop looking if your first selection was not to your liking.

make salad preparation a breeze. Box of cherry tomatoes. Low-sodium dip mixes such as Knorr (make with nonfat sour cream).

6. Boil-in-the-bag rice, white or brown, for always-perfect rice without having to use the highly processed and totally defibered instant rice. A bag of small new or red potatoes, for baking or microwaving. A can of fat-free refried beans for a high-fiber burrito or as a dip.

7. Low-fat, low-sodium, low-sugar breakfast cereals that are high in fiber and vitamins. (Nutrigrain cereals, Alpen, Post Grape-Nuts, Quick Oats, Wheatena, Total, Kix, Cheerios, Wheaties, Kellogg's Bran Flakes, Nabisco Shredded Wheat, Kashi Seven Whole Grains & Sesame, Ralston High Fiber, Cream of Wheat.)

8. One-percent or nonfat milk (for children over two years), but not 2-percent low-fat milk, which is not really low in fat.

9. Seasonal, ripe fresh fruit. Do not buy fruit that was prematurely picked and is hard as a rock. If you discover when you get home that the fruit tastes like cardboard, return it to your grocer.

10. Applesauce.

11. Bagels, breadsticks, unsalted pretzels, matzo, pita (pocket) bread, corn tortillas, nonfat whole wheat tortillas, popcorn for an air popcorn popper, fat-free fig bars, dried fruit, rice cakes, low-salt water-packed tuna, low-fat or fat-free string cheese, canned reduced-salt black beans, and don't forget the Beano.

12. Dried spaghetti, linguini, macaroni, angel hair pasta. Non fat, reduced salt marinara sauce.

13. Frozen skinless chicken breasts, Boca Burgers, extra-lean hamburger meat.

14. All-purpose flour.

15. Fresh-squeezed orange juice. Bottled water.*

FOOD SHOULD NEVER BE LEFT AT ROOM TEMPERA-TURE FOR MORE THAN TWO HOURS. LEFTOVERS SHOULD BE PLACED IN SHALLOW CONTAINERS AND PUT DIRECTLY IN THE REFRIGERATOR OR FREEZER.

Prevention of Nutritional Losses from Foods

Storage, processing, and cooking of fresh vegetables can cause nutritional losses. As a generalization, minerals, carbohydrates, fats, protein, vitamin K, and niacin are stable (greater than 85-percent retention) during processing and storage of foods. The nutrients most affected by cooking at home are the B-complex vitamins and vitamin C, because these vitamins dissolve in water and are usually drained away in the cooking water. Prolonged cooking in too much water as well as cutting vegetables into small pieces before cooking (processing) tend to increase vitamin loss. A basic rule for maintaining the nutrient is to cook vegetables in water that weighs no more than one-third as much as the food. For example, if you were to cook a pound of vegetables you would need only one-third of a pound of cooking water. One pound of water is equivalent to one pint, so one-third of a pound of water would amount to less than a cup. If cooking water does not cover the vegetable, steam from the boiling water will still cook it completely. It is important to limit the cooking water only if it is to be discarded. If it is saved to be eaten in soup, it makes no difference—the vitamins remain.

To further reduce all vitamin losses, cook your food no longer than is necessary to suit your taste. Food should be cooked as soon before serving as possible, since the nutritional value of food is highest at that time.

Steaming brings less water into contact with vegetables than boiling. But steam still wets the vegetables and the water drips back into the pan. Steaming and boiling in a small quantity of water are nearly equal in removing vitamins.

---

*Keeping healthy beverages in individual self-serve bottles may make them more appealing. Individualized water bottles are great for school lunches and on trips.

Microwaving is a rapid method of cooking and causes minimal vitamin loss.

Storing cooked vegetables for a day or longer in the refrigerator and then reheating results in losses of vitamin C between 25 to 50 percent. Vitamins in foods are also destroyed when stored in the freezer. The colder the refrigerator or freezer, the smaller the loss will be. Concentrated frozen orange juice refrigerated one year loses only 5 percent of the vitamin C. As a rule, however, there can be a significant loss of nutritional value when a food is stored longer than a few months in the freezer. Freezing slows destruction of nutrients but does not completely stop the destruction.

Vitamin A is reasonably stable in almost all food products and processes, but a notable exception is dehydrated foods exposed to air. Extended cooking of green, yellow or red vegetables can lower the vitamin A by 15 to 35 percent, but cooking high-fiber foods such as carrots probably increases the absorption of vitamin A.

Folic acid losses average only 10 percent during baking, but prolonged cooking of meat destroys this B vitamin.

Vitamin D is sensitive to light, and that is why milk should be stored in opaque containers such as cartons rather than in clear glass bottles.

TIPS TO BOOST VITAMINS AND MINERALS IN YOUR DIET:

1. Purchase only the freshest vegetables and fruits because vitamins are lost when produce is wilted, bruised, or old.

2. Darker-colored vegetables are generally richer in nutrients. Dark green salad leaves, for example, provide more vitamin A and iron than lighter ones. Orange carrots have more vitamin A than paler, yellow carrots. Yellow corn is more nutritious than white corn.

3. Pay attention to "sell before" expiration dates on milk and cottage cheese containers. Select the "youngest" product to assure freshest flavor and best maintenance of B vitamins.

4.   Avoid overcooking meat and fish. Medium or medium-rare rather than well-done meat or seafood contains more B-1 (thiamine). *An exception is hamburger meat. All ground meat should be cooked well-done, to kill any contaminating bacteria.*

5.   Refrigerate leftover vegetables as soon as possible and use them within a day or two.

6.   Potatoes, onions, carrots, and sweet potatoes keep best in a cool place (about 50°F).

7.   Ripen tomatoes at room temperature and then refrigerate when ripe. Use as soon as they are ripe, because tomatoes lose vitamin C with aging.

8.   Fresh vegetables should be used soon after purchase. Vitamins and flavor are lost when vegetables are kept too long in the refrigerator.

Complex Carbohydrate Recipes

GRAINS, RICE, POTATOES, PASTA, BREAD, TORTILLAS, COUSCOUS, AND POLENTA (4 SERVINGS PER DAY)

BASIC MASHED POTATOES

6 medium potatoes
¾ cup warm nonfat milk
ground pepper

Wash and peel potatoes and cut into quarters. Put in a pan and add enough water to cover them. Bring to a boil, then reduce heat to a simmer for about 20 minutes or until potatoes are tender but not mushy. Drain well. Mash with a potato masher or mixer, and add *warmed* nonfat milk. Beat in ground pepper to taste. You may wish to add a small amount of salt, "Butter Buds," or a salt substitute.

To add flavor, whisk in nonfat yogurt or buttermilk, season with chives or scallions, or add nonfat chicken broth for a buttery flavor.

BAKED POTATO

Russet potatoes are best for baking. Do not wrap them in foil, because the covering traps moisture, which will steam rather than bake the potatoes. Pierce the skin with a fork or knife in a few places before baking. This will permit the steam to escape, thus producing dry, fluffy potatoes. Thick-skinned potatoes may actually burst if baked without piercing. Baking nails can speed the baking process. Insert one lengthwise into each potato. Bake for 45–60 minutes in a 400°F oven. Test for doneness by squeezing the potato. It should give slightly. It's best to eat potatoes with their skins, which are rich in fiber,* iron, calcium, potassium, zinc, and B vitamins.

---

*Insoluble fiber, the kind in whole grains and beans, is known to help prevent colon cancer and to reduce the risk of heart attacks in adults. Most nutritionists recommend an adult diet that includes 20–35 grams of fiber a day. That is the equivalent of two large bowls of wheat bran cereal. The average adult American consumes less than half that much. Sneaking fiber into the diet isn't difficult. For example, half a cup of blackberries contains about 2 grams of fiber while half a cup of blueberries contains 1 gram of fiber. Add berries to your cereal for that extra treat. For the child over four, air-popped popcorn is another delicious source of nutritional fiber.

MICROWAVING POTATOES

Pierce the potatoes several times with a fork. Set them on a dish or double thickness of paper towel, placing a single potato in the center of the oven, and two or more in a circle or spoke pattern. Cooking times vary depending on the power of your microwave. Here are some starting suggestions. For one 8-oz. potato allow 5 minutes; for two potatoes of the same size, 7 minutes; for four potatoes, 13 minutes. After removing them from the microwave, let them stand for 5 minutes before eating.

NEW POTATOES WITH DILL SAUCE

6 medium new potatoes (medium-size red potatoes)

In about an inch of water, bring potatoes to a boil, then cover and simmer for approximately 20 minutes. When done, let potatoes cool, then slice into ¼-inch rounds. Place in serving bowl and cover with dill sauce. Serve hot.

DILL SAUCE

4 oz. low-fat or nonfat cottage cheese (small curds)
2 oz. nonfat milk
½ tsp dry mustard
½ tsp prepared horseradish (not creamed)
½ tsp dill weed

Blend cottage cheese and milk in blender or food processor for about 30 seconds or until smooth and creamy. Place mixture in a cup and stir in mustard powder until dissolved. Add horseradish and dill weed. You may substitute chives or chopped scallions for dill weed if desired.

BAKED POTATO LATKE-TOTS
(Recipe contributed by Mrs. Maddy Witner)

3 large russet potatoes, peeled and grated
1 medium onion, peeled and grated

1 egg
1 tsp salt
½ tsp pepper
½ tsp baking powder (mixed with flour)
2 Tbs flour
1½ Tbs canola oil
½ lemon
Pam
Nonstick mini-muffin tin

Grate onion and potatoes in a food processor or hand grater. Place in seive and drain well. Add the grated potatoes and onion to a bowl. Stir in the half lemon. Add a beaten egg, flour with baking powder, salt, pepper, and then the canola oil.

Spray mini-muffin tin generously with Pam. Spoon potato mixture into each cavity pressing gently to fill the cavity. Bake at 435°F in oven for 20 minutes. Check for browness. Continue baking until brown and crisp (up to 5 minutes longer). Remove from oven and invert nonstick muffin tin. Potato Latke-Tots should fall out easily onto a serving dish. Serve hot with powdered sugar, apple sauce, or non-fat sour cream. Receipe makes aproximately 36 Latke-Tots.

POTATO LATKES (PANCAKES)

3 medium (about 8 oz. each) russet potatoes,
     washed and peeled
1 medium onion
2 egg whites
1–2 Tbs flour
2 tsp sugar
¾ tsp baking powder
½ tsp salt
canola oil
½ lemon

Cut potatoes and onion into small pieces and add to food processor*

---

*Purists claim that you produce a better latke if the onion and potato are grated with a grater.

or blender along with egg whites. Pulse blend for about 25–30 seconds or until grated, but do not overblend to a thin soup! Be certain that all chunks of cut potato are grated. Pour grated mixture into a large strainer and drain the excess water. Put drained mixture in a large bowl and immediately stir in the juice of half a lemon. This will prevent the grated potatoes from oxidizing to a brown color. Add flour, sugar, and baking powder. Mix thoroughly.

Heat a 10- or 12-inch nonstick frying pan, at medium setting, with 3 Tbs canola oil. The oil will form a large bead. When hot, add to pan a heaping tablespoon per pancake of latke mixture (about three latkes per tablespoon of oil). Fry covered for 1½ minutes, tilting the pan to distribute the oil. Turn pancakes with a spatula and cook covered another 2–4 minutes without adding more oil. When both sides are golden brown, remove latkes from pan and place on brown paper (such as a grocery bag) and allow the paper to absorb some of the surface oil. Meanwhile, add more oil to the pan and follow the above instructions until the latke batter is gone. Then serve immediately with applesauce or powdered sugar dusted over the top of each latke.

SEE POTATOES, pages 52–53.

BASIC PREPARATION FOR VARIOUS KINDS OF RICE

All the recipes below call for 1 cup of dry rice with 2 cups of water. This makes about 3 cups of rice.

CONVERTED RICE: Although the directions on the box call for 2½ cups of water, use 2 cups. Bring the water to boil in a pan and add the rice. Stir briefly. Cover and reduce heat to low. *Do not disturb or remove cover.* This means no peeking! Cook for 30 minutes. Remove cover and admire your perfect rice.

LONG GRAIN BROWN RICE: Bring the water to a boil and add rice. Mix briefly and cover. Reduce heat to low and simmer for 45 minutes. *Don't remove cover until time's up!*

WILD RICE: Same as above. When you uncover, if there's any unabsorbed water, drain it or let the rice stand uncovered for a few minutes.

Cooked rice will keep for about a week in the refrigerator. It reheats well if you add a few teaspoons of water. It is easy to vary the flavor of any rice by cooking it in a low- or no-salt broth at the start and by adding spices or herbs such as parsley, cilantro, or dill to the freshly cooked grains. Substitute rice for pasta or use it as a base for shrimp, lean goulash, or stew. Pilaf is one of the most familiar rice dishes.

MEAT, RICE & KETCHUP

½ lb. extra lean ground beef
1½ cups of cooked white rice
½ cup of ketchup
green peas

Optional: ½ chopped onion
2 garlic cloves
1½ tsp olive oil
red pepper flakes
black pepper

This dish was one of my children's favorites for breakfast, lunch, dinner, or snack. It's nutritious and loved by children of all ages. Even my grandson, Cody, eats it.

Brown the ground beef in a nonstick frying pan. Tilt the pan and pour off any juices or fat. Stir in the rice and ketchup. Add a handful of green peas (thawed if frozen) and stir in lightly.

For more sophisticated palates, sauté half a chopped onion and 2 garlic cloves in olive oil. Cook until soft and then continue recipe as above. For spicier flavor, add a pinch of red pepper flakes and some black pepper.

For those parents who want to prepare a quick rice dish, be sure to read the Nutrition Facts before buying a box of a ready-to-prepare mix. Many are loaded with salt. For example, the popular Rice-A-Roni Chicken & Vegetables has 1,470 mg of sodium in one small serving. *Nutrition Action*, a health letter by the Center for Science in the Public Interest, checked on its contents and found only nine peas, 1½ teaspoons of carrot slivers, 1 teaspoon of tomato particles, and even less chicken in a 2-cup serving. *Nutrition Action* calls Rice-A-Roni "Rice-A-Salt," and recommends Marrakesh Express CousCous or Terrazza Pasta & Beans as healthier alternatives, because they cut out about 90 percent of the sodium.

SEE RICE, page 53

POLENTA

Polenta is a corn mush made from corn flour. It's a staple among the poorer farmers in Europe and a fancy side dish among the upper classes in America. It's delicious for breakfast, lunch, dinner, or snacks.

> ½ cup polenta cornmeal
> 2 cups water
> ⅓ cup shredded reduced-fat or nonfat
>   mozzarella or jack cheese
> 1 tsp sugar (optional)

In a pot: Soak cornmeal 15 minutes in ½ cup of water. Pour mixture into a pot of 1½ cups boiling water. Reduce heat to low and simmer for 20 minutes. Stir constantly to avoid sticking or scorching. Add shredded cheese and mix well with polenta until melted. Mix in the sugar if desired.

In a double boiler: The problem of sticking or scorching is avoided with a double boiler. Pour cornmeal slowly—to avoid lumping—into 2 cups of water on top of a double boiler. Mix well and cook for about 35 minutes, stirring occasionally. Stir in shredded cheese and mix until melted. Add sugar if desired.

Variations: Polenta is often served with a sprinkling of Parmesan cheese, with spaghetti-meat sauce, VERACRUZANA SAUCE, or with a chicken and tomato sauce dish.

VERACRUZANA SAUCE

> 2 onions (sliced thinly and separated into rings)
> 1 green pepper (quartered, seeded and cut cross-
>   wise into thin strips)
> 2 garlic cloves (minced)
> 1 can tomatoes (l lb. low sodium brand or fresh)
> 1 Tbs capers (drained)
> 1 Orange (juiced)
> ½ tsp oregano (crumbled)
> ½ tsp cumin (ground)
> 1 bay leaf

2 Tbs cilantro, fresh chopped or 1 tsp dried cilantro
1 dried red chili pepper, crushed
1 can pimientos (4 oz.)

Sauté onion rings in non-stick skillet, over medium heat, until soft but not browned and then stir in green pepper and garlic. Keep stirring for another 1–2 minutes. Break up tomatoes with a fork and add to mixture along with orange juice, capers, pimientos and herbs. Bring to a boil. Cover, reduce heat, and simmer for about 1 hour. May be frozen in Ziploc bags and stored for later use. This sauce is fantastic over chicken, rice, or broiled red snapper or any white fish.

SEE CORN, page 55

SPECIAL CREAM OF WHEAT*

⅓ cup Quick Cream of Wheat or Wheatena
1¾–2 cups nonfat milk
2 egg whites
1 egg yolk (optional)
½ tsp vanilla extract
1 Tbs brown sugar
raisins (optional)

Bring milk to rapid boil and slowly sprinkle in Cream of Wheat or Wheatena,† stirring constantly. Return to boil, then reduce heat and cook for 2½ minutes or until thickened, stirring frequently. Combine 2 egg whites (and one yolk if desired) in a cup, beat in brown sugar and vanilla extract. Stir this mixture into the Wheatena or Cream of Wheat and simmer for one more minute, stirring constantly. Add raisins if desired.

SEE WHEAT, page 56

---

*Oatmeal has more calcium, magnesium, zinc, folate, niacin, thiamin and copper than Cream of Wheat.
†Wheatena is a whole grain cereal while Cream of Wheat (farina) is mostly refined grain. There are more nutrients in whole grain cereals. Besides providing fiber as an aid in preventing constipation, whole grains are more likely to provide the vitamins, minerals, phytoestrogens, lignans, antioxidants and other unknown factors that are lost when grains are refined. For more information refer to Chapter 13.

BUCKWHEAT PANCAKES

¼ cup buckwheat flour
½ cup rolled oats
¼ tsp baking soda
¼ tsp baking powder
½ cup nonfat yogurt
½ cup buttermilk
1 tsp vanilla extract
1 Tbs apple juice concentrate
2 egg whites, beaten stiff

Combine buckwheat flour and rolled oats with the baking soda and powder. Add yogurt, buttermilk, the vanilla extract, apple juice concentrate and mix well. Gently fold the beaten egg whites into the mixture. Thin batter with a little milk if necessary.

Cook on a non-stick preheated griddle or skillet. About ¼ cup of pancake batter makes a six-inch-diameter pancake. Pour batter quickly and then lower heat slightly. Turn the cakes when small air bubbles break on the top. Serve with crushed fresh fruit or berries on top. Maple syrup is also popular as a pancake topping but fresh fruit and berries add more fiber and vitamins.

The Log Cabin Brand Maple Syrup had a seductive advertising gimmick when I was a child. The container was the shape of a log cabin. I'd beg my mother to buy that brand so I could play with the empty container. When she wasn't looking, I'd pour some of the syrup in the sink to empty it more quickly. The syrup was too sweet and I really didn't like it very much.

QUICK OATMEAL

1½ cups water
⅔ cup oatmeal (1-minute variety)
½ apple
¼ cup raisins
½ tsp cinnamon

In a small saucepan bring water to boil, stir in oatmeal. Reduce heat to medium low and stir exactly 1 minute. Cover with tightly fitting lid and let stand 3–4 minutes. Add remaining ingredients and stir lightly. Serves 3–4 depending or age and appetite. May serve with nonfat milk, if desired.

Variation: add banana slices.

SEE OATS, page 58

KASHA VARNISHKAS

No guarantees for this recipe since it has not been kid-tested outside of Russia. If you are adventuresome and enjoy new tastes this might be a bright new addition to your repertoire.

> 1 large onion, chopped
> 1 cup kasha (buckwheat groats)
> 1 egg
> 1½ cups chicken broth (low-salt type)
> ½ tsp lite salt
> 4 tsp canola or extra-virgin olive oil
> 2 cups (4 oz.) bow tie noodles

Place the egg in a sauce pan and beat lightly. Add kasha and stir until all the kernels are coated. Heat the egg-coated kasha grains in a non-stick pan that has first been coated with 2 tsp of the canola or olive oil, for about 2–3 minutes over low heat or until each grain is separate and dry. Now set aside Kasha and sauté onions in another non-stick pan with 2 tsp canola or olive oil.

Bring chicken broth to a boil in a saucepan. Add Lite salt and onions. Mix well and then add the Kasha grains. Stir for a few seconds, cover, and over low heat simmer for 10–15 minutes or until all broth is absorbed.

Prepare bow tie noodles according to package directions, drain, and combine the noodles with the kasha and onions. Mix well and cook gently until heated thoroughly. Serve piping hot. This is traditionally served as a side dish with a meat course.

MILLET PILAF

½ cup millet
1¼ cup chicken broth (low-salt)
1¼ cup chopped scallions
⅓ cup grated low or nonfat mozzarella or Jack cheese
black pepper to taste

Add millet to boiling chicken broth. Reduce heat to low and simmer covered for 30-40 minutes, stirring 1-2 times. When done, mix in chopped scallions and top with grated cheese. Add pepper to taste.

Variation: Mix in nonfat sour cream or nonfat yogurt.

BASIC BARLEY RECIPE

1 pound pearl barley (about 2½cups)
½ tsp salt
3 quarts water

Combine the barley, salt and water in a large saucepan. Bring to a boil over high heat. Reduce heat and simmer about 20 minutes or until the barley is tender but still crunchy.

Drain well, cool to room temperature or serve hot. Yields about 8 cups.

SEE ETHNIC GRAINS, page 59

More Complex Carbohydrate Recipes

FRUITS AND VEGETABLES (4 SERVINGS PER DAY)

STEAMING VEGETABLES

This method is good for many kinds of fresh vegetables: Use a 2-quart saucepan with a tight-fitting lid.* Add ½ cup water to the pan, drop in the vegetables, cover, bring to boil over high heat. Then reduce heat to the lowest setting and simmer until the vegetables can be pierced with a fork, but are not soft. You want the finished vegetables to be firm but not crunchy. Serve plain or dusted with Parmesan cheese or garlic or onion powder. In the categories below, begin timing when you turn the heat down to a simmer.

String beans: Cut off ends, cut beans into 1½-inch lengths, cook approximately 7 minutes.

Broccoli: Cut off thick ends, break into flowerettes, cook about 5 minutes.

Cauliflower: Cut flowerettes off central stem. Cook approximately 7 minutes.

Carrots: Cut into ¼-inch rounds. Cook about 7 minutes.

Zucchini or yellow squash: Cut into ¼-inch rounds. Cook about 3–5 minutes.

STIR-FRIED VEGETABLES

Stir-frying is the most versatile technique for cooking vegetables, and the most fun.

BROCCOLI

The microwave is the working mother's best friend. To make a quick side dish of broccoli, place fresh broccoli florets in a covered bowl with 2 tablespoons of water. Microwave for about 2–3 minutes. Season with squeezed lemon or sprinkle with a small amount of parmesan cheese.

---

*You can also use an inexpensive metal steamer that fits inside a pan and suspends the vegetables over the water.

ASPARAGUS

Young, thin, fresh asparagus is more tender and flavorful. Select only green spears that are about the same length and thickness so they'll all cook at the same rate. Cut away the thick ends, then scrape and wash each spear.

Place one bunch fresh, unwilted asparagus across the bottom of a large frying pan. Add about one cup of water, cover, bring to a boil, and immediately reduce the heat to a simmer for 1-3 minutes. Don't overcook. As with broccoli, if you overcook asparagus, it loses its dark green color and turns yellow-green.

COLESLAW

Now that you can buy preshredded cabbage, it's easy to make your own coleslaw and not be held hostage to the store-bought high-fat kind.

> 3 Tbs vinegar (there are many varieties, each with
> a slightly different flavor—experiment and find
> your favorite)
> 4 tsp sugar
> 3 Tbs nonfat sour cream*
> 1½ cups shredded green cabbage (optional—mix
> green and red cabbage)
> black pepper to taste
> ⅛ tsp salt (optional)

Combine vinegar, sugar and nonfat sour cream in a mixing bowl and mix until smooth. Add the cabbage and toss to coat well. Add pepper and salt if desired. Refrigerate at least one hour to enhance flavor. Coleslaw tastes best served cold.

---

*Naturally Yours Fat Free Sour Cream has an excellent natural taste that won't be disappointing.

VEGETABLE SOUP

Soup is a wonderful vegetable delivery system. Here is a basic recipe, but don't be afraid to innovate using your leftover vegetables. For the younger child, use a potato masher on the vegetables once the soup is cooked. As your child adapts to lumpy foods, you can omit this step.

6 cups chicken or beef nonsalt broth
2 carrots, diced
2 leeks, whole
1½ cups celery, diced
1 onion
3 cloves garlic, minced (optional)
2–3 Tbs basil, fresh, chopped
pepper to taste—but hold the salt!

Combine all ingredients and bring to a boil. Reduce heat and simmer for 20 minutes. Your basic preparation should now be ready. At this point you may add other vegetables such as cauliflower, broccoli, zucchini, summer squash, spinach, tomato, string beans, etc. cut into small pieces, about 2 cups total.

Variation: You may also add cooked white beans, boiled rice, and barley. Reduce some of the basic vegetables so the soup won't be too thick.

VEGETABLE SAUTE

Three-year-olds like this sauté, but try it on even younger children. Put it on your plate and see if your child reaches for a taste.

1 yellow onion, chopped
1 clove garlic, sliced
1 sweet red pepper, seeded and cut into ¼-inch strips
8 medium mushrooms, sliced
2 medium zucchinis, sliced ⅛-inch thick

¼ lb. snow pea pods
2 cups cooked brown rice
2 tsp Parmesan cheese

Sauté onion in non-stick pan until soft and slightly browned. Add garlic and red pepper, sauté for two minutes more at medium heat. Add mushrooms and zucchini and sauté until zucchini is tender (about 5 minutes). Stir frequently, being careful not to break up vegetables. Add pea pods and sauté about two more minutes.

Serve over two cups of cooked brown rice. Sprinkle with 2 tsp Parmesan.

GREEN SALAD WITH VEGETABLES
(for children over two years old)

A salad like the one below used to be time-consuming to prepare, but now ready-cut and washed fresh salad greens come packaged in sealed bags at most supermarkets. Salads like this should be served daily. The younger child may reject it at first, but make it a standard fare.

¼ head iceberg lettuce
3–4 leaves butter lettuce
3–4 leaves red leaf lettuce
2 Tbs garbanzo beans (canned, no sodium added)
2 Tbs red kidney beans (canned, no sodium added)
1 carrot, peeled and sliced to ¼-inch rounds
1–2 stalks celery, sliced to ¼-inch crescents
2 scallions, sliced to 1¼-inch segments (use the
   greens as well as the bulbs.)

Tear all the lettuce into bite size pieces, add the remaining ingredients, and toss with low-fat dressing.

A nutritious bowl of fresh greens can quickly turn unhealthy when it's smothered in high-fat, high-salt salad dressing. Read labels carefully or prepare your own salad dressing.

HUNGARIAN BUTTER LETTUCE SALAD
(Recipe contributed by Mrs. Geri Eszterhas)

1 head butter lettuce
1 large tomato, diced
1 red bell pepper, ribs and seeds removed, diced
1 cucumber, sliced
1 Tbs white or champagne vinegar
2 tsp sugar
1 cup water

Dissolve the sugar in vinegar and water and chill.

Wash lettuce well and tear leaves into large pieces. Arrange in salad bowl and add bell pepper chunks, tomato and cucumber. Pour large amounts of vinegar dressing over salad so that it is swimming in dressing.

Another delicious, easy to make, low-fat dressing can be made by combining 2 Tbs Dijon mustard, 1 tsp of honey, and a splash each of lemon and orange juice.

HUNGARIAN CUCUMBERS
(introduce to children over three years old)

3 large firm cucumbers, peeled and thinly sliced
1 small onion, thinly sliced
2 Tbs sugar
3 Tbs white or champagne vinegar
1 cup cold water
⅓ tsp garlic powder
1 ripe tomato, cut in wedges
1 bell pepper, ribbing and seeds removed, cut into
    thin wedges
sweet Hungarian paprika to garnish

Place sliced cucumbers and onion in a bowl. Dissolve sugar in vinegar and water and add to salad. Mix well. Sprinkle with garlic powder and stir. Garnish with pepper and tomato slices and sprinkle paprika lightly over top.

BAKED POTATO AND BROCCOLI

1 baked Idaho potato
2 Tbs fat-free sour cream
2 Tbs nonfat or low-fat shredded mozzarella cheese
2 Tbs salsa
1 cup steamed broccoli

This vegetable dish can serve as a stand alone after school snack or be a part of dinner. Bake the potato in the microwave and cut it in half. Cover it with sour cream, salsa and steamed broccoli.

SEE VEGETABLES, page 61–64

CAROL'S BANANA-STRAWBERRY SMOOTHIE
(Also good for breakfast on the run)

1 cup nonfat milk or nonfat yogurt
1 ripe banana
5 or 6 fresh or frozen strawberries
3 or 4 ice cubes, crushed
1 Tbs nonfat dry milk (optional)
¼ tsp vanilla extract
Blend in blender until smooth.

Other fruit combinations that make a delicious smoothie are: 3 oz. pineapple juice, four 1-inch chunks of pineapple, and 5 strawberries; 3 oz. orange juice (or half a peeled orange) and 1 peeled and cored apple: 3 oz. peach nectar (or half a peeled peach) and 5 strawberries. Find your own perfect blend through trial and error. Smoothies are low in fat and rich in fiber and they give you at least 2–3 servings of fruit.

BAKED APPLE

Large green baking apples, cored*
2 tsp apple juice
1 tsp brown sugar
⅛ tsp cinnamon

Place cored baking apples in baking dish. Spoon apple juice into the core cavity along with the brown sugar, mixed with the cinnamon. Bake at 375°F. for 45–50 minutes or until the skin turns brown and begins to separate from the apple. Serve either warm or cold. Top with nonfat yogurt or cold nonfat milk if desired.

*The large green apples are better for baking because they hold their shape better and do not turn into mush.

APPLESAUCE

2–2½ lbs. green apples, slightly tart*
½ cup water
a few drops lemon juice
cinnamon and raisins (optional)

Peel and core apples and cut into thin wedges. Place in non-stick saucepan with just enough water to cover. Applesauce will be too thin and watery if excess water is used. Add a few drops of lemon juice, cover and bring to a boil. Reduce heat and simmer for about 10 minutes, stirring occasionally. When apples become mushy, pour mixture into blender or food processor. Puree until fine. A potato masher may be used instead of an electric blender. Add some cinnamon and, if desired, raisins.

*The tartness of applesauce comes from these cruncy green apples. Choose a sweeter red apple if you prefer the sweeter, mushier taste and texture.

PEACH SHERBET
(a healthy sweet treat for toddlers and older children)

1 can (16 oz.) yellow cling peach halves (no sugar
    added) or 4–5 fresh ripe peaches in season.
4–5 ice cubes
1/2 cup nonfat milk
1 Tbs fresh lemon juice
1½ Tbs sugar (omit if regular canned peaches are
    used)

Chop ice cubes in food processor or blender until finely crushed. Add peaches with juices, milk, lemon juice, and sugar if used. Blend well. Pour into ice cube tray and freeze for 1–2 hours. Remove several cubes from tray per serving. Blend until mixture reaches snow cone consistency. Serve in sherbet glasses or small paper cups.

For variety, add some plain nonfat yogurt to frozen peach cubes. Blend until mixture becomes slushy.

BAKED PEARS FRENCH STYLE

3 Pears, peeled, cored and halved
¾ cup water
1½ Tbs sugar
1 tsp vanilla extract
cinnamon

Place halved pears, cut side down in a shallow baking dish. Over low heat simmer the water, sugar and vanilla until sugar is dissolved. Pour over pears and sprinkle cinnamon on top.

Bake at 350° for 25–30 minutes or until pears are tender. Serve alone, with sherbet or plain nonfat yogurt.

SEE FRUIT, pages 66–70

Protein Foods Recipes

MEAT, FISH, POULTRY, EGGS, BEANS, TOFU, AND LENTILS (2 SERVINGS PER DAY)

BASIC OMELET

Most children love omelets. They make a great snack, or can be the cornerstone of breakfast, lunch or dinner.

> 4 egg whites
> 1 egg yolk (optional)
> ¼ cup nonfat milk
> 6 drops Tobasco (optional)
> 2 tsp dehydrated, minced onion flakes
> ¼ tsp black pepper
> nonstick vegetable spray

Beat eggs with milk until frothy. Add Tobasco if desired. Add onion flakes and pepper. Mix lightly. Lightly spray the pan with non-stick vegetable spray. Pour into heated non-stick pan over medium heat. Cover and reduce to low heat. Cook for 5-7 minutes or until eggs are set. Eggs will be more tender if they're cooked slowly over low heat. This is true for any egg dish, including sunny-side-up.

Variations: After 5 minutes of cooking, add 1 Tbs chili salsa, tomatillo sauce, or nonfat shredded cheese to the center of omelet. Fold omelet in half and cook for another 3–5 minutes. Pour extra sauce on top just before serving.

LOUIS'S DRENCH TOAST

2 egg whites
1 egg yolk
2 Tbs nonfat milk
1 Tbs brown sugar
¼ tsp cinnamon
½ tsp vanilla
nonstick vegetable cooking spray (such as Butter
    Flavor Pam)
bread slices, slightly stale if available

Combine egg whites, yolk milk, sugar, cinnamon, and vanilla in a bowl. Mix well with egg beater or whisk. Soak bread in mixture until soggy. Spray nonstick vegetable cooking spray lightly over a non-stick pan. Fry on prepared hot nonstick pan until brown on one side. Turn and brown the other side. Serve hot.

SCRAMBLED EGGS WRAPPED IN A TORTILLA

3 corn or nonfat wheat tortillas
2 egg whites
1 egg yolk (optional)
1 Tbs nonfat milk
2 Tbs chili salsa
nonstick vegetable cooking spray (such as Butter
    Flavor Pam)

Lightly spray non-stick pan with a non-stick vegetable cooking spray. Scramble eggs and milk in a non-stick pan at medium heat. In another pan, heat both sides of a tortilla until soft, then remove from pan. Place scrambled eggs in center of tortilla and top with chili salsa. Roll up tortilla and eat while hot.

SEE EGGS, page 50-51.

HUMMUS
(Use this Garbanzo bean spread as you would use peanut butter)

8oz canned non salt garbanzos
½ cup 1% low-fat or nonfat cottage cheese
½ clove chopped garlic
1 Tbs fresh lemon juice
¼ tsp ground coriander.
3–4 drops Tabasco

Combine all ingredients in blender or food processor and blend for 30–40 seconds or until smooth. This makes an excellent spread over water crackers, bagels, bread, and for the older child, celery. It also mixes well with tuna.

SEE PEANUT BUTTER, page 46-47.

CHESTNUT STUFFING

Although chestnut stuffing is primarily a recipe enjoyed by older children and adults, it's not too early to introduce this whenever you wish to prepare a stuffing. Many young children adore stuffing, so beginning with a wholesome low-fat one makes nutritional sense.

1½ lb. chestnuts
1 large apple, peeled, cored and chopped
8 oz. can water chestnuts, drained
thyme
6 celery stalks, diced including leaves
½ lb. mushrooms, sliced
½ cup chopped scallions (bulbs and greens)
4–5 cups bread crumbs, unseasoned or stale bread
    (4 slices yields one cup)

Make criss-cross slits over chestnuts and boil in water for 30 minutes. Drain and cool before removing shells and skins. Remove and discard any moldy blemished areas. Blend chestnuts in food processor or blender with apple, water chestnuts and thyme. Stir celery, mushrooms and scallions over medium heat in a non-stick pan until soft. Add to chestnut mixture then stir in bread crumbs and enough water to bring it to a pasty, but not soggy consistency. Mix all ingredients together thoroughly. Makes enough stuffing for a 10–20 lb. turkey or 2–3 chickens.

SEE CHESTNUTS, page 48.

LENTIL SOUP

Unlike dried beans, lentils do not require soaking and long cooking times.

> 1 16-oz. package of lentils
> 2 medium onions, sliced
> 2 medium carrots, sliced
> 1 cup sliced celery
> ½ tsp pepper
> ½ tsp thyme leaves
> 2 bay leaves
> 8 cups water

Rinse lentils in running cold water and discard any small rocks or shriveled lentils. In a 5 quart Dutch oven or sauce pot bring lentils and remaining ingredients to a boil over medium heat. Reduce heat to low, cover, simmer about 45 minutes or until lentils are tender. Discard bay leaves. Makes about 11 cups or 6 servings.

Most toddlers love soups, and this is a great way to introduce vegetables.

COOKING HINTS FOR PREPARING BEANS

▲   A one pound package of dried beans will yield 5 to 6 cups of cooked beans.

▲   A 15-oz. can of beans is equal to about 1⅔ cups when drained.

To soak beans: In a large bowl or pot combine rinsed beans and enough water to cover by 3 to 4 inches (about 10 cups of water to a pound of beans.) Let stand at least 8 hours or overnight. Drain the soaking water before proceeding with your recipe.

Quick-Soak Method: In a pot, combine rinsed beans with about 10 cups of water to a pound of beans. Bring to a boil and simmer for three minutes. Turn off the heat and set aside for at least an hour. Drain the soaking water before proceeding with your recipe.

BEAN CUISINE'S "THICK AS FOG SPLIT PEA SOUP"

(Since there's quite a bit of chopping and mincing in this recipe, I recommend a Cuisinart-type food processor to make life easier.)

> 1 box of Bean Cuisine "Thick as Fog Split Pea Soup"*
> 2 Tbs olive oil
> 2 cups chopped onions
> 2 cups chopped celery**
> 2 cups grated carrots
> 6 cloves minced garlic
> 6 cups low-salt, nonfat chicken broth (3 cans)
> 2 cups water
> ⅓ lb. boneless ham slice, cubed

*Product of Health House, Reno, Nevada 89509. If not available at your local grocer, contact manufacturer. Also try the "Bag O Beans" soup with chicken!
**Celery has a wonderful crunch, has few calories because it is mostly water, and therefore makes a wonderful low calorie snack for older children. Raw celery should not be given to young children because they can choke on it

Sauté vegetables in olive oil in soup pot until soft but not browned. Add chicken stock, water, ham, split peas, ¾ of the spice packet and bring to a boil. Simmer 2½–3 hours or until peas are soft.

To turn this soup into a tasty and filling lunch, add 1–2 Tbs of cooked rice to each serving bowl.

BLACK-EYED PEAS

1 lb. dried black-eyed peas, soaked overnight or
    quick soaked (see above)
8 cups water
2 cups chopped tomatoes
1 medium onion, chopped
2 ribs of celery, chopped
1 tsp salt
2 tsp dried basil
2 bay leaves
2 tsp chili powder*

Combine all ingredient in a pot. Bring to a boil, cover, and simmer for 1–1½ hours, stirring occasionally. Serve over rice.

*Use a mild and colorful chili powder like California chili powder. Sprinkle chili powder over eggs, dust over chicken fillets or shrimp before grilling.

BEAN DIP

2 cups cooked black beans
½ medium onion, chopped
1 tsp cumin
½ tsp salt
½ tsp ground pepper
3–4 Tbs fresh chopped cilantro

Combine all ingredients in a food processor or blender. Puree until smooth, adding water as necessary to thin.

FRIJOLES
(refried beans)

2 cups dried pinto beans
2 oz. low-fat or fat-free Jack cheese, shredded

Place 2 cups of washed beans in a heavy pan with enough water to cover beans by 2 inches (about 4 cups). Simmer for 3–4 hours or until beans are tender. Keep adding water as necessary to cover beans. Drain and mash beans when tender, to desired consistency. Fifteen minutes before serving, stir in cheese.

Frijoles make an excellent dip with nonfat tortilla chips. Traditionally, they are served with rice on enchilada dishes. (See page 212.)

SEE BEANS, pages 34–35

PREPARING AND COOKING FISH, MEATS AND POULTRY

Cholesterol varies little regardless of the leanness of a cut of beef, pork, or lamb, but fat content does. The following are some ways to cut down on the fat content of meats, fish and poultry.

Trim all visible fat from meat. Remove all skin from poultry before cooking. Keep in mind that white meat of chicken contains less fat than dark meat. Choose the leanest cuts of meat and avoid steaks that are well marbled. Marbling, remember, is the fat streaks that run through the steak.

Select only extra lean ground meat. If extra lean hamburger is not available, have the butcher grind a well trimmed piece of lean roasting meat such as round. This may actually be less expensive and leaner than the hamburger on the display counter at your supermarket. When buying canned tuna, select only the "reduced sodium" water packed tuna. Avoid the oil packed or regular water packed tuna.

When a recipe calls for browning, frying, or sautéing, brown under the broiler. Broil or bake meats or poultry on a rack to drain off fat. Drain hamburgers or other meats further by patting with a paper towel.

Discard any fat after cooking. This significantly decreases the fat content of your food.

Or sauté with water, a mixture of lemon juice and water or garlic juice and water on a non-stick pan. Another method is to use a non-stick vegetable spray over a non-stick pan. Take care to use a plastic spatula to prevent damage to the non-stick surface.

Fish should be broiled, baked or poached, not fried. Breaded fish can be browned under the broiler to simulate frying, but avoid Shake 'n Bake type of products because of their extremely high fat content. Do not overcook fish. Avoid covering meat or fish with fatty, rich sauces.

Finally, it is a good idea to eat smaller portions than you are used to of the meats highest in fat such as beef, pork, and lamb. You will begin to find yourself no longer desiring the large quantities of meat found in many American diets.

"FRIED" FILLET OF FISH

1 lb. white fish (fillet of any firm white-fleshed fish such as orange roughy, cod, haddock, and halibut)
1 Tbs Dijon style mustard
1 Tbs nonfat nonflavored yogurt
1½ cups corn flakes (crushed)
1 Tbs chives
1 Tbs parsley (chopped)
powdered California chili or any mild chili powder —
    may substitute with ground red pepper (use
    sparingly).

If you want to thaw frozen fish, place it in the refrigerator. Do not thaw it at room temperature, where it may be subject to bacterial contamination. If you wish to cook fish while it is still frozen, double the cooking time, but in this recipe, allow the fish to thaw.

Rinse the fish quickly with cold water and pat dry. Run your finger across each fillet to check for bones. If you feel the tips of any bones, pull them out with tweezers. Cut the fish in equal parts. Combine mustard, chives, parsley, chili (or pepper) with yogurt. Rub mixture onto all sides of fish and marinate in refrigerator for 15–20 minutes. Then coat the fish with generous amounts of crushed corn flakes. Apply non-stick vegetable spray over a baking sheet and place fish so fish are separated from each other. Bake in preheated oven at 375° for 10 minutes, or until done.

To test for doneness, use a fork to see if fish flakes easily. When you probe with the fork or knife tip, the fish should barely flake. The fish should be just opaque and no longer translucent. Fish will continue to cook by retained heat even after it is removed from the oven or pan, so it may be best to stop cooking it when it is just a shade underdone.

RED SNAPPER VERACRUZANA
(Enjoyed even by children who do not like fish!)

> 1 lb. red snapper or rock fish
> Sauce Veracruzana (See page 184)
> Cilantro, choped

Prepare Veracruzana sauce as directed. Pre-heat broiler for about 5 minutes. Place fish fillets on teflon or non-stick broiler pan or baking sheet. Boil for approxiamately 5 minutes without turning. Fish should flake and be opaque. Better to undercook slightly than to overcook. Over-cooking fish markedly decreases its flavor. With the aid of a pancake turner, carefull yslide fish to a heated platter. Now pour warm Veracruzana sauce over fish. Sprinkle with chopped cilantro and serve immediately.

SEE FISH AND SHELLFISH, pages 84–86.

BEAN, TURKEY, AND BROCCOLI DINNER

When children grow up eating whole wheat bread, beans, and brown rice they will keep these good habits as adults.

> ½ lb. ground turkey
> 1 onion, chopped
> 1 garlic clove, chopped
> 1½ cups dry macaroni
> 2½ cups low-sodium broth or water

1 15-oz.-can of low-salt kidney beans, drained
1 cup chopped ripe tomatoes
1½ tsp dried oregano
1 tsp chili powder
¼ tsp salt
¼ tsp ground pepper
½ cup grated mozzarella cheese

Brown ground turkey in non-stick skillet and add onion and garlic. Cook until onion is translucent but not brown. Turn heat to low and mix in macaroni, broth or water, beans, tomatoes, and spices. Cover and simmer about 20 minutes, stirring occasionally. Remove from heat and sprinkle on grated cheese. Cover and let the cheese melt. Serves 4 to 6.

LOW-FAT TURKEY GRAVY

Collect the pan drippings including the brown solids. Let the drippings sit until the fat rises. Remove the clear broth with a bulb baster.

2½ cups defatted turkey broth (supplement with low-salt canned chicken broth)
¼ cup all-purpose flour
¼ cup water (cold)

Combine defatted turkey broth and canned broth in a skillet and bring to a simmer. Combine the flour and cold water in a bowl. Mix thoroughly until smooth. Now add this mixture to the simmering broth, slowly, while stirring with a whisk. Stir constantly til the mixture thickens. Add small amount of seasoning such as Molly Mc Butter or Lite Salt. My wife adds Tobasco or Worcestershire sauce to gravy to improve its taste, but not too much because of the salt content.

TURKEY MEATBALLS

8 oz. ground turkey breast
2 egg whites
1½ Tbs ketchup
Preheat oven to 375˚. Combine all ingredients in a large mixing bowl.

Roll into small meatballs about one inch wide. Place on a non-stick cooking sheet that has been coated with nonstick vegetable cooking spray. Cook for about 20 minutes or until all are cooked through and lightly brown.

Meatballs go well with pasta, or sliced in a sandwich. Use a sourdough or French roll. Toppings such as pizza sauce, salsa or melted nonfat shredded mozzarella make meatball sandwiches a favorite.

KIM'S CHICKEN IN ORANGE SAUCE

4 chicken breast halves, boned and skinned
1 cup all purpose flour
¾ cup orange juice (the sweeter the orange juice, the better)
⅓ cup chablis
⅓ cup mushrooms, fresh, sliced
2 Tbsp. parsley, fresh, finely chopped
1 tsp. orange peel, finely grated
1 pinch rosemary
2 Tbsp. raspberry or champagne vinegar
fresh peeled and pitted orange slices for garnish

Pound or cut chicken to even thickness. Coat lightly in flour. Saute chicken without oil using a non-stick skillet. Brown both sides well. Now add orange juice, chablis, mushrooms, orange peel, parsley and rosemary to frying pan. Simmer mixture covered for 7 minutes. Transfer chicken to heated serving platter. Add vinegar to skillet and continue simmering unitl sauce is reduced by one-third. Stir frequently. Pour sauce over chicken. Garnish with orange slices.

SEE MEATS AND POULTRY, pages 86–92.

Meals for a Healthy Family

All CARMINE'S recipes were contributed by Chef Michael Ronis of CARMINE'S Restaurant, 200 West 44th Street, New York, NY 10036; Telephone: (212) 221-3800.

CARMINE'S BARBECUED CHICKEN

8 chicken legs
garlic powder
2 cups barbecue sauce

I. Place the chicken legs in a baking dish and sprinkle lightly with garlic powder. Cover the baking dish with a lid or aluminum foil and bake in a preheated 350° oven for 30 minutes.
2. Remove from the oven and cool until the chicken legs can be handled easily.
3. Remove and discard the skin and place the chicken legs back in the dish.
4. Pour ¼ cup of the sauce over each chicken leg. Cover and bake for 20 minutes more.
Makes 8 servings
Each serving contains approximately 135 calories

CARMINE'S CHICKEN CACCIATORE

2 large onions, finely chopped
2 garlic buds, finely chopped
3 tomatoes, peeled and diced
1 Tbs rosemary, crushed, using a mortar and pestle
2 tsp oregano, crushed, using a mortar and pestle
1 1/2 tsp olive oil
salt
freshly ground black pepper

4 whole chicken breasts, boned, skinned and cut
    into halves
1 6oz.-can tomato paste
1 cup dry Marsala wine
1 cup dry white wine

1. Combine the onions, garlic, tomatoes, rosemary and oregano and mix well. Spread the mixture evenly over the bottom of a baking dish.
2. Heat the olive oil in a skillet. Lightly sprinkle both sides of the chicken breasts with salt and pepper and place them in the skillet and brown evenly on both sides.
3. Arrange the chicken breasts on top of the tomato-onion mixture in the baking dish and bake, covered, in a preheated 350 degree oven for 10 minutes.
4. Combine the tomato paste, white wine and Marsala and mix well. Pour over the tops of the chicken breast halves and continue to bake, covered, for 20 more minutes.
5. To serve, place each chicken breast half on a plate. Mix the sauce in the baking dish well and spoon over the chicken. (Take all the chicken, coarsely chop and add to any macaroni with the sauce.)
Makes 8 servings.
Each serving contains approximately 125 calories

CARMINE'S CHICKEN PIZZA

SAUCE:
1 large onion, finely chopped
2 garlic buds, finely chopped
1½ tsp oregano, crushed, using a mortar and pestle
¼ tsp salt
½ tsp freshly ground black pepper

4 whole chicken breasts, boned, skinned and cut
    into halves
1½ tsp olive oil

1 cup grated part skim mozzarella cheese

1. Combine the onion and garlic and cook, covered, over very low heat until soft, stirring frequently to prevent scorching. Add all other sauce ingredients and bring to a boil. Reduce the heat and simmer, uncovered, for 1 hour, stirring occasionally.
2. Heat olive oil in a skillet and cook the chicken breasts until they are lightly browned on both sides.
3. Arrange the chicken breast halves in a baking dish and spoon the sauce evenly over the tops. Sprinkle 2 tablespoons of the cheese over each chicken pizza and bake, uncovered, in a preheated 400° oven until the cheese is melted and lightly browned.

Makes 8 servings
Each serving contains approximately 190 calories.

CARMINE'S CHICKEN ENCHILADAS

3 onions, finely chopped
2 garlic buds, finely chopped
1 tsp salt
2 Tbs chili powder
1 tsp ground cumin
1 28 oz.-can no-sodium-added tomatoes, undrained
2 cups diced cooked chicken
1 cup grated sharp reduced-fat cheddar cheese
8 corn tortillas, warm

I. Combine the onion and garlic and cook, covered, over very low heat until soft, stirring frequently to prevent scorching.
2. Add the salt, chili powder, and cumin and mix well. Pour the juice from the tomatoes into the pan and then chop the tomatoes and add them to the mixture in the pan.
3. Continue to cook, covered, for 10 minutes. Pour half of the sauce in a bowl. Add the chicken and ½ cup of the grated cheese to the remaining sauce in the pan and mix well.
4. Spoon ⅛ of the mixture in the center of each tortilla and roll the tortilla around it. Place the enchiladas, fold side down, in a baking dish. Spoon the remaining sauce evenly over the tops of the enchiladas and then sprinkle 1 tablespoon of the remaining grated

cheese over each enchilada. Bake, covered, in a preheated 350°
oven for 30 minutes.

Makes 8 servings

Each serving contains approximately 230 calories.

VANDA'S SPAGHETTI PIE
(Recipe contributed by Vanda Braun)

6 oz. (uncooked weight) Spaghetti, cooked al dente
   and drained
¼–⅓ cup mozzarella cheese (low or nonfat), grated
1 whole egg
1 egg white (beaten with whole egg in a bowl)

SAUCE:
1 lb. ground round, extra lean
½ cup green peppers, chopped
1 onion, medium, chopped
3 oz.-can no-sodium-added tomato paste
8 oz.-can no-sodium-added stewed tomatoes
1 tsp Oregano
2 tsp Garlic powder
1 cup low-fat or nonfat cottage cheese

To hot spaghetti add cheese and mix well. Allow to cool a few minutes.
Stir in beaten egg. Spread spaghetti mixture into a 10-inch non-stick
or glass pie pan and shape into crust.

Prepare sauce by browning ground meat with green pepper and
onion in a non-stick skillet over medium heat.

Mix in tomato paste, stewed tomatoes, oregano and garlic powder.
Spread cottage cheese over spaghetti mixture and over this spread
the meat mixture. Bake in preheated oven at 350° for 20–30 minutes.
Remove from oven and sprinkle mozzarella cheese on top. Return to
oven for about 5 minutes or until cheese melts.

BEAN BURRITO

1 can fat-free refried beans
2 Tbs fat-free sour cream
2 Tbs fresh salsa
1 container nonfat mozzarella cheese, shredded
1 package corn or nonfat whole wheat tortillas

Heat the refried beans in your microwave until hot. Put 2½ Tbs in the center of a tortilla. Sprinkle about 1 Tbs of shredded cheese over the beans. Place the tortilla with refried beans and cheese in the microwave for 20 seconds or until the cheese is soft. Remove from the microwave, add the salsa and nonfat sour cream. Fold one end of the tortilla and wrap it like a blinz or crepe.

CHICKEN OR TURKEY ENCHILADAS

2½ cups shredded broiled or baked skinless chicken or turkey breasts.
4 oz. canned green chopped chiles (optional)
8 oz. chile salsa (reduced-salt variety)
8 oz. tomatillo sauce (reduced-salt variety)
6 oz. shredded low-fat Swiss, low-fat or nonfat Monterey Jack cheese
6 oz. corn tortillas or nonfat wheat tortillas.

To prepare corn tortillas so they will not crack when rolled, wrap them with a damp kitchen towel. Cover with foil and place in heated oven at 350° for about 10 minutes. This will soften the tortillas. This can also be done more quickly in the microwave, without the foil.

Mix shredded chicken or turkey with chili salsa in a pan and simmer covered for about 15 minutes. Place about ⅓ cup of well mixed chicken or turkey in the center of the tortilla. Roll up the tortilla and place folded side down on a non stick baking dish. Pour tomatillo sauce over tortillas and sprinkle with non or low-fat shredded cheese on top. Bake at 350° for about 15 minutes or until the cheese melts. Serve on heated dishes with low-fat or non fat refried beans (frijoles) and Spanish rice. Freeze leftover enchiladas. They can be reheated and served for lunch or as an after school snack.

Two Super Soups

CREAMY POTATO SOUP

Creamy Potato Soup Mix is a product of Bear Creek Country Kitchens. 325 W. 600 S. Heber City, UT, 84032. Questions or comments call 1-800-516-7286.

This soup can be prepared in a jiffy and is low in salt and fat. It may be your vehicle to deliver your toddler a variety of vegetables.

> ⅔ cup Creamy Potato Soup Mix
> 2 cups water
> peas, broccoli, corn, bay shrimp,* or leftover vegetables.

Chopped up clams and white fish turn this soup into a chowder.

Add soup mix to boiling water. Simmer 15–20 minutes. Add any of the above vegetables, shell fish, or fish and simmer for another 15–20 minutes. Add pepper and only a little salt. The vegetables add the needed fiber to the soup as well as other important nutrients.

---

*Avoid shrimp or clams if there is a strong family history of food allergy or eczema.

MEDITERRANEAN BLACK BEAN SOUP

This recipe is included to illustrate how easy it is to convert a high-salt, "ready-mix" to a delicious, wholesome, low-fat, high-fiber, reduced-sodium meal.

MANISCHEWITZ HOMESTYLE SOUP MIX

The label reads: "With Manischewitz Homestyle Soup Mix, you can make nutritious entrees (in just one pot) that your whole family will love! We have combined a carefully selected blend of beans with savory herbs and rice to help you create a delicious homemade soup."

The original recipe on the box follows:

> 1 box Manischewitz Homestyle Mediterranean
> Bean Soup
> 1 onion, chopped
> 7 cups water
> 1 15-oz. can chopped tomatoes or tomato sauce
> 1 cup celery, chopped
> salt and pepper to taste

In large pot, add water, bean package, onion, tomatoes and celery. Bring to a boil, reduce heat, cover and simmer 1½ hours or until beans are tender. Stir occasionally. Add seasoning and rice packet and continue simmering for ½ hour. Serve topped with chopped scallions or a dollop of sour cream. Makes six 1 cup servings.

If meat is desired: Brown ½–1 lb. ground beef or other meat choice and add to soup for last ½ hour of cooking.

Now here is how you modify the recipe and make it truly nutritious:

> 1 box Manischewitz Homestyle Mediterranean
> Bean Soup
> 1 onion, chopped
> 6 cups water (instead of 7 cups)
> 1 15-oz. can no-salt-added stewed tomatoes
> (instead of chopped tomatoes or tomato sauce)
> 1 cup celery, chopped
> 1 cup of sliced carrots (added to recipe)
> a pinch of red pepper flakes (instead of salt and
> pepper to taste)

In a large pot, add water, bean package, onion, tomatoes and celery. Bring to a boil, reduce heat, cover and simmer 1½ hours or until beans are tender. Stir occasionally. Add ⅓ packet of the seasoning instead of the whole packet, and all of the rice. Continue simmering for ½ hour. Serve topped with chopped scallions, but skip the dollop of sour cream. Makes six 1 cup servings.

If meat is desired: Brown ½–1 lb. extra lean ground beef or ground turkey and add to soup for last ½ hour of cooking.

▲ ▲ ▲

The food industry doesn't spend billions of advertising dollars to promote good food choices. They are bombarding your children with food and candy advertisements during the TV cartoon hours, thus shaping poor food preferences. As a parent you must take responsibility for what you and your children eat. To help you do that, videotape your child's favorite TV programs and delete the advertisements. Keep a library of videotapes. Kids love reruns. This is the first proactive step needed to capture or recapture your child's mind. Nutrition goes well beyond the belly!

One-third of all meals eaten by children are not at home—mostly school lunches. Become active in your PTA and school lunch program. Have other members of your group read this book, and they will learn why truly good nutrition is one of the most important gifts a parent can give a child. The common sense of your concerns and recommendations will become clear. You will win allies to promote healthier foods in school and at after school activities.

Parents must become more involved in the food selections made for our children. Insist and demand that the lunches served in school should be the gold standard or model for optimal nutrition. Give a copy of this book to any member of your community who is involved in making these far reaching decisions. Habits begin at an early age, and we as adults all know how difficult it is to make changes in food choices. Your efforts will go a long way to eliminate those diseases of advancing age that we needlessly endure. They need not be inevitable. Our next generation of adults should not have their quality of life sacrificed by eating habits that lead to early heart disease, colon and prostate cancer, gallbladder disease, diverticulosis, diabetes, and stroke.

CHAPTER EIGHTEEN

FAST FOODS

Let's face it. Your children are going to be eating "fast foods," and you probably will join in. As I said earlier, this isn't a perfect world, and to survive, compromise must be part of your menu. This section is not for those readers who believe they have total control of their children's diets and never eat at fast food joints. However, you still might enjoy reading about how us weak ones deal with the pressures to eat high fat, high sodium, low fiber inexpensive foods.

THESE NUTRITIONAL FACTS ARE INCLUDED TO HELP YOU BECOME A MORE INFORMED CONSUMER

McDonald's

DEADLY	MAYBE	BETTER CHOICE
Big Mac	Quarter Pounder	Grilled Chicken Deluxe (w/o mayo)
560 calories+31 grams fat	420 calories+21 grams fat	300 calories+5 grams fat

McDonald's (continued)

DEADLY	MAYBE	BETTER CHOICE
Chicken McNuggets (9)	Cheeseburger	Hamburger
430 calories+26 grams fat	320 calories+13 grams fat	260 calories+9 grams fat
Large French Fries	Small French Fries	Grilled Chicken Salad (with Fat-Free Herb Vinaigrette)
450 calories+22 grams fat	210 calories+10 grams fat	120 calories+1.5 grams fat
Sausage Biscuit	Egg McMuffin	Hotcakes
470 calories+31 grams fat	290 calories+12 grams fat	340 calories+9 grams fat
Cheese Danish	Cinnamon Roll	Lowfat Apple Bran Muffin
410 calories+22 grams fat	390 calories+16 grams fat	300 calories+3grams fat

Burger King

DEADLY	MAYBE	BETTER CHOICE
WHOPPER with Cheese	WHOPPER Jr (without mayo)	BK Broiler Chicken (without mayo)
760 calories+48 grams fat	320 calories+15 grams fat	370 calories+9 grams fat

Wendy's

DEADLY	MAYBE	BETTER CHOICE
Big Bacon Classic	Garden Veggie Pita	Grilled Chicken
580 calories+30 grams fat	400 calories+17 grams fat	310 calories+8 grams fat
Chicken Caesar Fresh	Jr. Hamburger	Small Chile Stuffed Pitas
490 calories+18 grams fat	270 calories & 10 grams fat	190 calories+6 grams fat

Hardee's

DEADLY	MAYBE	BETTER CHOICE
Blueberry Muffin	Cheeseburger	Sub
400 caloies+17 grams fat	500 calories+29 grams fat	370 calories+5 grams fat
Big Country Breakfast	Sausage Deluxe Burger	Pancakes
850 calories+57 grams fat	500 calories+30 grams fat	280 calories+2 grams fat
Frisco Burger	Hash Rounds Potatoes	Hamburger
760 calories+50 grams fat	30 calories+14 grams fat	260 calories+10 grams fat
New York Patty Melt	Big Fries	Regular Fries
780 calories+51 grams fat	500 calories+23 grams fat	230 calories+11 grams fat

Taco Bell

DEADLY	MAYBE	BETTER CHOICE
Taco Salad with Salsa	Taco Salad w/Salsa	Tostada without Shell
850 calories+52 grams fat	420 calories+22 grams fat	300 calories+15 grams fat
Big Beef Burrito	Grilled Chicken Burrito	Bean Burrito Supreme
520 calories+23 grams fat	410 calories+15 grams fat	380 calories+12 grams fat
Nachos Bell Grande	Mexican Rice	Pintos n' Cheese
770 calories+39 grams fat	190 calories+9 grams fat	190 calories+9 grams fat

Carl's Jr.

DEADLY	MAYBE	BETTER CHOICE
Super Star Hamburger	Jr. Hamburger	Charbroiled BBQ Chicken Sandwich
790 calories+46 grams fat	330 calories+13 grams fat	280 calories+3 grams fat

Pizza Hut

DEADLY	MAYBE	BETTER CHOICE
Pepperoni Lover's thin Pizza	Cheese Pizza	Veggie Lovers Pizza
(2 slices)	(2 slices)	(2 slices)
770 calories+32 grams fat	406 calories+20 grams fat	380 calories+16 grams fat

Subway

This fast food chain boasts of "7 subs with 6 grams of fat or less." This is true if you don't add mayo and cheese. But check out the sodium. The turkey breast sub has over 1400 mg! So if this is your selection, please don't make it worse by adding pickles. Subway is on the right track, but now they need to reduce the sodium in their lunch meats.

Arby's

DEADLY	MAYBE	BETTER CHOICE
Philly Beef 'n' Swiss	Giant Roast Beef	Light Roast Beef Deluxe
755 calories+47 grams fat	544 calories+26 grams fat	294 calories+10 grams fat
Deluxe Baked Potato	Italian Sub	Light Roast Turkey
736 calories+36 grams fat	671 calories+ 39 grams fat	260 calories+6 grams fat

CHAPTER NINETEEN

READING FOOD LABELS

▲ ▲ ▲

Now that you are fortified with a strong understanding of nutrition, it's time to go shopping and make intelligent food choices. The food label may help you, but only if you understand the special vocabulary used, and the little deceptive tricks employed by those who want you to buy their products. Once you learn the lingo, you will become a skillful shopper. To be able to see through the hype and half-truths of a sales pitch is empowerment that gives both strength and joy to any consumer.

Definitions

SERVING SIZE: The serving size is the first bit of information listed under the Nutrition Facts label. This amount is set by the FDA and not the manufacturer. Serving size is often an idealized amount rather than what you or most people would eat.

PERCENT DAILY VALUES (DV): These numbers are based on a 2000-calorie diet. This is of little value for the parent looking for guidelines for their child or adolescent who may consume fewer or more than 2000 calories per day. Even so, the acceptable amount of fat listed is excessive. Total fat should be 45 grams or less for those consuming a 2000-calorie diet. For teenagers consuming a 2500 calorie diet, total fat should be kept below 55 grams. Children consuming 1500 calories a day should limit their fat to 35 grams or less.

LOW FAT: No more than three grams of fat per serving of an *individual food*. The labeling law is different for a box that contains a *whole meal*.

If a main dish or whole meal is labeled "low fat" it means that it contains no more than 30 percent of its calories from fat, and *that is not low-fat!* Keep in mind that 30 percent is listed as a maximum! In the real world most consumers turn the maximum into the minimum. *A truly low-fat meal is one that is no more than 20 percent of calories from fat.* The decision to use 30 percent to represent low-fat was a political one and not based on our present nutritional knowledge. Almost all nutritional studies have demonstrated that the heart benefits of a reduced fat diet *are not demonstrated at 30 percent of calories from fat!* The studies *do* show that 20 percent of calories from fat or less *does* decrease cardiovascular disease. A diet containing 20 to 25 percent of calories from fat is not extremely low-fat and has been shown not to be harmful to the growth and development of young children or adolescents.*

LOW IN SATURATED FAT: No more than one gram of saturated fat per *individual serving* or less than 10 percent of calories from saturated fat *in a meal or main dish*.

LIGHT OR "LITE": The fat content or calories must be cut in half. The label should tell which one. Light can also mean half the usual sodium content.

LEAN: The USDA defines lean as less than 10 grams of fat in the meal; less than 4 grams of saturated fat, and less than 95 mg of cholesterol (per 100 grams or 3½ oz.).

EXTRA-LEAN: Less than 5 grams of fat in a meal or main dish; less than 2 grams of saturated fat, and less than 95 mg of cholesterol (per 100 grams or 3½ oz.).†

CHOLESTEROL FREE: Less than 2 mg of cholesterol and no more than 2 mg of saturated fat per serving.

---

*J. *Pediatr* 1998; 133: 28–34.
†Labels are sometimes confusing (deceptive?). For example: Extra-lean ground beef contains 16 grams of fat per 100 grams or 3-1/2 ounces. Refer to earlier section comparing beef cuts.

FOR MEALS AND MAIN DISHES, LOOK FOR NO MORE THAN 2 GRAMS OF FAT AND LESS THAN 1 GRAM OF SATURATED FAT FOR EVERY 100 CALORIES. THUS A 250-CALORIE MEAL SHOULD CONTAIN NO MORE THAN 5 GRAMS OF FAT AND LESS THAN 2½ GRAMS OF SATURATED FAT.

GOOD SOURCE: Must contain at least 10 percent of the Daily Value of the nutrient.

HIGH SOURCE: Must contain at least 20 percent of the Daily Value of the nutrient.

"Good source" or "High source" could be used deceptively by suggesting this is a healthy food. For example, if a meal contains a vegetable like broccoli, the package may claim "Contains broccoli, a good source of folic acid" but have a high fat or salt content.

CALORIES: The total calories per serving.

CALORIE-FREE: Fewer than 5 calories per serving

LOW CALORIE: 40 calories or less per serving and per 50 grams of food.

REDUCED CALORIES: A product altered to contain 25 percent fewer calories than the comparable food without reduced calories.

CALORIES FROM FAT: The calories from fat, which you wish to keep low. One gram of fat is equal to 9 calories. If Total Fat on the nutrition label is 10 grams, then the calories from fat is (9×10) 90 calories.

Unless you're a mathematician this figure won't help the typical shopper too much. Instead the label should contain the value of *percent calories from fat.* That would rapidly give some much-needed nutritional information. The percent of calories from fat should ideally be no more than 20 percent.

TOTAL CARBOHYDRATE: This part of the label does not offer too much information because it does not separate complex carbohydrates from simple carbohydrates (sugar).

SUGARS: The amount of naturally occurring as well as added sugars; omits some of the other sugars such as corn syrup. The amount of sugar, therefore, can be a larger amount than stated. There is no Daily Value (DV) recommendation for sugar on the label.

SUGAR FREE: Less than half a gram per serving.

SODIUM: Try to keep the milligrams of sodium to as much as or less than the Calories on the Nutrition Facts label. That is, if there are 100 calories per serving, the sodium should be 100 mg or less per serving. Try to avoid prepared meals that contain more than 450 mg of sodium per serving.

> **A 2000-calorie diet should contain less than 2000 mg of sodium.**
> **A 1500-calorie diet should contain less than 1500 mg of sodium.**
> **A 1000-calorie diet should contain less than 1000 mg of sodium.**

SODIUM FREE: Less than 5 mg per serving

LOW SODIUM: Less than 140 mg per serving and per 50 grams of food.

VERY LOW SODIUM: Less than 35 mg per serving and per 50 grams of food.

SODIUM, LITE OR LIGHT: If the sodium content of a low-calorie, low-fat food has been reduced by half.

FRESH FROZEN: Freshly frozen, frozen fresh. *A conflict of meanings!*

A SOURCE OF: One serving must contain at least 10 to 19 percent of the adult daily requirement of the named nutrient.

REDUCED OR LESS: Contains at least 25 percent less of the named substance than the food usually contains.

MORE: One serving contains at least 10 percent more of the Daily Value (DV) than the food it is being compared with.

INGREDIENTS: Ingredients are listed by weight, from the most to the least. If corn syrup, molasses, sugar, maltose, and/or fructose are high on the list, the food probably is loaded with simple sugars. When oil, butter, hydrogenated fats or oils, cheese, or lard are represented high on the list, the food may have excessive amounts of saturated fats and cholesterol. When the ingredients label says, "May contain one or more of the following: soybean oil and/or palm oil," it means either one may be substituted for the other (usually depending upon which one is less expensive or more available at the moment). Look for the words, salt, sodium, soy sauce, sodium bicarbonate, seaweed, and sea salt as indicators that you are dealing with a high-salt food.

MAKING FOOD CHOICES: USING THE NEW FOOD LABEL

To gather the most practical information from the Nutrition Facts and Ingredients labels, approach each food with a few basic questions.

1. *How many grams of fat are present per serving? Try to keep it below 3 grams per serving. If this is not possible, compare products and select the one with the least fat.*

2. *Next, look for the sodium content per serving. Use the rule of thumb: 1 gram of sodium for each calorie per serving. This may be difficult when buying cheese, pizza, soup, and other intrinsically high sodium foods. Here, the compromise rule may be expanded to read: 2 grams of sodium for each calorie per serving. Check different brands and select the one with the least sodium.*

3. *The fiber content of the food is the next important issue. If fiber is not listed, it means there is no significant fiber in the product. When choosing a cereal for your child (or for yourself) look for one that has 3 grams or more of fiber per serving (but not too high in sodium, fat, or simple sugar).*

4. *Check the Nutrition Facts and Ingredients labels for the amount of simple sugar. Avoid cereal products that say "frosted" and be careful when the label reads, "lightly sweetened." Select cereals that contain no more than 5 grams of* added sugar *per serving. Remember that juice is 100 percent sugar and water.* The container may say no sugar added, *but that does not mean it is without sugar. Fruit "drinks" and sodas should be avoided. Instead choose a beverage such as orange juice, or one that contains the entire fruit, blended, such as pear, apricot, guava, and papaya. These juices contain more nutrients than apple juice.*

5. *Finally check for vitamin and mineral content. Specifically look for vitamin C, folic acid, calcium, and iron.*

Breakfast Foods

OATMEAL

Oatmeal is a great source of fiber. The slow cooking oatmeal (about 15-20 minutes) has 4 grams of fiber compared to the 3 grams found in the instant type.

QUAKER INSTANT OATMEAL
(with real apple and cinnamon)

Nutrition Facts
Serving Size 1 packet
Servings Per Container 10

Amount Per Serving

Calories 130

Calories from Fat 15

Total Fat 1.5 grams

Saturated Fat 0.5 grams

Cholesterol 0 mg

Sodium 120 mg

Total Carbohydrate 27 grams

Dietary Fiber 3 grams

Soluble Fiber 1 gram

Sugars 11 grams

Protein 3 grams

Vitamin A 0%   Vitamin C 0%

Calcium 0%   Iron 0%

If you are sensitive to sulfite, this product contains sulfur dioxide, sodium sulfite, and sodium bisulfite.

QUAKER OATS
(Old Fashioned)

Nutrition Facts
Serving Size ½ cup
Servings Per Container 13

Amount Per Serving

Calories 150

Calories from Fat 25

Total Fat 3 grams

Saturated Fat 0.5 grams

Polyunsaturated Fat 1 gram

Monounsaturated Fat 1 gram

Cholesterol 0 mg

Sodium 0 mg

Total Carbohydrate 27 grams

Dietary Fiber 4 grams

Soluble Fiber 2 grams

Insoluble Fiber 2 grams

Sugars 1 gram

Protein 5 grams

Vitamin A 0%   Vitamin C 0%

Calcium 0%   Iron 0%

Select cereals with not more than 3 grams of fat per serving. And at least 3 grams of fiber per serving.

QUAKER TOASTED OATMEAL HONEY NUT

Nutrition Facts

Serving Size 1 cup
Servings Per Container 9

Amount Per Serving	with ½ cup skim milk
Calories 150	230 calories
Calories from Fat 25	25 calories

Total Fat 2.5 grams

Saturated Fat 0.5 grams

Polyunsaturated Fat 0.5 gram

Monounsaturated Fat 1 gram

Cholesterol 0 mg

Sodium 200 mg

Total Carbohydrate 39 grams

Dietary Fiber 3 grams

Soluble Fiber 1 grams

Insoluble Fiber 2 grams

Sugars 13 grams

Protein 5 grams

Vitamin A 10% Vitamin C 10%

Calcium 2%   Iron 25%

COLD CEREAL

Let's compare cereals. It may be time to change what you're buying your child.

CHEERIOS
Toasted Whole Grain Oat Cereal

> By adding sugar to the Cheerios, 2 grams of dietary fiber was eliminated by the manufacturer, thus reducing the nutritional value of the cereal. Wouldn't it be just as easy to add a teaspoon of sugar to regular Cheerios and keep the much-needed fiber? Better yet, instead of sugar as a sweetener, try blueberries, sliced strawberries, apples, peaches, or any seasonal fruit.

Nutrition Facts

Serving Size 1 cup
Servings Per Container 14

Amount Per Serving*	with ½ cup skim milk
Calories 110	150 calories
Calories from Fat 15	15 calories
Total Fat 2 grams	
Saturated Fat 0.5 grams	
Cholesterol 0 mg	
Sodium 280 mg	
Total Carbohydrate 22 grams	
Dietary Fiber 3 grams	
Soluble Fiber 1 grams	
Insoluble Fiber 2 grams	
Sugars 1 gram	
Other Carbohydrates 18 grams	
Protein 3 grams	

Thiamin %	Riboflavin %
Niacin %	Calcium %

*Amount in cereal. One half cup skim milk contributes an additional 40 calories, 65 mg sodium, 200 mg potassium, 6 grams total carbohydrate (6 grams sugars) and 4 grams protein. If 1%, 2%, or whole milk were used, it would increase the fat content of the meal.

> *Cheerios is one of the more popular cereals offered to infants as a "teething" food. Note that the sodium content is high. Avoid high-sodium foods at any age, but especially during infancy.*

FROSTED CHEERIOS
"Low Fat"

Nutrition Facts

Serving Size 1 cup
Servings Per Container 13

Amount Per Serving*	with ½ cup skim milk
Calories 120	160 calories
Calories from Fat 10	10 calories
Total Fat 1 gram	
Saturated Fat 0 grams	
Cholesterol 0 mg	
Sodium 210 mg	
Total Carbohydrate 25 grams	
Dietary Fiber 1 gram	
Sugars 13 grams	
Protein 2 grams	

Thiamin %	Riboflavin %
Niacin %	Calcium %

*Amount in cereal. One half cup skim milk contributes an additional 40 calories, 65 mg sodium, 200 mg potassium, 6 grams total carbohydrate (6 grams sugars) and 4 grams protein. If 1%, 2%, or whole milk were used, it would increase the fat content of the meal.

RAISIN BRAN

Nutrition Facts
Serving Size 1 cup
Servings Per Container 10

Amount Per Serving*	with ½ cup skim milk
Calories 190	230 calories
Calories from Fat 10	10 calories
Total Fat 1 grams	
Saturated Fat 0 grams	
Cholesterol 0 mg	
Sodium 300 mg	
Potassium 340 mg	
Total Carbohydrate 47 grams	
Dietary Fiber 8 grams	
Soluble Fiber 1 grams	
Insoluble Fiber 7 grams	
Sugars 20 grams	
Protein 4 grams	

Thiamin %	Riboflavin %
Niacin %	Calcium %

*Amount in cereal. One half cup skim milk contributes an additional 40 calories, 65 mg sodium, 200 mg potassium, 6 grams total carbohydrate (6 grams sugars) and 4 grams protein. If 1%, 2%, or whole milk were used, it would increase the fat content of the meal.

The type of dietary fiber that reduces cholesterol is called soluble fiber, which, here, is one gram. Insoluble fiber helps prevent constipation. Many labels lump the two together, thus making it near impossible to know which type is present. Both types are important.

> When I was a child, Rice Krispies were my favorite. What I liked most about them was the box they came in. I especially enjoyed the cartoon characters, Snap, Crackle, and Pop. The Rice Krispies got too soggy in milk, but I tolerated them only because I enjoyed reading the cartoons on the box. I also hated Cracker Jacks, but loved the toy.

POST SHREDDED WHEAT

Nutrition Facts

Serving Size 1 cup
Servings Per Container 10

Amount Per Serving*	with ½ cup skim milk
Calories 190	230 calories
Calories from Fat 10	10 calories
Total Fat 1 gram	
Saturated Fat 0 grams	
Cholesterol 0 mg	
Sodium 10 mg	
Total Carbohydrate 44 grams	
Dietary Fiber 5 grams	
Sugars 12 grams	
Other Carbohydrates 27 grams	
Protein 4 grams	

Thiamin %	Riboflavin %
Niacin %	Calcium %

*Amount in cereal. One half cup skim milk contributes an additional 40 calories, 65 mg sodium, 200 mg potassium, 6 grams total carbohydrate (6 grams from milk sugar, lactose), and 4 grams protein. If 1%, 2% or whole milk were used, it would increase the fat content of the meal.

POST FROSTED SHREDDED WHEAT

Nutrition Facts

Serving Size 1 cup
Servings Per Container 10

Amount Per Serving*	with ½ cup skim milk
Calories 190	230 calories
Calories from Fat 10	10 calories
Total Fat 1 gram	
Saturated Fat 0 grams	
Cholesterol 0 mg	
Sodium 10 mg	
Potassiun 170 mg	
Total Carbohydrate 44 grams	
Dietary Fiber 4 grams	
Sugars 12 grams	
Other Carbohydrates 27 grams	
Protein 4 grams	

Thiamin %	Riboflavin %
Niacin %	Calcium %

*Amount in cereal. One half cup skim milk contributes an additional 40 calories, 65 mg sodium, 200 mg potassium, 6 grams total carbohydrate (6 grams from milk sugar, lactose), and 4 grams protein. If 1%, 2% or whole milk were used, it would increase the fat content of the meal.

RICE KRISPIES

Nutrition Facts

Serving Size 1 ¼ cups
Servings Per Container 12

Amount Per Serving*	with ½ cup skim milk
Calories 120	160 calories
Calories from Fat 0	
Total Fat 0 gram	
Saturated Fat 0 grams	
Cholesterol 0 mg	
Sodium 350 mg	
Total Carbohydrate 29 grams	
Dietary Fiber 0 grams	
Sugars 3 grams	
Other Carbohydrates 25 grams	
Protein 2 grams	

*Amount in cereal. One half cup skim milk contributes an additional 40 calories, 65 mg sodium, 200 mg potassium, 6 grams total carbohydrate (6 grams from milk sugar, lactose), and 4 grams protein. If 1%, 2% or whole milk were used, it would increase the fat content of the meal.

POST GRAPE-NUTS FLAKES
Whole Wheat & Barley Cereal

Nutrition Facts

Serving Size ¾ cups
Servings Per Container 18

Amount Per Serving*	with ½ cup skim milk
Calories 100	140 calories
Calories from Fat 10	10 calories
Total Fat 1 gram	
Saturated Fat 0 grams	
Cholesterol 0 mg	
Sodium 140 mg	
Total Carbohydrate 24 grams	
Dietary Fiber 3 grams	
Sugars 5 grams	
Protein 3 grams	

Thiamin %	Riboflavin %
Niacin %	Folate 25%
Iron 45%	Calcium 15%
Zinc 10%	Copper 8%
Vitamin A 15%	

*Amount in cereal. One half cup skim milk contributes an additional 40 calories, 65 mg sodium, 200 mg potassium, 6 grams total carbohydrate (6 grams from milk sugar, lactose), and 4 grams protein. If 1%, 2% or whole milk were used, it would increase the fat content of the meal.

Although Rice Krispies have been around for years and the brand has sustained its popularity—even in candy bars such as Nestle's Crunch, as a cereal it falls short nutritionally because it has zero fiber, not to mention its high sodium content. Select a cereal that has at least 3 grams of fiber, and resist getting junky foods that have toys in the box. TV is full of these seductive advertisements, and your child has been primed to reach for candies that masquerade as food.

POST 100% BRAN

Nutrition Facts

Serving Size ⅓ cup

Servings Per Container 17

Amount Per Serving*	with ½ cup skim milk
Calories 80	120 calories
Calories from Fat 5	5 calories

Total Fat 0.5 grams

Saturated Fat 0 grams

Cholesterol 0 mg

Sodium 120 mg

Total Carbohydrate 23 grams

Dietary Fiber 8 grams

Potassium 270 mg

Soluble Fiber 1 gram

Insoluble fiber 7 grams

Sugars 7 grams

Other Carbohydrates 8 grams

Protein 4 grams

Thiamin %	Riboflavin %
Niacin %	Iron %

Calcium %

*Amount in cereal. One half cup skim milk contributes an additional 40 calories, 65 mg sodium, 200 mg potassium, 6 grams total carbohydrate (6 grams from milk sugar, lactose), and 4 grams protein. If 1%, 2% or whole milk were used, it would increase the fat content of the meal.

KASHI[1] SEVEN WHOLE GRAINS & SESAME

Nutrition Facts

Serving Size ¾ cup

Servings Per Container 12

Amount Per Serving*	with ½ cup non-fat milk
Calories 90	130 calories
Calories from Fat 10	10 calories

Total Fat 1 gram

Saturated Fat 0 grams

Cholesterol 0 mg

Sodium 70 mg

Total Carbohydrates 24 grams

Dietary Fiber 8 grams

Sugars 6 grams

Protein 3 grams

Thiamin %	Riboflavin %
Niacin %	Iron %

Calcium %

*Amount in cereal. One half cup skim milk contributes an additional 40 calories, 65 mg sodium, 200 mg potassium, 6 grams total carbohydrate (6 grams from milk sugar, lactose), and 4 grams protein. If 1%, 2% or whole milk were used, it would increase the fat content of the meal.

[1]*Kashi Company, P.O. Box 8557, La Jolla, CA 92038-8557*

READING FOOD LABELS — BREAKFAST FOODS

WHEATIES
(made with 100% Whole Wheat)

Nutrition Facts
Serving Size 1 cup
Servings Per Container 17

Amount Per Serving*	with ½ cup skim milk
Calories 110	150 calories
Calories from Fat 10	10 calories
Total Fat 1 gram	
Saturated Fat 0 grams	
Cholesterol 0 mg	
Sodium 220 mg	
Total Carbohydrate 24 grams	
Dietary Fiber 3 grams	
Sugars 4 grams	
Other Carbohydrates 17 grams	
Protein 3 grams	

Thiamin %   Riboflavin %
Niacin %   Iron %
Calcium %

*Amount in cereal. One half cup skim milk contributes an additional 40 calories, 65 mg sodium, 200 mg potassium, 6 grams total carbohydrate (6 grams from milk sugar, lactose), and 4 grams protein. If 1%, 2% or whole milk were used, it would increase the fat content of the meal.

TOTAL WHOLE GRAIN

Nutrition Facts
Serving Size ¾ cup
Servings Per Container 17

Amount Per Serving*	with ½ cup skim milk
Calories 110	150 calories
Calories from Fat 10	10 calories
Total Fat 1 gram	
Saturated Fat 0 grams	
Cholesterol 0 mg	
Sodium 200mg	
Total Carbohydrate 24 grams	
Dietary Fiber 3 grams	
Sugars 5 grams	
Protein 3 grams	

Vitamin A 15%	Vitamin C 25%
Vitamin D 25%	Vitamin E 100%
Thiamin 100%	Riboflavin100 %
Niacin100 %	Iron 100%
Calcium 40%	Vitamin B12 110%
Folic Acid 100%	Pantothenic Acid 100%
Magnesium 10%	Zinc 100%
Copper 4%	Vitamin B6 100%

*Amount in cereal. One half cup skim milk contributes an additional 40 calories, 65 mg sodium, 200 mg potassium, 6 grams total carbohydrate (6 grams from milk sugar, lactose), and 4 grams protein. If 1%, 2% or whole milk were used, it would increase the fat content of the meal.

233

KELLOG'S NUTRI-GRAIN CEREALS
Golden Wheat
Whole Grain Wheat-Corn Cereal

Nutrition Facts

Serving Size ¾ cup

Servings Per Container 12 milk

Amount Per Serving*	with ½ cup skim milk
Calories 100	140 calories
Calories from Fat 5	5 calories
Total Fat 1 gram	
Saturated Fat 0 grams	
Cholesterol 0 mg	
Sodium 220 mg	
Total Carbohydrates 24 grams	
Dietary Fiber 4 grams	
Sugars 0 grams	
Other Carbohydrates 20 grams	
Protein	

Thiamin %	Riboflavin %
Niacin %	Iron %
Calcium %	

*Amount in cereal. One half cup skim milk contributes an additional 40 calories, 65 mg sodium, 200 mg potassium, 6 grams total carbohydrate (6 grams from milk sugar, lactose), and 4 grams protein. If 1%, 2% or whole milk were used, it would increase the fat content of the meal.

Kellog's Nutri-Grain Cereals are nutritious breakfast cereals. Check the Nutrition Facts label and compare them with nutritional losers such as COCOA PUFFS or FROOT LOOPS.

Although Kellog's Cereal Bars are better than a doughnut, Carnation Instant Breakfast or the deadly Swanson Great Starts' sausage, egg, cheese, and biscuit, a better choice is Health Valley Healthy Tart, sweet cherry. It contains no fat and 3 grams of fiber.

KELLOG'S NUTRI-GRAIN CEREALS
LOW FAT CEREAL BARS
Strawberry, Blueberry, Apple-Cinnamon

Nutrition Facts

Serving Size 1 cup

Servings Per Container 8

Amount Per Serving

Calories 140
Calories from Fat 25
Total Fat 3 grams
Saturated Fat 0.5 grams
Cholesterol 0 grams
Sodium 110 mg
Total Carbohydrate 27 grams
Dietary Fiber 1 gram
Sugars 13 grams
Protein 2 grams

Vitamin A 15%	Vitamin C 0%
Folate 10%	Iron 10%
Calcium 2%	

CEREAL OR CANDY?

It is clear that 15 grams is sugar, but how much more sugar is there in the form of corn syrup and other sweeteners?
If it is 12 grams, then the actual sugar content is 27 grams and only one gram of complex carbohydrate! In other words, this is CANDY.

FROOT LOOPS

Nutrition Facts

Serving Size 1 cup
Servings Per Container 18

Amount Per Serving*	with ½ cup skim milk
Calories 120	160 calories
Calories from Fat 10	10 calories

Total Fat 1 gram
  Saturated Fat 0.5 grams
Cholesterol 0 mg
Sodium 150 mg
Total Carbohydrate 28 grams
  Dietary Fiber 1 gram
  Sugars 15 grams
  Other Carbohydrates 12 grams
Protein 2 grams

Thiamin %	Riboflavin %
Niacin %	Iron %
Calcium %	

*Amount in cereal. One half cup skim milk contributes an additional 40 calories, 65 mg sodium, 200 mg potassium, 6 grams total carbohydrate (6 grams from milk sugar, lactose), and 4 grams protein. If 1%, 2% or whole milk were used, it would increase the fat content of the meal.

COCOA PUFFS
FROSTED CORN PUFFS

Nutrition Facts

Serving Size 1 cup
Servings Per Container 13

Amount Per Serving*	with ½ cup skim milk
Calories 120	160 calories
Calories from Fat 10	10 calories

Total Fat 1 gram
  Saturated Fat 0 grams
Cholesterol 0 mg
Sodium 190 mg
Total Carbohydrate 27 grams
  Dietary Fiber 0 grams
  Sugars 14 grams
  Other Carbohydrates 13 grams
Protein 1 gram

Thiamin %	Riboflavin %
Niacin %	Iron %
Calcium %	

*Amount in cereal. One half cup skim milk contributes an additional 40 calories, 65 mg sodium, 200 mg potassium, 6 grams total carbohydrate (6 grams from milk sugar, lactose), and 4 grams protein. If 1%, 2% or whole milk were used, it would increase the fat content of the meal.

A rapid way to check the nutrition of a cereal is to use this rule of thumb: If the cereal has 3 grams of fiber or more, it's probably a reasonable choice.

LUCKY CHARMS

CAVEAT EMPTOR— BUYER BEWARE!

Nutrition Facts

Serving Size 1 cup
Servings Per Container 19

Amount Per Serving	with ½ cup skim milk
Calories 120	160 calories
Calories from Fat 10	15 calories

Total Fat 1 gram	
Saturated Fat 0 grams	
Polyunsaturated Fat 0	
Monounsaturated Fat 0	
Cholesterol 0 mg	
Sodium 210 mg	
Total Carbohydrate 25 grams	
Dietary Fiber 1 grams	
Sugars 13 grams	
Other Carbohydrates 11 grams	
Protein 2 grams	

Thiamin %	Riboflavin %
Niacin %	Iron %
Calcium %	

Ingredients: Whole oat flour (includes oat bran), marshmallows (sugar, modified corn starch, corn syrup, Dextrose, gelatin, artificial flavors, yellow #5 & #6, red #40, blue #1) sugar, corn syrup, wheat starch, salt, color added, trisodium phosphate, calcium carbonate, zinc & iron, Vitamin C, niacin, B6, B2, B1, Vitamin A, folic acid, B12, Vitamin D, Vitamin E added to preserve freshness.

It is not enough for a cereal to be low fat and low cholesterol to be considered nutritious. Don't be fooled by a "LOW FAT" or "NO CHOLESTEROL" label. I hope labels will soon be required to list the amount of complex carbohydrate per serving. Corn syrup, fructose, plus other monosaccharides should be listed under sugars.

RICE CHEX

Nutrition Facts

Serving Size 1 cup
Servings Per Container 16

Amount Per Serving	with ½ cup skim milk
Calories 120	160 calories
Calories from Fat 0	5 calories
Total Fat 0 grams	
Saturated Fat 0 grams	
Polyunsaturated Fat 0	
Monounsaturated Fat 0	
Cholesterol 0 mg	
Sodium 230 mg	
Total Carbohydrate 27 grams	
Dietary Fiber 0 grams	
Sugars 2 grams	
Other Carbohydrates 25 grams	
Protein 2 grams	

Thiamin %	Riboflavin %
Niacin %	Iron %
Calcium %	

This is another example of why "nonfat & no cholesterol" does not equal "healthy food." After all, two teaspoons of refined sugar can make the same claim. Feed your child RIGHT from birth and select cereals that will keep your child from growing healthy. To improve upon this cereal, add some high fiber fruit, such as sliced strawberries or fresh blueberries.

CAP'N CRUNCH

Nutrition Facts

Serving Size ¾ cup
Servings Per Container 17

Amount Per Serving*	with ½ cup skim milk
Calories 110	
Calories from Fat 0	
Total Fat 1.5 grams	
Saturated Fat 0.5 grams	
Cholesterol 0 mg	
Sodium 210 mg	
Potassium 35 mg	
Total Carbohydrate 23 grams	
Dietary Fiber 1 gram	
Sugars 12 grams	
Other Carbohydrates 11 grams	
Protein 1 gram	

Vitamin A 6%	Vitamin C 0%
Calcium 2 %	Iron 6 %

Here are a few examples of other breakfast food choices.

HOT CEREAL

STONE-BUHR* 4 GRAIN
(microwavable)

Nutrition Facts
Serving Size 1/3 cup
Servings Per Container 15

Amount Per Serving
Calories 140
  Calories from Fat 15
Total Fat 1.5 grams
  Saturated Fat 0 grams
Cholesterol 0 mg
Sodium 0 mg
Total Carbohydrates 31 grams
  Dietary Fiber 5 grams
  Sugars 0 grams
Protein 6 grams

Stone Ground Mills, Inc. Seattle, WA 98126

CREAM OF WHEAT
(½ minute stovetop cooking)

Nutrition Facts
Serving Size 3 Tbs. make 1 cup
Servings Per Container 24

Amount Per Serving
Calories 120
  Calories from Fat 0
Total Fat 0 grams
  Saturated Fat 0 grams
Cholesterol 0 mg
Sodium 0 mg
Total Carbohydrate 25 grams
  Dietary Fiber 1 gram
  Sugars 0 grams
Protein 3 grams

Vitamin A 0%	Vitamin C 0%
Calcium 10%	Iron 50 %

This low-fat, low-sodium, low-sugar cereal is an excellent way to start the day. To increase the fiber in this cereal, add raisins, berries, peaches, or your child's favorite fruit. Use non-fat milk for cooking. This will provide protein, calcium and Vitamins D and A.

GOLDRUSH SAN FRANCISCO SOUR DOUGH
PANCAKE & WAFFLE MIX*

Nutrition Facts

Serving Size 3 4" Pancakes

Servings Per Container 10

Amount Per Serving About

Calories 120

Calories from Fat 40

Total Fat 4.5 grams

Saturated Fat 1 gram

Cholesterol 0 mg

Sodium 540 mg

Total Carbohydrate 39 grams

Dietary Fiber 3 grams

Sugars 9 grams

Other Carbohydrates 11 grams

Protein 4 grams

Calcium 30%   Iron 15%

Thiamin 20%   Niacin 10%

Riboflavin 8%

Goldrush Products Co., San Jose, CA 95110

Just add water! Pancake Waffles and Fruit Fritters recipes on the box.

Pancake mixes are very appealing because they appear to be easy to prepare. The problem with most mixes is they often contain ingredients you may wish to avoid. For example, pancake mixes almost all have excessive sodium and partially hydrogenated oils.

Try the health-food stores for mixes high in whole grains, or better yet, make your own pancakes from scratch. It's really easy. See page 186 for my recipe for Buckwheat Pancakes.

EGGS

Nutrition Facts

Serving Size 1

Servings Per Container

Amount Per Serving

Calories 70

Calories from Fat 40

Total Fat 4.5 grams

Saturated Fat 1.5 grams

Cholesterol 210 mg

Sodium 65 mg

Total Carbohydrate 1 gram

Dietary Fiber 0 grams

Sugars 0 grams

Protein 6 grams

Vitamin A 6%	Vitamin C 0%
Calcium 2%	Iron 4 %

For the older child, don't forget the egg white omelet, (two egg whites with or without one yolk). French toast can be made by dipping whole wheat bread in the egg white and yolk mixture. Use a non-stick griddle and dust with powdered sugar when toast is done, if desired.

Avoid serving eggs with bacon, sausage or fried potatoes. If you must have bacon, use the lower fat Canadian bacon and limit it to special occasions.

The egg substitute Ener G Egg Replacer, found in many natural food markets, is for people who cannot use regular eggs in their diets and who want a replacer that's animal protein–free. It can be used to replace both whole eggs and egg whites in bakery goods, mayonnaise, and meringues. It is not designed to be used by itself in scrambled eggs or omelets. It contains potato starch, tapioca flour, leavening and carbohydrate gum. This mixture is particularly good in baked products such as muffins, cookies, and fruit breads.

EGG BEATERS

Nutrition Facts

Serving Size 1/4

Servings Per Container 4

Amount Per Serving About

Calories 30

Calories from Fat 0

Total Fat 0 grams

Saturated Fat 0 grams

Cholesterol 0 mg

Sodium 110 mg

Total Carbohydrate 1 gram

Dietary Fiber 0 grams

Sugars less than 1 gram

Protein 5 grams

Vitamin A 6%	Vitamin C 0%
Calcium 2%	Iron 6 %

KELLOGG'S EGGO WAFFLES

Nutrition Facts
Serving Size 2 Waffles
Servings Per Container 4

Amount Per Serving

Calories 220
   Calories from Fat 70

Total Fat 8 grams
   Saturated Fat 1.5 grams

Cholesterol 25 mg

Sodium 480 mg

Potassium 100 mg

Total Carbohydrate 32 grams
   Other Carbohydrate 28 grams
   Dietary Fiber 1 gram
   Sugars 3 grams

Protein 5 grams

Vitamin A 20%	Vitamin C 0%
Calcium 4%	Iron 2 %
Folate 10%	Vitamin B12 20%
Thiamin 20%	Riboflavin 20%
Vitamin B6 20%	

Note the 480 mg of sodium per 2 waffles. Check out the Special K Eggo Waffles. They have almost half the sodium per 2 waffles.

KELLOGG'S EGGO SPECIAL K

Nutrition Facts
Serving Size 2 Waffles
Servings Per Container 4

Amount Per Serving

Calories 120
   Calories from Fat 0

Total Fat 0 grams
   Saturated Fat 0 grams

Cholesterol 0 mg

Sodium 270 mg

Potassium 131 mg

Total Carbohydrate 25 grams
   Dietary Fiber 1 gram
   Sugars 4 grams

Protein 6 grams

Vitamin A 20%	Vitamin C 0%
Calcium 4%	Iron 20 %
Folate 10%	Vitamin B12 20%
Thiamin 20%	Riboflavin 20%
Vitamin B6 20%	Niacin 2%

SAFEWAY BUTTERMILK WAFFLES

Nutrition Facts
Serving Size 2 Waffles
Servings Per Container 6

Amount Per Serving*

Calories 220
   Calories from Fat 80

Total Fat 9 grams
   Saturated Fat 1 gram

Cholesterol 5 mg

Sodium 390 mg

Total Carbohydrate 30 grams
   Dietary Fiber 1 gram
   Sugars 6 grams

Protein 6 grams

THIS IS LOW IN CHOLESTEROL BUT IT IS NOT LOW IN FAT.

Look for frozen waffles or French toast that are low in fat, contain whole wheat or whole grains. Buy brands with at least 3 grams of fiber. If you can't find any at your usual grocery, add high fiber fruit as topping. Visit a local health food store and see whether they have a more nutritious product, but beware, not all foods sold by health food stores are necessarily healthy.

Snack Crackers

If you learn to read labels you can find many delicious snack crackers that have high nutritional value that children enjoy. Here are a few examples, but limit crackers to only a few, since the combination of grapes, juice, raisins, and crackers often leads to a poor appetite.

Reduced fat Triscuit Wafers have 3 grams of fat compared with 5 grams in Original Triscuit Wafers. For a product to be called reduced, it must contan 25% less than the named substance (fat). Reduced fat Triscuits contain 40% less fat than regular Triscuit crackers. Check the sodium content (180 mg.) Check the calories per serving (130 mg.) This is a good sodium to calorie balance.
Fiber content is 4 mg. This is more than is found in most crackers. However the label does not tell us of how much of the fiber is soluble or inslouble.

TRISCUIT
Baked Whole Wheat Wafers
Reduced Fat 40% Less Fat
Than Original Triscuit

Nutrition Facts
Serving Size 8 Wafers
Servings Per Container 8

Amount Per Serving

Calories 130
   Calories from Fat 25

Total Fat 3 grams
   Saturated Fat 0.5 grams
Cholesterol 0 mg
Sodium 180 mg
Total Carbohydrate 24 grams
   Dietary Fiber 4 grams
   Sugars 0 grams
Protein 3 grams

Vitamin A 0%	Vitamin C 0%
Calcium 0%	Iron 10 %

RY KRISP

Nutrition Facts
Serving Size 2 CRACKERS
Servings Per Container 17

Amount Per Serving

Calories 60
   Calories from Fat 10

Total Fat 1.5 grams
   Saturated Fat 0 grams
Cholesterol 0 mg
Sodium 90 mg
Total Carbohydrate 10 grams
   Dietary Fiber 3 grams
   Sugars 0 grams
Protein 1 gram

Vitamin A 0%	Vitamin C 0%
Calcium 0%	Iron 2 %

A nutritious cracker is an excellent after school snack. Serve them along with non-fat string cheese, cherry tomatoes, sliced cucumbers, raw carrots or celery and a favorite fruit, such as apple, banana or orange slices.

MANISCHEWITZ MATZO-CRACKER MINIATURES

Nutrition Facts

Serving Size 13

Servings Per Container 8

Amount Per Serving

Calories 110

Calories from Fat 0

Total Fat 0.5 grams

Saturated Fat 0 grams

Cholesterol 0 mg

Sodium 0 mg

Total Carbohydrate 25 grams

Dietary Fiber 1 gram

Sugars 1 gram

Protein 3 gram

Vitamin A 0%   Vitamin C 0%

Calcium 0%   Iron 7 %

These crackers are better than the popular PEPPERIDGE FARM'S Original Smiley GOLDFISH Crackers. Check the Nutritional facts label the next time you shop. A serving of GOLDFISH contains 6 grams of fat, 230 mg sodium, and no fiber! DON'T FEED THESE CRACKERS TO YOUR CHILDREN.

CHEEZ-IT (White Cheddar)

Nutrition Facts

Serving Size 26 Crackers

Servings Per Container 9

Amount Per Serving

Calories 150

Calories from Fat 70

Total Fat 7 grams

Saturated Fat 1.5 grams

Cholesterol 1 mg

Sodium 280 mg

Total Carbohydrate 18 grams

Dietary Fiber 1 gram

Sugars 1 gram

Protein 3 grams

Vitamin A 0%   Vitamin C 0%

Calcium 0%   Iron 6 %

CHEEZ-IT crackers should also be on the "no-no" list

QUAKER SALT-FREE RICE CAKES

Nutrition Facts

Serving Size 1
Servings Per Container 14

Amount Per Serving About

Calories 35

Calories from Fat 0

Total Fat 0 grams

Saturated Fat 0 grams

Cholesterol 0 mg

Sodium 0 mg

Total Carbohydrate 7 grams

Dietary Fiber 0 grams

Sugars 0 grams

Protein 1 gram

Ingredients: Whole Grain Brown Rice

To add more fiber, use a high fiber spread, such as low fat hummus

SNYDER'S OF HANOVER SOURDOUGH UNSALTED HARD PRETZELS

Nutrition Facts

Serving Size 1
Servings Per Container 15

Amount Per Serving About

Calories 100

Calories from Fat 0

Total Fat 0 grams

Saturated Fat 0 grams

Cholesterol 0 mg

Sodium 90 mg

Total Carbohydrate 22 grams

Dietary Fiber 1 gram

Sugars 0 grams

Protein 3 grams

PADERINOS REDUCED FAT TORTILLA CHIPS "ORIGINAL"
40% less fat than regular tortilla chips

Nutrition Facts

Serving Size 1oz (14 chips)
Servings Per Container

Amount Per Serving About

Calories 130

Calories from Fat 40

Total Fat 4 grams

Saturated Fat 0.5 grams

Cholesterol 0 mg

Sodium 125 mg

Total Carbohydrates 20 grams

Dietary Fiber 1 gram

Sugars 0 grams

Protein 2 grams

Ingredients: Corn, Rice, Corn & Canola oil, Salt.

Breads and Tortillas

All breads are high in sodium. Look for breads with a high fiber content. For example, Orowheat Light Bread has a fiber content of 5 grams per serving and no fat. Most breads contain only 1–2 grams of fiber per portion. Nutritional Facts do not always tell us how much of the fiber is cholesterol-lowering soluble versus colon-cancer-fighting insoluble fiber. Both components are important, and hopefully this will be corrected when Nutrition Facts are revised.

WONDER BREAD

Nutrition Facts

Serving Size 1 Slice
Servings Per Container 24

Amount Per Serving About

Calories 70
   Calories from Fat 0

Total Fat 1 gram
   Saturated Fat 0 grams
   Polyunsaturated Fat 0 gram
   Monounsaturated Fat 0 gram
Cholesterol 0 mg
Sodium 150 mg
Total Carbohydrate 14 grams
   Dietary Fiber 0 gram
   Sugars 1 gram
Protein 2 grams

Vitamin A 0%   Vitamin C 0%
Calcium 2%   Iron 4 %
Folate 6%

Children love white bread, white rice and white pasta, but whole grain foods are more nutritious. Try to introduce whole-grain foods 2-3 times a day. Milling grains removes the fiber-rich outer layer along with the B Vitamins and phytochemicals (the non nutritive substances that have subtle effects on health).

WHOLE WHEAT BREAD

Nutrition Facts

Serving Size 1 Slice
Servings Per Container 18

Amount Per Serving About

Calories 60
   Calories from Fat 10

Total Fat 1 gram
   Saturated Fat 0 grams
Cholesterol 0 mg
Sodium 120 mg
Total Carbohydrate 11 grams
   Dietary Fiber 2 grams
   Sugars 1 gram
Protein 3 grams

What happened to the fiber in WONDER BREAD?

PITA BREAD
(POCKET BREAD)

Nutrition Facts
Serving Size 1 pita

Amount Per Serving About

Calories 130

Calories from Fat 10

Total Fat 1 gram

Saturated Fat 0 grams

Polyunsaturated Fat 0.5 gram

Cholesterol 0 mg

Sodium 210 mg

Total Carbohydrates 27 grams

Dietary Fiber 2 grams

Sugars 1 gram

Protein 5 grams

Vitamin A 0%   Vitamin C 0%

Calcium 2%   Iron 6 %

La TORTILLA FACTORY KING SIZE CORN TORTILLAS

Nutrition Facts
Serving Size 2

Serving per container 6

Amount Per Serving About

Calories 120

Calories from Fat 9

Total Fat 1 gram

Saturated Fat 0.5 grams

Cholesterol 0 mg

Sodium 2 mg

Total Carbohydrate 25 grams

Dietary Fiber 2 grams

Sugars 0.5 gram

Protein 2 grams

Vitamin A 2%   Vitamin C 2%

Calcium 6%   Iron 4 %

La TORTILLA FACTORY* 99% FAT FREE WHOLE WHEAT PITA

Nutrition Facts
Serving Size 1 pita
Serving per container 10

Amount Per Serving About

Calories 60

  Calories from Fat 0

Total Fat 0 gram

  Saturated Fat 0 grams

Cholesterol 0 mg

Sodium 180 mg

Total Carbohydrate 12 grams

  Dietary Fiber 6 grams

  Sugars 0 gram

Protein 2 grams

Calcium 2%   Iron 6 %

Whole wheat pita bread contains about 6 grams of fiber.

For a quick snack, stuff 1/2 a pita bread with 1/2 cup of low-fat cottage cheese or non-fat refried beans.

Try a tortilla wrap: Place a tortilla between two dampened paper towels. Microwave on high until warm. Sprinkle Fat-free shredded mozzarella cheese (about 1 tablespoon) over the center of the warmed tortilla. Spoon salsa over cheese. Fold the tortilla like a "blinza" or crepe. Microwave for another 20 seconds. Enjoy this nutritious snack, but don't burn your mouth!

*LaTortilla Factory, 3654 Standish Ave. Santa Rosa, CA 95407. 800-446-1516

Butter and Other Spreads

COMPARE BUTTER WITH THE FOLLOWING SPREADS:

EXTRA VIRGIN OLIVE OIL
(Although not a "spread" it's included here so you can compare with butter)

AVOID BUTTER!
Select a spread that contains the least amount of saturated fat or transfatty acids and after studying the nutrition facts labels, select the brand with the most appealing flavor.

Nutrition Facts
Serving Size 1 Tbs.

Amount Per Serving About
Calories 120
Calories from Fat 120

Total Fat 14 grams
Saturated Fat 2 grams
Polyunsaturated Fat 1 gram
Monounsaturated Fat 10 grams
Cholesterol 0 mg
Sodium 0 mg
Total Carbohydrate 0 grams
Dietary Fiber 0 grams
Sugars 0 gram
Protein 0 grams

BUTTER

Nutrition Facts
Serving Size 1 Tbs.
Servings Per Container 32

Amount Per Serving About
Calories 100
Calories from Fat 100

Total Fat 11 grams
Saturated Fat 7 grams
Polyunsaturated Fat 0.5 gram
Cholesterol 30 mg
Sodium 90 mg
Total Carbohydrate 0 grams
Dietary Fiber 0 grams
Sugars 0 gram
Protein 0 gram

| Vitamin A 8% | Vitamin C 0% |
| Calcium 2% | Iron 6 % |

Olive oil is one of the preferred fats because it contains mostly monosaturated fat and no cholesterol, BUT IT'S NOT LOW FAT. Like all fats, use it sparingly. All oils contain the same number of calories.

PROMISE ULTRA SPREAD
Vegetable Oil Spread
70% Less Fat than margarine

Nutrition Facts

Serving Size 1 Tbs.
Servings per container 32

Amount Per Serving About

Calories 30

Calories from Fat 30

Total Fat 3.5 grams

Saturated Fat 0 grams

Polyunsaturated Fat 1 gram

Monounsaturated Fat 2 grams

Cholesterol 0 mg

Sodium 60 mg

Total Carbohydrate 0 grams

Dietary Fiber 0 grams

Sugars 0 gram

Protein 0 grams

PROMISE ULTRA
FAT FREE

Nutrition Facts

Serving Size 1 Tbs.
Servings per container 32

Amount Per Serving About

Calories 5

Calories from Fat 0

Total Fat 0 grams

Saturated Fat 0 grams

Polyunsaturated Fat 0 gram

Monounsaturated Fat 0 grams

Cholesterol 0 mg

Sodium 90 mg

Total Carbohydrate 0 grams

Dietary Fiber 0 grams

Sugars 0 gram

Protein 0 grams

Vitamin A 10% Vitamin C 0%

Calcium 0%   Iron 0 %

BENECOL LIGHT SPREAD

Nutrition Facts

Serving Size 1 container (8 grams)
Servings per container 21

Amount Per Serving About

Calories 30

Calories from Fat 30

Total Fat 3 grams

Saturated Fat 0 grams

Polyunsaturated Fat 1.5 gram

Monounsaturated Fat 1.0 grams

Cholesterol 0 mg

Sodium 65 mg

Total Carbohydrate 0 grams

Dietary Fiber 0 grams

Sugars 0 grams

Protein 0 grams

Vitamin A 10%   Vitamin D 10%

Calcium 0%   Vitamin E 4 %

Benecol is a relatively new spread on the market, but has been used in Finland for years and actually has a cholesterol lowering effect.

Benecol is a vegetable oil spread and it contains 1.5 grams of plant stanol esters. Stanols have been found to have a blood cholesterol lowering effect. A three gram serving of Benecol Light has only 30 calories campared to margarine which contains 11 grams of fat per serving, or 100 calories.

It is not recommeded for baking or frying.

I CAN'T BELIEVE IT'S NOT BUTTER 60% VEGETABLE FAT SPREAD

Nutrition Facts

Serving Size 1 Tbs.
Servings per container 32

Amount Per Serving About

Calories 80

Calories from Fat 80

Total Fat 9 grams

Saturated Fat 1.5 grams*

Polyunsaturated Fat 2 grams

Monounsaturated Fat 2 grams

Cholesterol 0 mg

Sodium 100 mg

Total Carbohydrate 0 grams

Dietary Fiber 0 grams

Sugars 0 grams

Protein 0 grams

Vitamin A 10% Vitamin C 0%

Calcium 0%   Iron 0 %

OLIVIO SPREAD* 75% VEGETABLE OIL

Nutrition Facts

Serving Size 1 Tbs.

Servings per container 32

Amount Per Serving About

Calories 100

Calories from Fat 100

Total Fat 11 grams

Saturated Fat 1.5 grams**

Polyunsaturated Fat 1.5 grams

Monounsaturated Fat 5 grams

Cholesterol 0 mg

Sodium 110 mg

Total Carbohydrates 0 grams

Dietary Fiber 0 grams

Sugars 0 grams

Protein 0 grams

Vitamin A 10%   Vitamin C 0%

Calcium 0%   Iron 0 %

*Liquid soybean & hydrogenated Canola oil blend. No trans fatty acids per serving.
**Olivio contains 1.5 grams of saturated fat; butter contains 7.0 grams.

FLEISCHMANN'S FAT FREE SPREAD

Nutrition Facts

Serving Size 1 Tbs.

Servings per container 23

Amount Per Serving About

Calories 5

Calories from Fat 0

Total Fat 0 grams

Saturated Fat 0 grams*

Cholesterol 0 mg

Sodium 130 mg

Total Carbohydrates 1 gram

Dietary Fiber 0 grams

Sugars 0 grams

Protein 0 grams

Vitamin A 10% Vitamin D 15%

Calcium 0%   Iron 0 %

*Distributed by NICOLA Corp. 17 Arlington St., Boston, MA 02116.

KRAFT MAYO REAL MAYONNAISE

Nutrition Facts

Serving Size 1 Tbs.

Servings per container

Amount Per Serving About

Calories 100

Calories from Fat 100

Total Fat 11 grams

Saturated Fat 2 grams

Cholesterol 5 mg

Sodium 75 mg

Total Carbohydrate 0 grams

Dietary Fiber 0 grams

Sugars 0 grams

Protein 0 grams

Compare the other spreads with Kraft Real Mayonnaise. Note especially the calories from fat.

KRAFT FAT FREE MAYO

Nutrition Facts

Serving Size 1 Tbs.

Servings per container 32

Amount Per Serving About

Calories 10

Calories from Fat 0

Total Fat 0 grams

Saturated Fat 0 gram

Polyunsaturated Fat 0 grams

Monounsaturated Fat 0 grams

Cholesterol 0 mg

Sodium 120 mg

Total Carbohydrate 2 grams

Dietary Fiber 0 grams

Sugars 1 gram

Protein 0 grams

Vitamin A 0%	Vitamin C 0%
Calcium 0%	Iron 0 %

KRAFT LIGHT MAYO

Nutrition Facts

Serving Size 1 Tbs.

Amount Per Serving About

Calories 50

Calories from Fat 45

Total Fat 5 grams

Saturated Fat 1 gram

Cholesterol 5 mg

Sodium 90 mg

Total Carbohydrate 2 grams

Dietary Fiber 0 grams

Sugars Less than 1 gram

Protein 0 grams

Vitamin A 0% Vitamin C 0%

Calcium 0% Iron 0 %

These are two examples of better-tasting low and nonfat spreads.

BEST FOODS DIJONNAISE CREAMY MUSTARD BLEND

Nutrition Facts

Serving Size 1 Tbs.

Servings per container 64

Amount Per Serving About

Calories 5

Calories from Fat 0

Total Fat 0 grams

Cholesterol 0 mg

Sodium 70 mg

Total Carbohydrate 1 gram

Dietary Fiber 0 grams

Sugars 0 gram

Protein 0 grams

Vitamin A 0% Vitamin C 0%

Calcium 0% Iron 0 %

Dairy and Dairy Substitutes

CREAM CHEESE

Nutrition Facts

Serving Size 1 oz to 30
Servings per container

Amount Per Serving About

Calories 100

Calories from Fat 90

Total Fat 10 grams

Saturated Fat 6 grams

Cholesterol 30 mg

Sodium 95 mg

Total Carbohydrate 1 gram

Dietary Fiber 0 grams

Sugars 0 gram

Protein 2 grams

Vitamin A 15%   Vitamin C 0%

Calcium 2%

LITE CREAM CHEESE

Nutrition Facts

Servings Size 1 oz (30 grams)

Amount Per Serving About

Calories 60

Calories from Fat 40

Total Fat 5 grams

Saturated Fat 3 grams

Cholesterol 10 mg

Sodium 160 mg

Total Carbohydrate 2 grams

Dietary Fiber 0 grams

Sugars 1 gram

Protein 3 grams

FAT FREE CREAM CHEESE

Nutrition Facts

Serving Size 1 oz

Amount Per Serving About

Calories 30

Calories from Fat 0

Total Fat 0 grams

Saturated Fat 0 grams

Cholesterol 0 mg

Sodium 150 mg

Total Carbohydrate 1 gram

Dietary Fiber 0 grams

Sugars 1 gram

Protein 5 grams

Vitamin A 8%   Calcium 8%

Compare the fat content and calories

WHOLE VITAMIN D MILK

Nutrition Facts

Serving Size 1cup (236 ml.)
Servings per container

Amount Per Serving About

Calories 160
　Calories from Fat 70

Total Fat 8 grams
　Saturated Fat 5 grams

Cholesterol 35 mg

Sodium 125 mg

Total Carbohydrate 13 grams
　Dietary Fiber 0 grams
　Sugars 12 grams

Protein 8 grams

Vitamin A 10%　Vitamin C 2%

Calcium 30%　　Iron 0 %

Vitamin D 25%

2% MILK
(Reduced Fat)

Nutrition Facts

Serving Size 8 fl oz.
Servings per container 4

Amount Per Serving About

Calories 130
　Calories from Fat 45

Total Fat 5 grams
　Saturated Fat 3 grams

Cholesterol 25 mg

Sodium 130 mg

Total Carbohydrate 13 grams
　Dietary Fiber 0 grams
　Sugars 13 gram

Protein 10 grams

Vitamin A 10%　Vitamin C 4%

Calcium 40%　　Iron 0 %

Vitamin D 25%

2% milk is not low-fat.

1% MILK
(Low Fat)

Nutrition Facts

Serving Size 8 fl oz.
Servings per container 4

Amount Per Serving About

Calories 130

Calories from Fat 20

Total Fat 2.5 grams

Saturated Fat 1.5 grams

Cholesterol 15 mg

Sodium 160 mg

Total Carbohydrate 16 grams

Dietary Fiber 0 grams

Sugars 15 gram

Protein 11 grams

Vitamin A 10%   Vitamin C 4%

Calcium 40%   Iron 0 %

Vitamin D 25%

These are the Nutritional Facts from a carton of Grade A pasteurized homogenized 1% low fat milk.

As you can see, milk is an excellent source of protein and calcium. There is no iron in milk or yogurt and that is why a diet too high in dairy contributes to anemia and because there is no fiber in milk, constipation is common in children who consume too much milk at the expense of vegetables and fruit. Note the sodium content of milk and other dairy products, and you will readily see why added salt is unnecessary to the diet. Two glasses of milk and two slices of white or whole wheat bread already contributes 670 milligrams of sodium to a child's diet.

Rice Dream has become a popular substitute for milk. Look carefully at the Nutritional Food Label and note that the protein content is only 1 gram per serving. This is in contrast with the 9 grams found in fat free milk! Children need protein and if Rice Dream is used as a substitute for milk, it is extremely important for the baby or child to get adequate protein from another source. The same is true for vitamim D and calcium. Milk is a rich source of both, while rice dream is deficient in both nutrients. If for some reason you are inclined to give rice dream to your child, be certain to use the enriched form (with vitamins A and D, and calcium.) Older children and young adults also need these nutrients. Between the ages of 10 and 21, the most calcium can be deposited in bone. It is a critical period because these are the years when sufficient calcium storage along with vitamin D, a reduced sodium diet and exercise can prevent or delay the onset of osteoporosis.

FAT FREE MILK (SKIM)

Nutrition Facts

Serving Size 8 fl oz.
Servings per container 4

Amount Per Serving About

Calories 90

Calories from Fat 0

Total Fat 0 grams

Saturated Fat 0 grams

Cholesterol less than 5 mg

Sodium 120 mg

Total Carbohydrate 12 grams

Dietary Fiber 0 grams

Sugars 12 gram

Protein 9 grams

Vitamin A 10%   Vitamin C 4%

Calcium 40%   Iron 0 %

Vitamin D 25%

VANILLA RICE DREAM

Nutrition Facts

Serving Size 8 fl oz.
Servings per container 4

Amount Per Serving About

Calories 130

Calories from Fat 20

Total Fat 2 grams

Saturated Fat 0 grams

Cholesterol 0 mg

Sodium 90 mg

Total Carbohydrate 28 grams

Dietary Fiber 0 grams

Sugars 12 grams

Protein 1 gram

Vitamin A 0%   Vitamin C %

Calcium 2%   Iron 0 %

Vitamin D 0%   Vitamin E 4%

Ingredients: Filtered Water, Brown rice, (partially milled) (Expeller Pressed Oleic, Safflower oil, Vanilla, Sea salt.

Beverages

GATORADE

WOW! I could have had a cup of salt water!

Nutrition Facts

Serving Size 8 fl oz.

Servings per container

Amount Per Serving About

Calories 50

   Calories from Fat 0

Total Fat 0 grams

   Saturated Fat 0 grams

Cholesterol 0 mg

Sodium 110 mg

Total Carbohydrate 14 grams

   Dietary Fiber 0 grams

   Sugars 14 grams

Protein 0 gram

This "sport drink" has enjoyed popularity as a "re-hydration" fluid. Many doctors recommend it for children who are vomiting or have diarrhea, in order to prevent dehydration. Gatorade may be good for the long distance runner, but it's not advisable to give this drink to either healthy or ill children. It's too high in sodium for the healthy child and its high sugar content may increase diarrhea.

V8 JUICE

Nutrition Facts

Serving Size 1 can (340 ml)

Servings per container 1

Amount Per Serving About

Calories 70

   Calories from Fat 0

Total Fat 0 grams

   Saturated Fat 0 grams

Cholesterol 0 mg

Sodium 880 mg

Total Carbohydrate 15 grams

   Dietary Fiber 2 grams

   Sugars 11 grams

Protein 2 grams

CAMPBELL'S TOMATO JUICE

Nutrition Facts

Serving Size 1 can (340 ml)

Servings per container 1

Amount Per Serving About

Calories 70

Calories from Fat 0

Total Fat 0 grams

Saturated Fat 0 grams

Cholesterol 0 mg

Sodium 1230 mg

Total Carbohydrate 13 grams

Dietary Fiber 2 grams

Sugars 9 grams

Protein 2 grams

This high sodium beverage should not be given to children. There are many other wholesome choices, such as fresh orange juice and other pure fruit juices. Don't forget water. It's an excellent beverage.

CAPRI-SUN "ALL NATURAL" FRUIT PUNCH JUICE DRINK

Nutrition Facts

Serving Size 1 Pouch

Servings per container 1

Amount Per Serving About

Calories 100

Calories from Fat 0

Total Fat **0** grams

Saturated Fat 0 grams

Cholesterol 0 mg

Sodium 20 mg

Total Carbohydrate 26 grams

Dietary Fiber 0 grams

Sugars 26 grams

Protein 0 gram

Vitamin A 10% Vitamin C 4%

Calcium 40% Iron 0 %

Vitamin D 25%

WHAT IS IN THIS POPULAR DRINK?
Ingredients: Water, high fructose corn syrup, pineapple, water extracted orange, grapefruit and peach juice concentrate, citric acid, natural flavor.

In other words,-pure sugar water! Avoid punch, and fruit "drinks." Kool Aid, Kool Aid Bursts, Hi-C, or soft drink mixes. These products are packaged and advertised heavily on TV to attract children. Protect your children from these beverages and send your child to school with a more nourishing beverage.

ORIGINAL APPLE TIME
(UNSWEETENED)

Nutrition Facts

Serving Size ½ cup

Servings per container 3

Amount Per Serving About

Calories 50

Calories from Fat 0

Total Fat 0 grams

Saturated Fat 0 grams

Cholesterol 0 mg

Sodium 0 mg

Total Carbohydrate 13 grams

Dietary Fiber 2 grams

Sugars 8 grams

Protein 0 gram

100% FRESH SQUEEZED
ORANGE JUICE

Nutrition Facts

Serving Size 8 fl oz

Servings per container 4

Amount Per Serving About

Calories 110

Calories from Fat 0

Total Fat 0 grams

Saturated Fat 0 grams

Cholesterol 0 mg

Sodium 0 mg

Potassium 440 mg

Total Carbohydrate 29 grams

Dietary Fiber 1 grams

Sugars 25 grams

Protein 1 gram

Vitamin C 160%   Folate 10%

Thiamin 6%   Magnesium 6 %

Copper 2%

The King of Juices! For those of you who are not able to get fresh O.J., the frozen juice or O.J. in a carton can be found in most grocery stores or supermarkets. Calcium fortified O.J. is also an excellent way to supplement your calcium intake.

"TWICE THE FRUIT" FAT FREE
YOGURT (SAFEWAY BRAND)

Nutrition Facts

Serving Size 1 (227 g)

Servings per container about 1

Amount Per Serving About

Calories 260

Calories from Fat 0

Total Fat 0 grams

Saturated Fat 0 grams

Cholesterol 5 mg

Sodium 160 mg

Total Carbohydrate 55 grams

Dietary Fiber 0 grams

Sugars 52 grams

Protein 11 gram

Vitamin A	Vitamin C 2%
Iron 0%	Calcium 40%

Note that the nutritional value of milk is about the same as yogurt except for the added sugar which accounts for the extra calories. Plain non-fat yogurt has the same amount of calories as non-fat milk. Milk has 15 grams of milk-sugar (lactose) versus 55 grams in this yogurt, which means that an extra 40 grams of sugar has been added. Try instead to add some fresh fruit or berries to plain yogurt. This will give you fewer refined sugar calories, more vitamins, and some fiber.

Calcium is reported in percent, but we usually think in terms of milligrams of calcium. This is confusing to most shoppers who are trying to provide sufficient calcium. In this case, 40% is equal to 320mg of elemental calcium.

Low Fat Frozen Yogurt contains about 3 grams of fat, of which two are from saturated fat. Regular Ben & Jerry's Ice Cream contains a whopping 28 grams of fat per serving. This Nutrition Facts label is included to illustrate how easy it is to find delicious low fat substitutes for traditionally high fat foods or desserts.

Remember that LOW FAT doesn't mean LOW CALORIE nor does it mean "healthy." It should not mean, "Now I can eat the whole thing."Keep your sugary dessert portions small, and never use, "non-fat" as permission to "pig out." Non-fat often means high sugar calories. And calories do count!
For those of you who are regular yogurt lovers, remember: fruit-flavored yogurt is made with jam, a poor source of nutrients. The jam adds the equivalent of 8-9 teaspoons of sugar per cup! Instead, add fresh fruit to plain yogurt.

BEN & JERRY'S CHERRY GARCIA
LOW FAT FROZEN YOGURT

Nutrition Facts

Serving Size 1/2 cup (89 g)

Servings per container 4

Amount Per Serving About

Calories 170

Calories from Fat 30

Total Fat 3 grams

Saturated Fat 2 grams

Cholesterol 20 mg

Sodium 80 mg

Total Carbohydrate 32 grams

Dietary Fiber 0 grams

Sugars 27 grams

Protein 4 grams

Vitamin A 2%   Vitamin C 0%

Iron 2%   Calcium 10%

Loaded with artery-clogging saturated fat.

NATURALLY YOURS FAT FREE SOUR CREAM

Nutrition Facts

Serving Size 2 Tbs.

Servings per container 15

Amount Per Serving About

Calories 20

   Calories from Fat 0

Total Fat 0 grams

   Saturated Fat 0 grams

Cholesterol 0 mg

Sodium 50 mg

Total Carbohydrate 3 grams

   Dietary Fiber 0 grams

   Sugars 2 grams

Protein 1 gram

Vitamin A 4%   Vitamin C 0%

Iron 0%   Calcium 4%

REGULAR SOUR CREAM

Nutrition Facts

Serving Size 2 Tbs.

Servings per container 4

Amount Per Serving About

Calories 60

   Calories from Fat 50

Total Fat 6 grams

   Saturated Fat 4 grams

Cholesterol 25 mg

Sodium 15 mg

Total Carbohydrate 1 gram

   Dietary Fiber 0 grams

   Sugars 1 gram

Protein 1 gram

Vitamin A 4%   Vitamin C 0%

Iron 0%   Calcium 2%

Experiment with the taste of the many new fat free sour cream choices.

KNUDSEN FREE FAT FREE SOUR CREAM

Nutrition Facts

Serving Size 2 Tbs.

Servings per container

Amount Per Serving About

Calories 35

   Calories from Fat 0

Total Fat 0 grams

   Saturated Fat 0 grams

Cholesterol less than 5 mg

Sodium 25 mg

Total Carbohydrate 6 grams

   Dietary Fiber 0 grams

   Sugars 2 grams

Protein 2 gram

Vitamin A 4%   Vitamin C 0%

Iron 0%   Calcium 4%

AMERICAN OR CHEDDAR CHEESE

Nutrition Facts

Serving Size 1 oz. or 1 slice

Servings per container 12

Amount Per Serving About

Calories 120

Calories from Fat 90

Total Fat 10 grams

Saturated Fat 6 grams

Unsaturated Fat 4 grams

Cholesterol 25 mg

Sodium 180 mg

Total Carbohydrate 1 gram

Dietary Fiber 0 grams

Sugars 0 grams

Protein 7 gram

Vitamin A 6%   Vitamin C 0%

Iron 0%   Calcium 20%

ALPINE LACE REDUCED FAT SWISS CHEESE
(25% Less Total Fat & 53% Less Sodium)

Nutrition Facts

Serving Size 1 oz.

Servings per container 12

Amount Per Serving About

Calories 90

Calories from Fat 50

Total Fat 6 grams

Cholesterol 20 mg

Sodium 35 mg

Total Carbohydrate 1 grams

Dietary Fiber 0 grams

Sugars 0 grams

Protein 8 gram

Vitamin A 6%   Vitamin C 0%

Iron 0%   Calcium 25%

Low-fat, reduced-fat, or fat-free cheese is an excellent source of calcium and protein.

HEALTHY CHOICE LOW-FAT MOZZARELLA CHEESE (STRING CHEESE)

Nutrition Facts

Serving Size 1 piece

Servings per container 10

Amount Per Serving About

Calories 50

Calories from Fat 0

Total Fat 1.5 grams

Cholesterol less than 5 mg

Sodium 220 mg

Total Carbohydrate 1 gram

Dietary Fiber 0 grams

Sugars 0 grams

Protein 8 grams

Vitamin A 4%   Vitamin C 0%

Iron 0%   Calcium 20%

Shredded nonfat or low-fat mozzarella cheese is excellent as a "melt" over an english muffin. To make pizza, put pizza sauce over the muffin, then cheese. Microwave until cheese melts.

LOW-FAT 1% COTTAGE CHEESE

Nutrition Facts

Serving Size ½ cup

Servings per container 10

Amount Per Serving About

Calories 72

Calories from Fat 9

Total Fat 1 gram

Cholesterol 4 mg

Saturated Fat 1 gram

Sodium 400 mg

Total Carbohydrate 3 grams

Dietary Fiber 0 grams

Sugars 1 gram

Protein 12 grams

Vitamin A 4%   Vitamin C 0%

Iron 0%   Calcium 2%

Although a bit high in sodium, this is an excellent high-protein after-school snack along with fresh fruit or berries for extra vitamins and fiber. It may come as a surprise to you that there is little calcium in cottage cheese.

Fruit

**FROZEN BIG VALLEY CALIFORNIA
MIXED FRUIT:**
(peaches, cantaloupe and honeydew
melon, red seedless grapes)

Nutrition Facts

Serving Size ¾ cup

Servings per container 18

Amount Per Serving About

Calories 60

Calories from Fat 0

Total Fat 0 gram

Cholesterol 0 mg

Sodium 0 mg

Total Carbohydrate 14 grams

Dietary Fiber 2 grams

Sugars 8 grams

Protein 1 gram

Vitamin A 20%   Vitamin C 150%

If or when seasonal fruit is not available, this is an excellent second choice. It is more nutritious than canned fruit.

TRADER JOE'S* DRIED PITTED CALIFORNIA BING CHERRIES**

Nutrition Facts

Serving Size ⅓ cup

Servings per container 6

Amount Per Serving About

Calories 140

Calories from Fat 0

Total Fat 0 gram

Cholesterol 0 mg

Sodium 0 mg

Total Carbohydrate 34 grams

Dietary Fiber 2 grams

Sugars 25 grams

Protein 1 gram

Vitamin A 2%   Vitamin C 0%

*Distributed and sold exclusively by Trader Joe's, So. Pasadena, CA91031
**Other dried fruit such as prune, apricot, pear, apple and peach are available at most supermarket and health food stores. Banana chips are deep fried and should be avoided. They are much closer to potato chips than bananas or dried fruit. One ounce of dried chips has nearly 10 grams of fat, mostly saturated, coming often from coconut oil. These chips are made from bananas that are picked green before the starch has had time to change to sugar. Sugar is added to make them taste sweet.

No preservatives. No artificial colors or flavors.
Great for snacks or to bake into muffins, breads and cookies (just as you would use raisins). They add flavor to home made trail mixes and fruit salads.

TRADER JOE'S DRIED BLUEBERRIES

Nutrition Facts

Serving Size ¼ cup

Servings per container 5

Amount Per Serving About

Calories 160

Calories from Fat 0

Total Fat 0 gram

Cholesterol 0 mg

Sodium 0 mg

Total Carbohydrate 38 grams

Dietary Fiber 5 grams

Sugars 20 grams

Protein 1 gram

Vitamin A 0%   Vitamin C 0%

Iron 2%   Calcium 2%

Ingredients: Blueberries, Fructose, Malic Acid, Sunflower oil.

Dried Fruit is high in fiber and are good for snacks or to bake into muffins, breads and cookies (just as you would raisins). I found the dried bing cherries more flavorful than the dried blueberries. Add dried fruit to cereals to enhance flavor and add fiber.

Compare Canned Vegetables for Nutritional Value

S & W PEELED TOMATOES
READY CUT

Nutrition Facts

Serving Size ½ cup
Servings per container 3½

Amount Per Serving About

Calories 25

Calories from Fat 0

Total Fat **0** gram

Cholesterol 0 mg

Sodium 190 mg

Potassium 150 mg

Total Carbohydrate 4 grams

Dietary Fiber 1 gram

Sugars 4 grams

Protein 1 gram

Vitamin A 20% Vitamin C 15%

Iron 15%   Calcium 4%

S & W PEELED TOMATOES
NO SALT ADDED
READY CUT

Nutrition Facts

Serving Size ½ cup
Servings per container 3½

Amount Per Serving About

Calories 25

Calories from Fat 0

Total Fat **0** gram

Cholesterol 0 mg

Sodium 30 mg

Potassium 150 mg

Total Carbohydrate 4 grams

Dietary Fiber 1 gram

Sugars 3 grams

Protein 1 gram

Vitamin A 20% Vitamin C 15%

Iron 10%   Calcium 0%

Buy the no-salt-added canned vegetables. When you have a choice, always try to select the brand with the least added sodium.

Always look for the reduced-sodium can. This can be an acceptable school snack. Compare this with Rice-a-Roni

RICE-A-RONI
(CHICKEN FLAVORED)

Don't look for the chicken. There isn't any.

Nutrition Facts

Serving Size 2½ cup or 1 cup prepared.

Servings per container 4

Amount Per Serving About

Calories 240 (310 prepared)

Calories from Fat 80 (prepared)

Total Fat 1 gram*

Saturated Fat 1 gram

Cholesterol 0 mg

Sodium 1090 mg (prepared)

Potassium 150 mg

Total Carbohydrate grams

Dietary Fiber 2 grams

Sugars 0 grams

Protein 7 grams

Folate 25%   Calcium 2%

Iron 10%

HEINZ
VEGETARIAN BEANS IN
RICE & TOMATO SAUCE

Nutrition Facts

Serving Size ½ cup

Servings per container 3½

Amount Per Serving About

Calories 140

Calories from Fat 0

Total Fat 0 gram

Cholesterol 0 mg

Sodium 480 mg

Total Carbohydrate 27 grams

Dietary Fiber 5 grams

Sugars 14 grams

Protein 6 gram

Vitamin A 2%   Vitamin C 0%

Iron 8%   Calcium 6%

Beware when you see an asterisk (*) on the Nutrition Facts label! If you use a magnifying glass, you will see on the bottom of the pacxkage an explanation of the asterisk. 1 gram of fat is actually 9 grams of fat when Rice-A-Roni is prepared as directed!! Pasta Roni has at total 7 grams of fat on the nutrition Facts label with that same asterisk. It should read 27 grams of fat when prepared!*

BUMBLE BEE TUNA SALAD
(mixed and ready to eat)
FAT FREE

Nutrition Facts

Serving Size 1 can

Servings per container 1

Amount Per Serving About

Calories 70

Calories from Fat 0

Total Fat 0 grams

Cholesterol 15 mg

Sodium 380 mg

Potassium 150 mg

Total Carbohydrate 10 grams

Dietary Fiber 0 grams

Sugars 5 grams

Protein 7 gram

Folate 25%   Calcium 2%

Iron 10%

Try the Bumble Bee Chunk Light Tuna in Water (easy to open cans). They only have 1 gram of fat, 15 grams of proteins and 350 mg. sodium. They make a good school lunch along with low sodium crackers, celery, cherry tomatoes and a piece of fruit.

DENNISON'S REDUCED FAT CHILI CON CARNE WITH BEANS

Nutrition Facts

Serving Size 1 cup

Servings per container 2

Amount Per Serving About

Calories 290

Calories from Fat 60

Total Fat 7 grams

Saturated Fat 2.5 grams

Cholesterol 35 mg

Sodium 940 mg

Total Carbohydrate 38 grams

Dietary Fiber 13 grams

Sugars 3 grams

Protein 19 grams

Vitamin A 20%   Calcium 10%

Iron 20% Vitamin C 0%

When shopping for chili or beans, look for the brand with the lowest sodium content. For example, Hormel Chili contains 1200 mg of sodium per serving!

The 50%-less-sodium garbanzo beans have only 230 mg of sodium per serving.

S & W GARBANZO BEANS
("ceci beans" or "chick peas")

AVOID THESE BEANS! Buy the 50%-less-sodium cans instead.

Nutrition Facts

Serving Size 1/2 cup

Servings per container 2

Amount Per Serving About

Calories 80

Calories from Fat 15

Total Fat **1.5** grams

Saturated Fat 0 gram

Cholesterol 0 mg

Sodium 460 mg

Total Carbohydrate 18 grams

Dietary Fiber 7 grams

Sugars 2 grams

Protein 6 grams

Vitamin A 0%   Calcium 6%

Iron 8%   Vitamin C 8%

S & W KIDNEY BEANS
PREMIUM DARK RED

Nutrition Facts

Serving Size 1/2 cup

Servings per container 2

Amount Per Serving About

Calories 100

Calories from Fat 5

Total Fat **0.5** grams

Saturated Fat 0 gram

Cholesterol 0 mg

Sodium 460 mg

Total Carbohydrate 23 grams

Dietary Fiber 6 grams

Sugars 8 grams

Protein 7 grams

The 50%-less-sodium kidney beans also have only 230 mg of sodium per serving.

Lunch

**MARUCHAN INSTANT LUNCH
RAMEN NOODLES
(chicken flavor)**

Nutrition Facts

Serving Size 1

Servings per container 1

Amount Per Serving About

Calories 280

    Calories from Fat 110

Total Fat 12 grams

    Saturated Fat 6 gram

Cholesterol 5 mg

Sodium 1260 mg

Total Carbohydrate 36 grams

    Dietary Fiber 4 grams

    Sugars 2 grams

Protein 6 grams

Along with "Top Ramen" I can't think of many foods that are nutritionally worse. The only ingredient missing is radioactivity. Ramen noodles are a common cause of afternoon school headaches. It is loaded with sodium and MSG. Hot dogs are another headache producer loaded with sodium and nitrites.

LUNCHABLES LEAN TURKEY BREAST, FUDGE SANDWICH COOKIE, AMERICAN CHEESE

Nutrition Facts

Serving Size 1 package

Servings per container 1

Amount Per Serving About

Calories 370

   Calories from Fat 180

Total Fat 20 grams

   Saturated Fat 8 gram

Cholesterol 50 mg

Sodium 1390 mg

Total Carbohydrate 33 grams

   Dietary Fiber 1 gram

   Sugars 10 grams

Protein 16 grams

By now you should be able to understand why lunchables are a poor choice. The fat and sodium content is enormous— and only one gram of fiber! Leave this one out of your child's lunch box.

Reduced-Fat Lunchables is a product made up of "98% Fat-Free" smoked turkey breast, cheddar cheese, and wheat crackers. Don't be fooled. It contains 9 grams of fat, 5 grams of which is saturated, plus a megadose of sodium at 1580 mg per serving! It also contains nitrite.

OSCAR MAYER WIENERS (MADE WITH TURKEY AND PORK)

Nutrition Facts

Serving Size 1 link
Servings per container 10

Amount Per Serving About
Calories 140
  Calories from Fat 120

Total Fat 13 grams
  Saturated Fat 4.5 gram
Cholesterol 45 mg
Sodium 440 mg
Total Carbohydrate 1 gram
  Dietary Fiber 0 grams
  Sugars 1 gram
Protein 5 grams

Ingredients: Mechanically separated turkey, pork, water, salt, contains less than 2% corn syrup, dextrose, flavor, sodium phosphate, sodiumerythrobate, sodium nitrite.

Take a look at the traditional frank your child is served to raise money for the school library. This food isn't exactly designed to enhance brain power.

If you think these ingredients are bad, check out John Morrell Skinless Polish Sausage. They contain 22 grams of fat per serving. Of that 8 grams are saturated fat, and 990 mg. of sodium to boot.

If you take Vitamin C before eating nitrite containing foods, you can protect yourself from those cancer producing nitrosamines.

If there must be a PTA "Hot Dog Day," at least use a low or non-fat frank. But they still contain nitrite and too much sodium.

HEALTHY CHOICE LOW FAT FRANKS

Nutrition Facts

Serving Size 1 frank
Servings per container 8

Amount Per Serving About
Calories 60
  Calories from Fat 15
Total Fat 1.5 grams
  Saturated Fat 0.5 gram
Cholesterol 20 mg
Sodium 430 mg
Total Carbohydrate 6 grams
  Dietary Fiber 0 grams
  Sugars 2 grams
Protein 6 grams

CELESTE PIZZA FOR ONE
(with sausage, green and red peppers, pepperoni, mushrooms, onions, and olives)

Nutrition Facts

Serving Size 1 Pizza

Servings per container 1

Amount Per Serving About

Calories 580

Calories from Fat 240

Total Fat 27 grams

Saturated Fat 9 gram

Cholesterol 25 mg

Sodium 1290 mg

Total Carbohydrate 49 grams

Dietary Fiber 6 grams

Sugars 6 grams

Protein 22 grams

Vitamin A 25%   Calcium 40%

Iron 15%   Vitamin C 11%

Note the high fat, high sodium load.

If your school lunch program offers pizza, get a copy of the nutrition facts from the provider. Beware the dietician who defends pizza because it is high in calcium and protein. There are healthier ways to get these nutrients.

The following Nutrition Facts on two frozen Healthy Choice lunches are examples to be compared with Swanson Hungry-Man frozen fried chicken and Safeway chicken pot pie.

HEALTHY CHOICE
CHICKEN & VEGETABLES
MARSALA

Nutrition Facts
Serving Size 1 meal

Servings per container 1

Amount Per Serving About

Calories 230

Calories from Fat 15

Total Fat 1.5 grams

Saturated Fat 0.5 gram

Polyunsaturated Fat 0.5

Cholesterol 30 mg

Sodium 440 mg

Total Carbohydrate 32 grams

Dietary Fiber 3 grams

Sugars 1 gram

Protein 22 grams

Vitamin A 10% Calcium 6%

Iron 10%   Vitamin C 6%

HEALTHY CHOICE
GINGER CHICKEN
HUNAN

Nutrition Facts
Serving Size 1 meal

Servings per container 1

Amount Per Serving About

Calories 350

Calories from Fat 20

Total Fat 2.5 grams

Saturated Fat 0.5 gram

Polyunsaturated Fat 1 gram

Monounsaturated Fat 1 gram

Cholesterol 25 mg

Sodium 430 mg

Total Carbohydrate 59 grams

Dietary Fiber 5 grams

Sugars 11 grams

Protein 24 grams

Vitamin A 15% Calcium 6%

Iron 15%   Vitamin C 0%

SWANSON HUNGRY MAN FRIED CHICKEN, MASHED POTATO, CORN & APPLE-CRANBERRY CRUMB DESSERT

Nutrition Facts

Serving Size 1 package

Servings per container 1

Amount Per Serving About

Calories 780

Calories from Fat 350

Total Fat 35 grams

Saturated Fat 12 grams

Cholesterol 105 mg

Sodium 1700 mg

Total Carbohydrate 74 grams

Dietary Fiber 8 grams

Sugars 15 grams

Protein 33 grams

SWANSON HOME STYLE "MAIN DISH" OVEN BAKED CHICKEN POT PIE

Nutrition Facts

Serving Size 7 oz

Servings per container 4

Amount Per Serving About

Calories 518

Calories from Fat 288

Total Fat 30 grams

Saturated Fat 7 grams

Cholesterol 16 mg

Sodium 550 mg

Total Carbohydrate 44 grams

Dietary Fiber 7 grams

Sugars 6 grams

Protein 14 grams

Vitamin A 25% Calcium 6%

Snacks

The single largest source of fat among people who eat high-fat diets is french fries. Hamburgers are second. Buy the leanest meat to make your hamburgers and stay clear of the Big Mac or the many other super-charged hamburger combinations. Check those "baked" French fries for fat content. Try those vegetarian burgers, such as wholesome Hearty Foods Burgers, Morningstar Farms Garden Vege and Garden Grain patties, Fantastic Foods Nature's Burger or Boca Burgers. They have little fat, good taste, and are enjoyed by most children when served on a fresh bun with ketchup, non-fat or reduced fat mayo, or fresh salsa. Parents are always looking for a special treat to put in their child's lunch box. Fresh fruit is always a safe choice. Before buying a treat, check the nutrition label. Here are a couple of suggestions.

ENTENMANN'S LIGHT FAT FREE BROWNIES

Nutrition Facts
Serving Size 1/10 Strip
Servings per container 10

Amount Per Serving About
Calories 120
Calories from Fat 0
Total Fat 0 grams
Saturated Fat 0 gram
Cholesterol 0 mg
Sodium 140 mg
Total Carbohydrate 29 grams
Dietary Fiber 1 gram
Sugars 23 grams
Protein 2 grams

SARA LEE FAT-FREE ANGEL FOOD CAKE

Nutrition Facts
Serving Size 1/5 Cake
Servings per container 5

Amount Per Serving About
Calories 180
Calories from Fat 0
Total Fat 0 grams
Saturated Fat 0 gram
Cholesterol 0 mg
Sodium 285 mg
Total Carbohydrate 43 grams
Dietary Fiber 1 gram
Sugars 14 grams
Protein 3 grams

The following are examples of "treats" to keep out of your child's lunchbox.

HOSTESS FROSTED DONETTES (CHOCOLATE COVERED)

Nutrition Facts

Serving Size 3

Servings per container 8

Amount Per Serving About

Calories 230

 Calories from Fat   120

Total Fat 14 grams

 Saturated Fat 9 gram

Cholesterol 0 mg

Sodium 210 mg

Total Carbohydrate 24 grams

 Dietary Fiber 0 grams

 Sugars 15 grams

Protein 2 grams

SARA LEE CHOCOLATE COVERED DONUTS

Nutrition Facts

Serving Size 2 Tbs.

Servings per container 11

Amount Per Serving About

Calories 300

 Calories from Fat   170

Total Fat 19 grams

 Saturated Fat 9 grams

Cholesterol 5 mg

Sodium 240 mg

Total Carbohydrate 30 grams

 Dietary Fiber 1 gram

 Sugars 8 grams

Protein 2 grams

ENTENMANN'S SOFTEE POWDERED CINNAMON POPETTES
(packaged especially for children!)

Nutrition Facts
Serving Size 3

Servings per container 7

Amount Per Serving About

Calories 240

  Calories from Fat 130

Total Fat 15 grams

  Saturated Fat 3.5 gram

Cholesterol 15 mg

Sodium 220 mg

Total Carbohydrate 24 grams

  Dietary Fiber 0 gram

  Sugars 12 grams

Protein 2 grams

HOSTESS' HO HO'S

Nutrition Facts
Serving Size 2 cakes

Servings per container 5

Amount Per Serving About

Calories 250

  Calories from Fat   110

Total Fat 12 grams

  Saturated Fat 8 grams

Cholesterol 20 mg

Sodium 150 mg

Total Carbohydrate 34 grams

  Dietary Fiber 1 gram

  Sugars 23 grams

Protein 2 grams

LUCKY'S HOME RUN CHERRY PIE

Nutrition Facts
Serving Size 1 (3 oz.)

Servings per container 1

Amount Per Serving About

Calories 110

  Calories from Fat   100

Total Fat 13 grams

  Saturated Fat 6 grams

Cholesterol 13.5 mg

Sodium 270 mg

Total Carbohydrate 36 grams

  Dietary Fiber 0 gram

  Sugars 16 grams

Protein 3 grams

HERSHEY'S SYRUP SPECIAL DARK

Nutrition Facts
Serving Size 2 Tbs.

Servings per container 11

Amount Per Serving About

Calories 110

  Calories from Fat   less than
                        ½ gram/serving

Total Fat 12 grams

  Saturated Fat 0 grams

Cholesterol 0 mg

Sodium 35 mg

Total Carbohydrate 27 grams

  Dietary Fiber 0 grams

  Sugars 22 grams

Protein 1 gram

▲ ▲ ▲

"What shall I feed my child?" is on the mind of every parent. It took many people to help me answer this question, some unknowingly and others very directly. The encouragement of my wife, Linda, to write *Feed Your Child Right from Birth through Teens* deserves special recognition. Her critical review of each page kept me focused. The lactation specialists Nancy Held, R.N., M.S., IBCLC; Chris Costello, R.N., CLE, of the Marin General Hospital Lactation Center; and Kristin Robertson, M.S., R.N., of the Pediatric Intensive Care Nursery contributed to the breastfeeding section. Paul Steinman, M.D., FAAP, of Fairfax, California, and many other pediatricians helped me clarify various points of view. Special thanks to Michael Ronis of Carmine's Restaurant in New York, Vanda Braun, Geri Eszterhas, Kim Norgaard, Maddy Wilner, and Linda Goldberg, R.N., N.P., for enhancing this book with their personal recipes. Cody Harrison, Carol Harrison, Cameron Briggs, Janelle Briggs, and Natalie Smyth deserve praise for volunteering to be my official recipe tasting team members. Katherine Kam; Martha Lawler, MFT; Susan I. Reinke, DVM; and Doris Ober helped make the text more readable, while the librarians Julie Kahl and Katherine Renick at Marin General Hospital worked overtime to help me retrieve references and research the literature. Sincere thanks to my friend Deborah Santana and my agent Barbara Ryan of Sterling Lord Literistic, Inc. for their belief in this project along with the staff of my publisher, M. Evans and Company, Inc., who added magic to my manuscript.

▲ ▲ ▲

Adolescent's Diet, 93
Aflatoxin, 46
Allergenic Foods, 17, 18, 32
Alpha-linolenic acid, 85
American Academy of Pediatrics, 7
Anemia, 100, 116
Appetite, Loss of , 42
ARA, 2, 20
Arborio, 55
Artificial sweeteners, 69
Atherosclerosis, 124, 142
Banana Puree, 32
Barley, 59, 114
Beano, 60
Beans, 49, 60. See also Folic Acid
Beta-carotene, 22, 61, 63, 64, 66, 141
Bottle feeding, 7, 41
Botulism, 17
Bowel movements, 19
Breakfast meals, 73, 74
Breast milk, 1, 2, 3, 14, 16, 20, 22,
  29, 32, 117. See high blood pres-
  sure. See also Folic Acid
Breastfeeding, 1, 8, 10, 14, 96. See
  also Nursing
  diet, effects on nursing, 1
  vomitting during breast feeding,
  10
Brown whole grain rice, 54
Buckwheat, 59
Calcium, 147-150
Campylobacter, 20
Carbohydrates, 97, 98, 110, 116
Cereals, dry, 75
Cereals, hot, 74, 75
Cheese, 21, 25, 45, 52, 76, 78, 148-
  149
  Cream Cheese, 45, 166
Chestnuts, 48

Chicken noodle soup. See Sodium
  and Salt
Colon Cancer, 86
Colostrum, 2. See also first milk
Constipation, 17
Controling your toddler's eating
  habits, 42
Cooking Fish , 203, 204
Cooking meat, 178, 203, 204
Cooking poultry , 203
Corn, 55, 56
Couscous, 59
Cow milk, switching the baby to, 20
Cretinism. See Folic Acid
DHA, 2, 20, 85
DHEA, 98
Diarrhea, 18, 20, 51
Diverticulosis, 127
E. coli, 20
Egg, raw, 23
Eggs, 17, 44, 50, 51, 97. See Folic
  Acid
Eggs, preparing eggs for your child,
  50
Eicosapentaenoic acid (EPA), 85
Energy, 108
Enriched rice, 54
Familia, 17
Fast Foods, 217
Taco Bell, 219
Pizza Hut, 220
Wendy's, 218
McDonald's, 217, 218
Carl's Jr., 219
Burger King, 218
Hardee's, 219
Subway, 220
Arby's, 220
Fats, 2, 120, 122

Fatty Foods, 45, 47, 49, 77, 89
FDA, 7
Fiber, 126
Fiber-rich foods, 126, 129. See also
  Beta-carotene
First milk, 2. See Colostrum
Fish, 77, 84, 85, 86. See Folic Acid
Fluorine. See Folic Acid
Folate. See Folic Acid
Folic acid, 144
Food Labels, 221–224
Food Pyramid, 163–169
Foods that are not recommended,
  20, 21, 23, 39, 72
Formulas, 6, 7, 12, 13, 16, 20, 22, 29,
  32
Fructose, 109
Fruit, 66, 70, 72
Fruits and Vegetables, 18
Galactose, 109
Garlic, 65
Grains, 49
Granola, 58
High blood pressure, 3, 21, 124
High salt foods, 39. See also Sodium
  and Salt
Hilocobacter pylori, 139
Homemade Baby Foods, 30, 31
Homemade Foods, preparing fruit,
  32, 33, 34, 35
Hypertension. See High blood pres-
  sure
Infant Formula Act, 7
Instant breakfast bars, 75
Iron deficiency, 99, 100, 101
Iron tablets, 102
Jaundice, 10
Juices, 22, 29, 70
Junk foods, 43, 45, 72
Kasha, 59
Keshan disease. See Folic Acid
Kitchen Condiments, 174, 175, 176
Kwashiorkor, 116
Lactose, 22, 29, 109. See Folic Acid
Lamb, 88
Laxative, natural , 19, 23
Legumes, 60
Linoleic acid, 85
Lipase, 2, 3

Loss of appetite in children, 38
Low-fat cooking, 173
Low-fat milk, 44
Low-fat recipes, 78
Maltose, 109
Meat and poultry, 86–92
Meats, 19, 35, 86–92
Metabolism, 108
Microwaving foods, 177
Milk, 43, 76. See Folic Acid
Millet, 59
Minerals
  Chlorine (Chloride), 153–153
  Copper, 161
  Fluorine (Fluoride), 158–160
  Iodine, 161–162
  Iron, 153–156
  Magnesium, 151
  Potassium, 150–151
  Zinc, 156
Muesli, 58
Non-pasteurized food, 23
Nonfat milk, 44, 74, 76, 98
Nutrition Facts, 225
Oats, 58
Olive oil, 121
Omega-3 fat, 84, 85, 86
Onions, 64, 65
Pacifier Habit, 41
Palatschincken, 76
Pancakes, 75, 76
Parboiled, 54
Peanut butter, 17, 46, 47
Picky Eaters, 40
Pizza, 76, 77
Pork, 88
Potatoes, 52, 53
Poultry. See also Meat
Precooked rice, 54
Preschooler. See toddlers
Prevention of Nutritional Losses, 176
Processed foods, 22
Prostate cancer, 86
Protein for your infant, 19
Proteins, 115–117
Prune juice, 23
Ramen noodles, 39
RDA, 70, 94, 99, 136, 137, 141. See
  beta-carotene

Reading Nutrition Labels, 225
  Beans, 273
  Beverages, 258, 259, 260, 261
  Breads and Tortillas, 245, 246, 247
  Butter and Other Spreads, 248, 249, 250, 251
  Cheese, 266, 267
  Cereals
    Cold Cereals, 228, 229, 230, 231, 232, 233, 234, 235, 236, 237
    Hot Cereals, 238
  Dairy and Dairy Substitutes, 254, 257
  Desserts, 279
  Eggs, 240
  Fruit, 268, 269
  Healthy Choice lunches, 278
  Lunch, 274, 275
  Mayonnaise, 252, 253
  Milk, 255, 256, 257
  Oatmeal, 226, 227
  Packaged Foods, 271, 272, 276
  Pancake and Waffle, 239
  Pizza, 277
  Quaker salt-free Rice Cakes, 244
  Snack Crackers, 242, 243
  Snacks, 280, 281, 282
  Sour Cream, 264, 265
  Vegetables, 270, 271
  Yogurt, 262, 263
Recipes, 173
  Applesauce, 195
  Baked Apple, 194
  Baked Pears French Style, 196
  Baked Potato, 179
  Baked Potato and Broccoli, 194
  Barley Recipe, 188
  Basic Mashed Potatoes, 179
  Basic Omelet, 197
  Bean Cuisine's "Thick as Fog Split Pea Soup," 201
  Bean Burrito, 212
  Bean Dip, 202
  Bean, Turkey, and Broccoli Dinner, 205
  Black-eyed peas, 202
  Broccoli, 189

Buckwheat Pancakes, 186
Carol's Banana-Strawberry Smoothie, 194
Carmine's Barbecued Chicken, 208
Carmine's Chicken Cacciatore, 208
Carmine's Chicken Enchiladas, 210
Carmine's Chicken Pizza, 209
Creamy Potato Soup, 213
Chicken or Turkey Enchiladas, 212
Chestnut Stuffing, 199
Coleslaw, 190
Fried Fillet of Fish, 204
Frijoles, 203
Green Salad With Vegetables, 192
Hummus, 199
Hungarian Butter Lettuce Salad, 193
Hungarian Cucumbers, 193
Kasha Varnishkas, 187
Lentil Soup, 200
Louis's Drench Toast, 198
Low-Fat Turkey Gravy, 206
Manischewitz Homestyle Soup Mix, 214
Meat, Rice & Ketchup, 183
Millet Pilaf, 188
New Potatoes With Dill Sauce, 180
Peach Sherbet, 195
Polenta, 184
Potato Latkes, 181
Quick Oatmeal, 186
Scrambled Eggs Wrapped in a Tortilla, 198
Special Cream of Wheat, 185
Steaming Vegetables, 189
Turkey Meatballs, 206
Vanda's Spaghetti Pie, 211
Vegetable Saute, 191
Vegetable Soup, 191
Veracruzana Sauce, 184
Rejecting food, 38, 39
Rice, 53, 54
  preparation of, 182

Rye, 57
Salmonella, 23, 51
Salmonella-shigella, 20
Salt. See also Sodium. See hypertension
Sausages, 89
Scurvy, 138, 139
Seafood, 77
Selenium, 126, 147, 160–161
Semisolid foods for your baby, 15
Shellfish, 84
Snacks, 39, 44, 46
Snacks for older children, 71, 78
Snacks for preschoolers, 45
Soda, 96
Sodium. See also Salt. See Hypertension
Soups, 36
Soy, 12
Soybeans, 60
Spinach, 19
Starch, 109
Steaming vegetables, 176
Storing foods, 176, 177
Stork Myth, 28
Sucrose, 109
Sugar, 27, 28, 112
Sugar and hyperactive children, 28
Tap water and your baby's health, 22
Tapeworms, 20
Toddlers, 37

Toxoplasmosis, 20
Trail mix, preparing, 69
Trichinosis, 20
Turkey, 91
Unhealthy foods in the diet, 40
USDA Food Guide Pyramid. See Folic Acid
Vegetable fat, 47
Vegetables, 61, 64, 177. See Folic Acid
Vegetables for your preschooler, 48, 49
Vitamin A, 140
Vitamin B-12, 87
Vitamin C, 138, 139
Vitamin D, 133, 143, 144.
Vitamin E, 126, 142
Vitamins, 130–135
Vitamins and Birth Defects, 102
Vitamins and minerals in your diet, 177
Vitamins B-6, 87
Vitamins, Fat Soluble, 132
Vitamins, in Breast Milk, 22
Vitamins, Water Soluble, 131
Water, feeding your baby, 22
Weaning, 13, 14
Wheat, 56, 57
Whole grain cereals, 127, 128
Whole grain rice, 54
Wild rice, 55

Tofu, 49, 51, 52. See Folic Acid
Tomato, 22, 61–62